THE REST WRITE BACK

Studies in Critical Social Sciences Book Series

Haymarket Books is proud to be working with Brill Academic Publishers (www.brill.nl) to republish the *Studies in Critical Social Sciences* book series in paperback editions. This peer-reviewed book series offers insights into our current reality by exploring the content and consequences of power relationships under capitalism, and by considering the spaces of opposition and resistance to these changes that have been defining our new age. Our full catalog of *SCSS* volumes can be viewed at https://www.haymarketbooks.org/series_collections/4-studies-in-critical-social-sciences.

THE REST WRITE BACK

Discourse and Decolonization

EDITED BY
ESMAEIL ZEINY

Haymarket Books
Chicago, IL

First published in 2019 by Brill Academic Publishers, The Netherlands.
© 2019 Koninklijke Brill NV, Leiden, The Netherlands

Published in paperback in 2020 by
Haymarket Books
P.O. Box 180165
Chicago, IL 60618
773-583-7884
www.haymarketbooks.org

ISBN: 978-1-64259-194-1

Distributed to the trade in the US through Consortium Book Sales and
Distribution (www.cbsd.com) and internationally through Ingram Publisher
Services International (www.ingramcontent.com).

This book was published with the generous support of Lannan Foundation and
Wallace Action Fund.

Special discounts are available for bulk purchases by organizations and
institutions. Please call 773-583-7884 or email info@haymarketbooks.org for
more information.

Cover design by Jamie Kerry and Ragina Johnson.

Printed in United States.

10 9 8 7 6 5 4 3 2 1

Library of Congress Cataloging-in-Publication Data is available.

Contents

Foreword: Whose Rest is Best? (Un)Learning Binaries from Subalternity

Arjuna Parakrama

I am happy and privileged to be associated with this timely and innovative collection of essays that seeks to explore difficult yet crucial questions relating to the production and dissemination of norms and paradigms of knowledge as well as the entrenching of modalities of rationality and explanation which span the globe today.

That said, my own approach to these key issues, though inflected by similar concerns, has begun to take a slightly different direction. It is this tentative footpath that I offer here as both tribute to and expression of solidarity with this project.

In 1969 a Palestinian poet writes devastatingly about the limits of writing back as imposed from within as well as without. The challenge is not of inventing or returning to a different vocabulary, grammar and syntax, but that even these perceived alternatives are not radically different. The articulate opponents of the colonial project at the time of decolonization are also its subjects.

> My country that was home
> Has become an argument
> Don't blame the rifle
> When it died without leaving a will
>
> On a cloud I wrote:
> Own with censorship –
> And they confiscated the sky.[1]

There is no rest, and whatever rest there is *cannot* be restful (NRIP), nor *should* it be. The "de" in decolonization is also always-already too final, and may also be seen as annoyingly definitively multiple and hopelessly fraught. For Beseisso, in translation (as always resistance hangs out in the trajectories of translation) there was a home – incredibly hard to translate into my language this deceptively simple word – replaced by an argument in this vestigial realm of settler colonialism.

---

1 Mouin Beseisso (trans. Ibrahim Abu-Nab and Martin Walker)

Decolonization as used to mark a moment and more in the historiography of colonialism is well-argued here, but its replacement with other forms of globalized capital coupled with more or less localized exploitative systems – only seemingly antagonistic to each other, but deep structurally congruent, of course – needs to be stubbornly, persistently spelt out in more mainstream locations as well. In this sense too, there is no rest for the weary, no resting on the laurels of this exciting publication. If not, we run the danger, oft-repeated, of replacing one term in a binary with another. In this context, "decolonized" is rejected as incomplete and even false in comparison with "indigenous" (which has thankfully replaced "native" in progressivist discourse), as the newish touchstone of authenticity and inherent value.

The *Keywords for Today* entry for "indigenous" is instructive as a cautionary tale, which has clear implications for the critical decolonization debate, especially as it is provoked into positing an overarching and cumulated other who were/are relatively at least outside the episteme(s) of colonialism.

> The link between the more specialized and selective current meaning with the more general past use of *indigenous* is its meticulous relationship as the European Other, though 'indigenous peoples' is also a political construct that, in theory at least, can also refer to a small number of distinct marginalized groups living in the European continent, and it is deliberately less pejorative than its now discredited near-synonym, native....
>
> The range of contemporary uses of this term mirrors the current geopolitics of selective inclusivity. Peoples of the world are now divided into two categories: the indigenous and everyone else. What appears on the surface to be a scrupulous acknowledgement of radical difference has also become a debilitating homogenization that lumps together (South Asian) Adivasis [literally original/beginning dweller/inhabitant] with Australian Aborigines and Kalaallit of Greenland, for instance. While this may lead to mobilization and sharing in common causes at the political level, it effaces and distorts differences that are as stark as those that obtain between 'indigenous' and 'non-indigenous' peoples."[2]

Thus, the indigenous (less ubiquitous than "the rest" certainly) tend to be homogenized, where the formula is of "(a) radical-difference-from-us who are

---

2   MacCabe Colin and Holly Yanacek (eds.). *Keywords for Today: A 21st Century Vocabulary.* (New York: Oxford University Press, 2018), 198ff.

fundamentally individualist even when collective, combined with (b) they-are-all-the-same because they are undifferentiated both within their group and among all such groups reflects the great difficulty of engaging productively and equally with a fundamentally different worldview, while recognizing that this worldview is itself internally differentiated, without descending into unexamined racism appearing as benevolence."

I would argue that the point is to recognize the multiple and multiply diverse ways in which an alternative meta-narrative is at work which is far more insidious and ubiquitous than the vestiges of an almost defunct settler colonialism, or a self-evident neo-colonial state apparatus, or even the façade of a globalized free market, and the ever-waning ever-defiant remnants of the (socialist?) welfare state, in which knowledge production does not allow for a simplistic good-bad/us-them/colonized-decolonized/west-rest binary. This binary would be neat and would allow us to tidy up our home, in Beseisso's sense, but, I would argue, it has no real explanatory power today.

One way to see this is to be meticulous about who and how this articulation of the other (as rest and/or as excluded) is made, which in turn excludes, devalues and rests non-elites within its contours and shores. And so on, even in the second and third iterations of this entirely salutary if self-congratulatory accounting of colonialism's continuing cost on post-neo-colonial peoples.

Hence, this accounting is as much about complicity as it is about exploitation and betrayal. We have seen many brilliant analyses of the creation of colonial mindsets in the former colonies through education, culturation, governance, even nationalist freedom struggles, and so on, but the heavy emphasis has been on imposition, force-feeding, lack of real choices, and both ideological and physical power. However, local elites' active complicity and even counter-manipulation of the colonial project for their own ends has received far less attention, for obvious reasons, if one is attentive to who is saying what to whom here.

Thus, I believe, the question should not be so much "Why have 'western' (Are they really? We may be giving up too much here in an attempt to claim that our hands are clean as upwardly mobile non-western or wannabe intellectuals) modes and grammars of thought and norms of rationality etc., persisted in decolonized post-colonial space, but, rather, "How can it not be so, since so little has changed, especially in who is writing back and forth to whom and in which languages?"

Another approach to this predicament would be to explore it from the perspectives of those who remain inside-outside even the post-colonial discursivities, and in this sense are even more the other of the knowledge-wallah elites than their European counterparts with whom they have regularly stimulating

academic discussions over cappuccinos at international conferences and published debates. Gayatri Spivak has scrupulously re-described the changing yet
distinctive positionality of "the subaltern"[3] as not having (structured) access to
lines of upward social mobility, where their identity is qualitatively different,
and meta-narratives (especially such as nationalism) do not clinch easily.

It is in this last point that I find the most powerfully potential for a far-
reaching critique of the western versus non-western polarization. One feature
of subalternization (which *process* for me is more provisional and fragile, but
of course less theoretical than subaltern as *being*, and hence more useful to
understand and explain such radically different worlds within this world) is
that the larger national narrative does not cohere, is not *natural* as it is for (the
rest of) us. This is an irrefutable critique of the self-evidence of our love of our
country (that is home – but is it a country that is home, or is it our home writ
small that should qualify?), that can even render the bigger nationalist and de-
colonialist debates suspect, however politically and academically interesting
and important they may seem.

---

3 See, for instance, Gayatri Chakravorty Spivak, "Scattered Speculations on the Subaltern and
   the Popular" in her *An Aesthetic Education in the Era of Globalization*. (Harvard University
   Press, 2012), 429–442, and Gayatri Chakravorty Spivak. *Nationalism and the Imagination*.
   Seagull Books, 2010.

Acknowledgements

First and foremost, I would like to thank the contributors who have worked diligently during the editorial process of this volume. Their contributions made it possible for this collection to accentuate and concretize the developing concern with "epistemic colonization." I would also like to thank Peivand Zandi who was kind enough to copyedit the entire volume. I am grateful to the editorial and production staff at Brill whose hard work saw this volume reach completion. Last but certainly not least, I would like to thank The Institute of Malaysian and International Studies (IKMAS), The National University of Malaysia (UKM) for their constant support throughout this project.

Notes on Contributors

Dustin J. Byrd

is an Associate Professor of Religion, Philosophy, and Arabic at Olivet College, in Michigan, USA. He is a specialist in the Critical Theory of Religion, the Frankfurt School, and contemporary Islamic thought. He has recently published a monograph entitled *Islam in a Post-Secular Society: Religion, Secularity and the Antagonism of Recalcitrant Faith* (Brill, 2016), as well as *Unfashionable Objections to Islamophobic Cartoons: L'affaire Charlie Hebdo* (Cambridge Scholars Publishing, 2017). Recently he co-edited the book *Ali Shariati and the Future of Social Theory: Religion, Revolution, and the Role of the Intellectual* (Brill, 2017, with Seyed Javad Miri).

Ciarunji Chesaina

is a Professor of Literature at the University of Nairobi. She holds a PhD and Master of Arts in Literature from the University of Leeds. She also holds a Master of Education degree in Child Psychology from Harvard University. Professor Chesaina has published widely in Literature and Women's Studies. Her books include *Oral Literature of the Kalenjin* (East African Publishers, 1991), *Oral Literature of the Embu and Mbeere* (East African Publishers, 1997), *Joy Comes in the Morning* (The Asis Publishers, 2017), and *Run Gazelle Run* (The Asis Publishers, 2018). Currently, she is working on a novel entitled *Diazipporah* and a critical work entitled *Cultural Dimensions of the Proverb*.

Hiba Ghanem

has recently earned her Doctorate from Lancaster University, UK. She currently teaches Comparative Literature and English Literature at the Lebanese University. Her research focuses on the concept of justice in Middle Eastern and World Literature. She is the author of "The 2011 Egyptian Revolution Chants: A Romantic-Mu'tazili Moral Order" in *The British Journal of Middle Eastern Studies*.

Mladjo Ivanovic

is an Assistant Professor of Philosophy at Northern Michigan University. His research focuses on moral, political and environmental challenges tied with the forceful displacement and migration of people, particularly by examining both the sociohistorical and environmental contexts of human vulnerability and exclusion (contexts such as gender, race, poverty, violence, colonialism, environmental degradation, climate change, etc.). He is also engaged with NGO communities in Serbia, Greece and Turkey, and serves as an advisor for various student organizations that deal with humanitarianism and social justice.

Masumi Hashimoto Odari

is a Senior Lecturer and Chairperson in the Department of Literature at the University of Nairobi. She holds a Master of Arts and PhD in Literature from the University of Nairobi. She is also an Advocate of the High Court of Kenya as well as a Member of the Chartered Institute of Arbitrators. Dr. Odari has published widely in various international journals. Her books include *Daisaku Ikeda and Africa: Reflections by Kenyan Writers* (Nairobi University Press, 2001, co-edited with Henry Indangasi), *Daisaku Ikeda and Voices for Peace from Africa* (Kenya Literature Bureau, 2008, co-edited with Henry Indangasi), and *Value Creating Education in Kenya: Building a Humane Society* (Kenya Literature Bureau, 2018, co-edited with Henry Indangasi and Anna Mwangi).

Arjuna Parakrama

is Senior Professor of English and Cadre Chair at the University of Peradeniya. Before this he was Dean/Arts at Colombo University where he taught for over 15 years. He has published widely on language standardization and the politics of language, subaltern studies, Lankan English and teaching English in Sri Lanka, conflict transformation and discourse theory. He has been awarded a Guggenheim research grant, as well as senior fellowships from the Carnegie Council on Ethics and International Affairs, and the US Institute of Peace. He was a Fulbright New Century Scholar in 2007/8.

JM. Persánch

has graduated with two BAs in English and Hispanic Philology at the University of Cádiz, where he later received his first Ph.D. in Comparative U.S. Latino Studies with distinctions. Whilst he was graduating, he studied abroad at the University of Birmingham in the United Kingdom and he was an instructor of Spanish and non-degree seeking student at Amherst College in the United States. He later received his second Ph.D. in Peninsular Studies at the University of Kentucky. He is currently a visiting Assistant Professor of Spanish at Western Oregon University, Editor of Nuestra Andalucía, an external reviewer for academic journals, Founding Director and Presenter of the Persona, Personae Interview Series Project and Community Outreach Project Director.

Andrew Ridgeway

is a graduate student studying English literature at the University of Vermont, where his research examines rhetoric, affect and circulation through the lens of Marxist psychoanalysis.

Rudolf J. Siebert

was born in Frankfurt a.M, Germany. He studied history, philosophy, psychology, sociology, theology at the University of Frankfurt, the University of Mainz the University of Münster, and the Catholic University of America, Washington D.C. Siebert created and is a specialist in the critical theory of religion, or dialectical religiology. He has taught, lectured and published widely in Western and Eastern Europe, the United States and Canada, Israel and Japan. He is a Professor of Religion and Society, Founder and Director of the Center for Humanistic Future Studies at Western Michigan University, Founder and Director of the 42-year-old international course on the Future of Religion in the IUC, Dubrovnik, Croatia, and Founder and Director of the 20-year-old international course on Religion in Civil Society, in Yalta, Republic of Crimea. Siebert has written 30 books and 500 articles. His major works are the three-volume Manifesto of the *Critical Theory of Society and Religion: The Wholly Other, Liberation, Happiness, and the Rescue of the Hopeless* (Brill, 2010), *From Critical Theory to Political Theology: Personal Autonomy and Universal Solidarity* (Peter Lang, 1994) and *The Critical Theory of Religion: Frankfurt School* (Mouton De Gruyter, 1985).

Esmaeil Zeiny

is a Research Fellow at the Institute of Malaysian and International Studies (IKMAS), National University of Malaysia (UKM). He has received his PhD in Postcolonial Literature in English from the National University of Malaysia. His research interests lie at the intersection of literary studies, political theory, and cultural studies. His work addresses questions about identity, representation, colonialism and postcolonialism. He has recently co-edited *Seen and Unseen: Visual Cultures of Imperialism* (Brill, 2018, with Sanaz Fotouhi) and *Reconstructing Historical Memories* (UKM Press, 2018, with Richard Mason).

Introduction: The Rest and Decolonial Epistemologies

Esmaeil Zeiny

As one of the decisive historical occurrences of the twentieth century, the disintegration of European colonies in Africa and Asia altered the world entirely. Between 1945 and 1965, more than three-dozen countries gained independence in both Asia and Africa. This disintegration of European colonies in Africa and Asia may have ended formal colonization, but colonization has not completely ended as we are still battling the vestiges of colonization in thoughts, actions and practices. As Grosfugel beautifully reminds us, 'one of the most powerful myths of the twentieth century was the notion that the elimination of colonial administrations amounted to decolonization of the world.'[1] It is extremely an arduous task to decouple a discussion of colonialism from contemporary episodes that conjure up colonialism such as the 2017 white supremacist movement in Charlottesville, Virginia where hundreds of white supremacists took to the streets and chanted hateful and racist slogans to supposedly defend "white civil rights" demonstrating their levels of intolerance, bigotry and xenophobia. Inherent in the idea of defending "white civil rights" is the belief in what Smith (2006) identified as the three key pillars of white supremacy logics: slavery, genocide and orientalism.[2] In fact, these logics are the continuing traits of western imperialism through which the desire to enslave and objectify non-whites accompanied by the efforts to annihilate their humanity, knowledge systems and languages and identities is conspicuous. Another instance that speaks of the West's desire to rekindle the narratives of empires with a sense of longing for a supposedly better past is the conservative and pro-Brexit British Member of Parliament, Heather Wheeler's tweeting of the map of the world showing former British colonies highlighted in red with the words 'Empire goes for the gold' during the Olympic Games Rio 2016.

Decolonization may have ended formal colonization, but discursive norms have perpetuated to exert dramatic impact, demonstrating themselves in new ways with various longings at different times. The fact that the current

---

1   Ramón Grosfoguel, "The Epistemic Decolonial Turn: Beyond Political-Economy Paradigms." *Cultural Studies*, 21 (2–3) (2007): 219.

2   Andrea Smith, "Heteropatriarchy and the Three Pillars of White Supremacy," in *Color of Violence: The Incite! Anthology*, ed. Incite! Cambridge, Mass.: South End Press, 2006.

world is witnessing the perpetration and perpetuation of colonial inequities and structures of power and epistemology is emblematic of the continuum in the history of colonialism. What is disparate now is just the gravity, scope and method of these colonial practices. The disintegration of European colonies in Asia and Africa along with the consequent perpetration and perpetuation of colonial practices had a dramatic impact upon the uprising of national-ist movements, increased the national historical consciousness, and brought about a worldwide sentiment against colonialism. Since then, discussions and debates over the interrelated issues of Eurocentrism, Orientalism, imperialism, and racism have exhausted themselves. They all have been concerned with the issue of decolonization as a process to emancipate the colonized people from the political, economic, social and intellectual dependency. In today's postco-lonial world, however, colonialism is no longer identified through the politi-cal, economic, and territorial conquest and occupation; it has morphed into invisible patterns of power relations and wormed its way through a delicate deviation of marginalizing the non-western authors, thinkers, concepts and theories.[3] This is "coloniality" which refers to 'long-standing patterns of power that emerged as a result of colonialism, but that define culture, labor, intersub-jective relations, and knowledge production well beyond the strict limits of colonial administrations.'[4] Therefore, coloniality survives the end of direct co-lonialism. This coloniality continues the colonial matrices of power that reside in the lives, minds, imaginations, languages and epistemologies of (formerly)-colonized people and has been extended to other non-western locales that were not directly colonized. Torres reflects the same sentiment and argues that coloniality is:

> maintained alive in books, in the criteria for academic performance, in cultural patterns, in common sense, in the self-image of peoples, in aspirations of self, and so many other aspects of our modern experi-ence. In a way, as modern subject we breathe coloniality all the time and every day.[5]

This explains why the current education system in almost all of the colonized countries is based on western ethos, values, theories and intellectual traditions.

---

3   Syed Farid Alatas. *Alternative Discourses in Asian Social Science: Responses to Eurocentrism*. Delhi: Sage, 2006.
4   Nelson Maldonado-Torres, "On Coloniality of Being: Contributions to the Development of a Concept." *Cultural Studies*, 21 (2–3) (2007): 243.
5   Ibid., 243.

This sort of coloniality, which is the marginalization of non-western authors, concepts and theories, can be traced back to the 17th century *Enlightenment* when it was deemed as the 'project of establishing objective foundations for knowledge that was taken up by such thinkers as Descartes, Locke and, later, Kant.'[6] These scholars sought to institute *reason* as an abstract methodology and as the foundation for justification of knowledge.[7] Emanating from this, emerged the idea that knowledge cannot be comprehended as oral, particular, local and timely in favor of the comprehension of knowledge that was written, abstract, universal and timeless.[8] Whereas these thinkers' perspectives became central to the Enlightenment epistemology, any other epistemological orientations were considered uncivilized, irrational, superstitious, and were therefore marginalized.[9] Christian missionaries were also the initial agents to present European culture, religion, values and knowledge system as the superior and universal way. Through their proselytizing mission, they inculcated the idea of inferiority of non-Europeans and their culture, and universalized the notion of a superior European modernity. This created 'the conditions to build and control a structure of knowledge, either grounded on the word of God or the word of Reason and Truth.'[10] This is how they performed, what Ndlovu-Gatsheni terms as, 'epistemicides.'[11] Having performed these epistemicides, Ndlovu-Gatsheni argues, 'the constructors and drivers of global coloniality that included Christian missionaries, proceeded to make their own patterns of producing knowledge and modes of knowing to be the only legitimate and scientific ways of understanding the world.'[12] These cultural invasions and epistemicides continue to this day.

This coloniality is a structure of discrimination and benefit that keeps maneuvering through time, claims geographic territories and is continued

---

6   Jeanne Kerr, "Western Epistemic Dominance and Colonial Structures: Considerations for Thought and Practice in Programs of Teacher Education." *Decolonization: Indigeneity, Education & Society*, 3 (2) (2014): 88.

7   Richard J. Bernstein. *Beyond Objectivism and Relativism: Science, Hermeneutics, and Praxis.* (Philadelphia: University of Pennsylvania Press, 1983), 115–117.

8   Stephen Toulmin. *Cosmopolis: The Hidden Agenda of Modernity*. New York: The Free Press, 1990.

9   Daneil Carey & Lynn Festa. *The Postcolonial Enlightenment: Eighteenth-century Colonialism and Postcolonial Theory.* (New York: Oxford University Press, 2009), 8.

10   Walter D. Mignolo. *The Darker Side of Western Modernity: Global Futures, Decolonial Options.* (Durham: Duke University Press, 2011), xv.

11   Sabelo J. Ndlovu-Gatsheni, "Why Decoloniality in the 21st Century?" *The Thinker*, February (48) (2013).

12   Sabelo J. Ndlovu-Gatsheni. *Epistemic Freedom in Africa: Deprovincialization and Decolonization.* (Routledge, 2018), 194.

through material and discursive epistemic practices in social and institutional locations. As a systematic structure of power, coloniality and its epistemological architecture reside at the heart of the current world order that can be described as imperialistic, colonialist, Euro-American-centric, violent and racially hierarchized. This world order carries the task of naturalization, normalization and universalization of certain ways of thinking and producing knowledge that are given the name Euro-American-centrism. At the heart of this world order lies epistemic racism. This racism is the hierarchization in accordance with the binarical notions of primitive/civilized, the denigration and marginalization of non-western and their concepts, theories and systems of knowledge, and the accentuation of western philosophy in order to catapult it to the level of universality. This actively disparaging and obstructing non-western approaches to knowledge are what Spivak terms as "epistemic violence."[13] It occurs when power and desire appropriate and condition the production of knowledge, and subjugate the victim through a mechanistic mode. Epistemic violence silences the potential locales of knowledge. It goes even a step further and functions as "palimpsestic" that aims to alter the historical and social narrative consciousness, to erase the original and rewrite it with something considered more appropriate.[14] Imperialism functions covetously as an epistemological *a priori* within knowledge production; and thus denigrates and dismisses non-western epistemology because it is regarded as insufficient, inadequately elaborated and naïve. This subjugation of non-western epistemology is a way of forming and retaining the colonial subject merely as a heterogeneous 'Other.' Thus, decolonization has not yet succeeded in removing coloniality as the legacy of colonialism. In fact, one of the most crucial questions that has constantly engaged scholars and activists throughout the non-western world is how to extricate the non-west from this sort of coloniality or epistemic racism.

This is by no means a new question as the idea that knowledge is also colonized and needs to be decolonized has been an issue of concern since the early seventies. The pioneering formulation came from Syed Hussein Alatas' (1972) concept of "captive mind" during the heated debates triggered by dependency theory.[15] He argues that whereas other forms of dependency such as the political and economic dependency are almost always resisted, knowledge

13   Gayatri Chakravorty Spivak, "Can the Subaltern Speak?" in *Marxism and Interpretations of Culture*, ed. Cary Nelson &Lawrence Grossberg, (Basingstoke: Macmillan Education, 1988), 271–313.
14   Ibid.
15   Syed Hussein Alatas, "The Captive Mind in Development Studies." *International Social Science Journal*, xxiv (1) (1972): 9–25.

dependency not only remained intact after the disintegration of the European colonies but also expanded and promoted. His "captive mind" which arises from the 'overdependence of the western intellectual contribution in the various fields of knowledge'[16] captures our attention about the production and distribution of knowledge described as colonial knowledge and its powerful consequences on the non-western people. Syed Hussein Alatas puts that the western predominance of the production and distribution of knowledge generates a "captive mind" defined as 'uncritical and imitative mind...whose thinking is deflected from an independent perspective.'[17] To diffuse this academic dependency, he proposes the decolonization of knowledge by producing an autonomous Asian social science tradition. Another prominent pioneer scholar who links the coloniality of power in the political and economic spaces with that of knowledge is Anibal Quijano. While introducing the concept of 'coloniality,' Quijano (1992) critiques the complicity between modernity/rationality the central point of which is the 'exclusionary and totalitarian notion of Totality...that negates, exclude, occlude the difference and the possibilities of other totalities.'[18] This "Totality" would silence history, subjugate subjectivities and subalternize knowledge. Resulting from these two pioneer scholars' works are the projects of "decolonization of knowledge," "epistemic disobedience" and "delinking"[19] that open up feasibilities of decoloniality in reconstructing and restituting muted histories, repressed subjectivities and subalternized knowledge and languages.

Over the past decade, decoloniality became the prevailing term coupled with the notion of coloniality and the extension of coloniality of power (economic and political) to coloniality of knowledge. It is borne out of the realization that the world order is asymmetrical and is preserved by the colonial matrices of power including its epistemologies that push the non-western endogenous and indigenous knowledges to the periphery. Decoloniality in this context is premised on the concept of coloniality of knowledge which zeroes in on extracting epistemological issues and politics of knowledge generation,

---

16   Syed Hussein Alatas, "The Autonomous, the Universal and the Future of Sociology." *Current Sociology*, 54 (1) (2006): 8.

17   Syed Hussein Alatas, "The Captive Mind and Creative development." *International Social Science Journal*, (36) (1974): 692.

18   Walter D. Mignolo, "Delinking: The rhetoric of modernity, the logic of coloniality and the grammar of de-coloniality," in *Globalization and the Decolonial Option*, ed. Walter D. Mignolo & Arturo Escobar. (Routledge, 2010), 305.

19   'Delinking' as a concept was introduced and formulated by Egyptian Sociologist Samir Amin (1985) at the level of economic and political delinking. It was advanced by Anibal Qijano in his 1992 article 'Coloniality and modernity/rationality' and was developed further by Walter D. Mignolo.

investigating how knowledge has been exploited to help imperialism and colonialism and 'how knowledge has remained Euro-American-centric.'[20] It is within this vein that decoloniality requires epistemic disobedience and delinking. A delinking that 'leads to de-colonial epistemic shift and brings to the foreground other epistemologies, other principles of knowledge and understanding and, consequently, other economy, other politics, other ethics.'[21] This delinking disrupts and ruptures the hegemonic ideas of knowledge and understanding through denaturalizing the notions and 'conceptual fields that totalize a reality.'[22] It excoriates the so-called universality of a specific ethnicity located in a particular part of the globe, i.e. the West. This delinking critiques the coloniality of knowledge and provides a vision towards the co-existence of many worlds. It builds a politics of knowledge that moves towards what Mignolo terms as a 'pluri-versal world as a uni-versal project'[23] where a 'new inter-epistemic communication' occurs.[24] Delinking is, therefore, crucial because it not only critiques Eurocentrism but it also brings about changes in the terms and contents of the conversation between the West and the non-west; a conversation that has ruled the world for the last five hundred years.

This delinking implies epistemic disobedience that leads us to a set of decolonial projects 'that have in common the effects *experienced* by all the inhabitants of the globe that were at the receiving end of global designs'[25] of colonization. The 'epistemic disobedience...[that] takes us to a different place, to a different "beginning" (... in the responses to the "conquest and colonization" of America and the massive trade of enslaved Africans), to spatial sites of struggles and building...'[26] "Epistemic disobedience"[27] (Mignolo, 2009), "epistemic de-linking"[28] (Mignolo, 2007, 2010) and "epistemic reconstruction" (Quijano, 2007) in this context are all forms of decoloniality that question

---

20   Ndlovu-Gatsheni, "Why Decoloniality in the 21st Century?" 11.
21   Mignolo, "Delinking: The rhetoric of modernity," 307.
22   Ibid., 313.
23   Ibid., 317.
24   Ibid., 307.
25   Walter D. Mignolo, *The Darker Side of Western Modernity: Global Futures, Decolonial Options.* (Durham: Duke University Press, 2011), 45.
26   Ibid.
27   For a comprehensive study of "epistemic disobedience" please see Walter D. Mignolo's "Epistemic Disobedience, Independent Thought and De-Colonial Freedom." *Theory, Culture & Society,* 26 (7–8) (2009): 1–23; and "Epistemic Disobedience and the Decolonial Option: A Manifesto." *TRANSMODERNITY: Journal of Peripheral Cultural Production of the Luso-Hispanic World,* 1(2) (2011).
28   For a detailed study of 'delinking,' please see Walter D. Mignolo's "Delinking." *Cultural Studies,* 21 (2) (2007): 449–514.

the historical dominance of colonial knowledge production and distribution, and contemporary power structures. They are decolonial methodologies that present options for 'confronting and delinking from [...] the colonial matrix of [epistemological] power.'[29] Anchored within such discourse, decoloniality 'struggles to bring into intervening existence an-other interpretation that brings forward, on the one hand, a silenced view of the event and, on the other, shows the limits of imperial ideology disguised as the true (total) interpretation of the events.'[30] This sort of decoloniality destructs the coloniality of knowledge, shifts the geography of reason and geopolitics of knowledge production that instigate the reproduction of racial, gender, and geopolitics of hierarchies but it never aims to replace the 500 years of Western epistemic hegemony. Decoloniality unearths articulations of decolonial epistemologies and reminds the West that "the Rest" has a mind of its own, philosophies of its own and a growing boosting economy of its own. One of the most crucial questions that I believe should be asked before going further with "decoloniality" is "how valid is the West/Rest bifurcation in the current world order?" This binary has never been valid and has been false in and of itself. The "West and the Rest" seems to have involved the principle of "take the best and leave the Rest" as if the West is the best and the Rest is rotten and unpolished. The "West" has been used to describe a society formed by such processes as industrialization, secularization, urbanization, democratization and any sort of development; and what was otherwise would fall under the general idea of the "Rest." This is indicative of the fact that "the West" and "the Rest" have been more than a geographical entity. They have been western constructed notions in which the potentials of "the Rest" have either been overlooked or suppressed, and located outside the epistemic locale. Whereas "Europeans," "Western," and "White" were the hallmarks of epistemic sources, the non-western people, scholars and intellectuals were left outside this epistemic locale. This was the case in the history of coloniality of knowledge. The binary opposition of "the West and the Rest" does not have the same potency that it had once possessed. The Rest[31] now engages in a constructive dialogue with the West and brings them the realization that the West is not the sole epistemic locale from which the globe is described, conceptualized and hierarchized.

---

29   Mignolo, *The Darker Side of Modernity*, xxvii.

30   Walter D. Mignolo, *The Idea of Latin America*. (Malden, MA: Blackwell Publishing, 2005), 35.

31   In using the term 'the Rest,' I have no intention whatsoever of bolstering the false West/Rest bifurcation. I am using it to exhibit that what they termed 'the Rest' is now rising and reclaiming its voice, agency and authority. Thus, my use of the term bears positive connotations.

Decoloniality is, therefore, a double-faced concept that points towards the analytic of coloniality and towards constructing decolonial epistemologies. The first step towards constructing decolonial epistemologies is decolonization of the current western epistemology through delinking. It is through this delinking and epistemic disobedience that "writing-back" emerges and leads us to a "different place" and a "different beginning." The writing-back paradigm involves "revisioning" the view of colonial history offered by the colonial centers, reconstruction of the region and the nation according to the non-western writers' experience, and "rewriting' of canonical stories' in order to undermine the 'assumption of authority, 'voice,' and control of the word' on the part of the Empire.[32] Writing-back interrogates European discourses, investigates the means through which Europe imposed and sustained its codes in the colonial domination of so much of the rest of the world, and finally dismantles the hegemonic discourse of European writing. What is significant in disrupting this European hegemonic discourse is 'rereading and rewriting of the European historical and fictional record' in the construction and reconstruction of regional or national.[33] In the world of literature, writing-back is a counter-discourse 'in which a post-colonial writer takes up a character or characters, or the basic assumptions of a…[western] canonical text, and unveils those assumptions, subverting the text for post-colonial purposes.'[34] Some prime examples of the canonical counter-discourse involve texts such as Chinua Achebe's *Things Fall Apart* (1958) that challenges the European racist assumptions, its cultural superiority, and its economic exploitation of the colonized that exist in European literature such as Joseph Conrad's *Heart of Darkness* (1902); the Caribbean author Jean Rhys' novel *Wide Sargasso Sea* (1966) which revisions Charlotte Bronte's *Jane Eyre* (1847) wherein Rhys gives a voice to Bronte's Caribbean silent madwoman in the attic; and J.M. Coetzees' *Foe* (1986) which can be considered as a write-back to Daniel Defoe's *Robinson Crusoe* (1719).

That "writing-back" is an act of resistance, a recreation and narration of alternative histories raise two important questions: (a) is it an act of textual revenge? and (b) can it stand on its own as it seems to be a product of binary opposition between colonial/postcolonial discourses? To begin with, I reckon it wreaks havoc on our understanding of writing-back paradigm to see it as merely an oppositional strategy or a sheer antinomy between the non-west and the West. What has been oftentimes disregarded is the important role of

32   Bill Ashcroft, Gareth Griffiths and Helen Tiffin. *The Empire Writes Back: Theory and Practice in Postcolonial Literatures.* (New York and London: Routledge, 1989), 97.
33   Helen Tiffin, "Post-colonial Literatures and Counter-Discourse." *Kunapip,* 9 (13) (1987): 18.
34   Ibid., 22.

dialogue that the "writing-back" paradigm bears. Borrowing the term *counter-discourse* from Richard Terdiman (1985),[35] Helen Tiffin (1987) highlights the dynamic qualities of this dialogue between peripheral and metropolitan texts in the "writing-back" contexts. A counter-discourse, argues Tiffin (1987), is dynamic and by no means seeks to 'subvert the dominant with a view to taking its place.'[36] The "writing-back" paradigm speaks either of the racism and oppression of the colonizers or the cultural better-ness of the natives than the ones depicted by the colonizers. It is a reclamation of voice, narrative autonomy and agency. "Writing-back" is not a writing in pursuit of revenge when it is considered a path of decoloniality because decoloniality is against any sort of essentialism and fundamentalism. If the "writing-back" exposes and erodes the stereotypes borne out of essentialism, then the paradigm cannot allow a denigration or superiority of a culture or a group of people. Grosfoguel (2007) corroborates this sentiment and argues that decoloniality 'is not an essentialist, fundamentalist, anti-European critique. It is a perspective that is critical of both Eurocentric and Third World fundamentalist, colonialism and nationalism.'[37] He continues that 'what all fundamentalisms share (including the Eurocentric one) is the premise that there is only one sole epistemic tradition from which to achieve Truth and Universality.'[38] Within this spirit, "writing-back" is not just writing to the metropolis or European colonial centers; the current paradigm also involves fixing the gaze on local forms of oppression and social problems that are seen parallel to classical colonialism.

That is how "writing-back" initiates and engages in a conversation with the West and paves the way for, what Mignolo terms, an 'inter-epistemic and dialogical, [and] pluri-versal' world[39] – a world where epistemic diversity or a dialogue amongst different epistemic traditions is of significance. On the other side of this "writing-back" spectrum is the objection that these texts are just simply reacting and resisting against the dominant ideology. They are marginalized into the idea that they cannot stand on their own and 'are relegated to the status of a mere reaction to imperial textuality, and become a kind of second-class creativity that derives its impetus from Western canon.'[40] It is difficult to

---

35   Richard Terdiman. *Discourse/Counter-Discourse: The Theory and Practice of Symbolic Resistance in Nineteenth-Century France.* Ithaca and London: Cornell University Press, 1985.
36   Tiffin, "Post-colonial Literatures and Counter-Discourse," 18.
37   Grosfoguel, "The Epistemic Decolonial Turn," 212.
38   Ibid.
39   Mignolo, "Delinking: The rhetoric of modernity," 353.
40   Barbara Schmidt-Haberkamp, "The Writing-Back Paradigm Revisited: Peter Carey, Jack Maggs, and Charles Dickens, Great Expectations," in *Fabulating Beauty: Perspectives on the Fiction of Peter Carey*, ed., Andreas Gaile, (Rodopi: Amsterdam-New York. 2005), 247.

deny their relationality and intertextuality but it is also hard to reconcile with the notions of inferiority given to "writing-back" texts. It is important not to reduce the "writing-back" texts to a less creative and reactionary mode. While this relationality is significant to the understanding of the "writing-back" paradigm, it is by no means illustrative of its inferior position. Such hierarchical modalities of knowledge, suggests Aamir Mufti (2005), should be replaced with a 'global comparativism' that comes from the realization that 'societies on either side of the imperial divide now live deeply imbricated lives that cannot be understood without reference to each other.'[41] Reading the "writing-back" texts in this way brings to the surface its inherent dialogical potentiality, which is conducive in understanding that no single center is privileged in establishing norms. "Writing-back" frustrates the emboldening of fallacious narratives that serve to rewrite history and erase the historically sidelined voices. It is not simply a response or writing back to an imperial text but, as Tiffin (1987) argues, to the 'whole of the discursive filed within which such a text operated and continues to operate in post-colonial worlds.'[42] "Writing-back" is, therefore, not just a rewriting or a revisioning of an imperial text; it is rather a construction of decolonial epistemologies.

This brief introduction forms the backdrop of this volume and helps the readers understand how *The Rest Write Back* constructs decolonial epistemologies. This volume draws from the existing scholarship and brings together a uniquely diverse range of global voices that either examine the "writing-back" paradigm or write back with the intention of creating a conversation in order to construct decolonial epistemologies. For instance, Dustin J. Byrd's 'Must Non-Europeans Think Like Us? A Critique of Modern Thoughtlessness in Western and Resten Societies' is a write-back to the historian Niall Ferguson's book *Civilization: The West and the Rest* (2011). By examining the 'night side' of the six killer applications that led the West to dominate the Rest of the world as argued by Niall Ferguson, Byrd exposes the negative and destructive aspects of such developments. Through this unmasking, he exhibits how those six killer applications led to 'metaphysical pessimism, extreme nihilism, and pervasive thoughtlessness.' Byrd puts forward a proposition to shun away from this thoughtlessness in the West and comes up with a way to resist this thoughtlessness in the Resten societies without falling into 'nationalist identity politics or religious extremism.' He believes that the West and the Rest need to construct a new pattern of dialogue through an inter-civilizational discourse which is the sine qua non for making a world where the superior/

---

41   Aamir Mufti, "Global Comparativism." *Critical Inquiry,* 31 (2) (2005): 478.
42   Tiffin, "Post-colonial Literatures and Counter-Discourse," 23.

inferior race, episteme and epistemic locale has no momentum. Within the same line of inter-civilizational dialogue for securing a better world, Rudolf J. Siebert in 'End or Continuation of World History: The European, Slavic and American World – a New Paradigm?' writes of a new paradigm with which the European, Slavic and American World can compete against one another in ending neo-colonialism, racism, predatory capitalism, urban and rural slums, class struggle, the battle of the sexes, Eurocentrism, Orientalism, imperialism, cultural superiority, economic exploitation, poverty, epidemics, and personal and national inequality. Siebert illustrates how these Worlds could prepare for the arrival of a more peaceful, democratic *world republic* in which the Rest and its philosophy can no longer be excluded.

Within the same spirit of producing a paradigm or an alternative way to engage in a conversation for a decolonial epistemology, Mladjo Ivanovic in the next chapter 'Echoes of the Past: Colonial Legacy and Eurocentric Humanitarianism,' steps into an untrodden path of the discourse of humanitarianism. Ivanovic makes it a point to show that the current western humanitarian aid, shaped by the philosophical and value system of Europe and North America system, is nothing short of a continuation of the colonial project. It is no secret that the West uses this humanitarian aid system as an extension of their foreign policy. Their intervention is replete with corruption, discrimination, racism and many other issues that are symptoms of the core illnesses of the current humanitarian system. Ivanovic reveals these shortcomings of humanitarian discourse and practices and through analytical dimension he attempts to 'tease out the epistemic forces, cultural habits, forms of knowledge, skills and expertise that were folded into the ontological organization and form of subjectivity that is at the center of humanitarian attention and "solidarity."' This chapter also illustrates how the encounters between the Western humanitarian agent and Non-Western 'other' takes place. Finally, Ivanovic concludes the essay by proposing an alternative way of 'thinking about responsibility and solidarity.'

Some of the essays in this volume depart from the tradition of "writing-back" to the European colonial center and focus their gaze on local forms of oppression that are seen parallel to classical colonialism. Esmaeil Zeiny's 'Women Refashion Iran: Decolonizing the Rehistoricized Narratives' examines the post-9/11 diasporic Iranian women's autobiographies that present an alternative history of Iran and Iranians. He contends that many of these autobiographies, which write back both to the empire and their own state, are replete with generalizations, selectivity and out-of-context accounts. He calls for decolonization of these rehistoricized narratives and presents instances of counter-discourses that reverse the stereotypical representation of Iran and

Iranian women. This chapter is also a write-back to the narratives that portray Iranian women as submissive and victims of a patriarchal society. He brings this decolonization to its ultimate destination through portraying how Iranian women have been refashioning the country. 'African Literature: Leadership, Plight of the Majority and Hope' by Masumi Hashimoto Odari and Ciarunji Chesaina is another essay in this volume that lends itself to such a reading and departs from the "writing-back" tradition. It explores how the African writers-on behalf of the African masses- write back to the authorities in both colonial and neo-colonial periods through poetry and novels. This essay brings to the surface not only the writings-back to the colonial/imperial center but to the local leaders whose leadership of 'greed and vested interest' take the African masses back to the colonial period. It brings to light the political leaders' 'betrayal of masses' hope' in bringing humane welfare and justice in post-independence Africa.

If there is one characteristic that I could use to lump together all of these essays emerging from different parts of the world, is that they form part of a counter-discourse which has been an essential component of discourse of decoloniality. In her essay 'Aesthetic Hospitality: Mustafa Sa'eed as Guest in Tayeb Salih's *Season of Migration to the North*,' Hiba Ghanem studies the Sudanese author, Tayeb Salih's (1969) masterpiece and argues that it is a counter-discourse of postcolonial discourses on relationship of power. Critics have also pointed out that Salih's novel writes back not only to Conrad's *Heart of Darkness* but also to Shakespeare's *Othello* and *King Lear*. Ghanem, however, studies it from another perspective and uses Derrida's hospitality in investigating the role of the migrant as a guest in the novel. She brings to the fore how the category of the "guest" rewrites the postcolonial categorization of master/slave through the hospitality practices of eating, drinking and poetry recitation. In 'The Rest in the White West: After the Empire is Buried, *Shadows of Your Black Memory* Are Born,' JM. Persánch takes us to another counter-discourse through the last years of Spanish rule in Equatorial Guinea. He explores how the Equatorial Guinean-Spanish writer Donato Ndongo upsets the binarical opposition from within the West in his novel. He investigates how the novel *Shadows of Your Black Memory* can be presented as a counter-discourse to the empire's narratives and as a source of 'resistance, dignity and pride' for the Rest. This chapter also bears a succinct analysis of power relations between the West and the Rest where Persánch argues that the West's new policies, especially those of America's, are shifting the discourse of "the West and the Rest" to "the West vs. the Rest."

The desire to rekindle the narratives of empires with a sense of longing for a supposedly better past is the main subject that the next chapter explores.

Andrew Ridgeway's 'The Topography of Nostalgia: Imaginative Geographies and the Rise of Nationalism' is a study of nativism, right-wing populism, and anti-immigrant sentiment. He illustrates how nostalgia shapes these emerging sentiments. Drawing on Svetlana Boym's (2007) distinction between 'restorative nostalgia' and 'reflective nostalgia,' he argues for a new version of "imaginative geographies" that highlights the 'violent history of colonialism.' Within this vein, he analyzes the Israeli occupation of Palestine and the militarization of the U.S-Mexican border, through the lens of postcolonial literature, to investigate how the current expression of nationalism instigate political nostalgia. This chapter examines Teju Cole's (2012) *Open City* and Gabriel García Márquez's (1967) *One Hundred Years of Solitude* in order to illustrate how literature ruptures the epistemological framework that maintains nationalism.

It is the collective intention of this volume to present ways for "decoloniality" and "epistemic disobedience" in order to continue interrogating the colonial legacies, the contemporary power structure and the geopolitics of knowledge production. These essays provide the readers with decolonial methodologies that confront and delink from the colonial matrix of power. As a complementary collection to Ashcroft, Griffiths and Tiffin's *'The Empire Writes Back'* (1989), Kishore Mahbubani's *'Can Asians Think?'* (1998) and Hamid Dabashi's (2015) *'Can Non-Europeans Think?'* this collection is questioning the epistemic racism underlying the normalization of particular ways of seeing, thinking and producing knowledge that is given the name Eurocentrism. The chapters in here have taken up the task of decolonizing epistemologies through different disciplines as varied as history, philosophy, literature, and critical studies. Thus, at the crux of this collection lies the effort to add to the scholarship of creating new matrixes of knowledge by revealing subjugated knowledge elucidated and elaborated by the authors.

Bibliography

Achebe, C. *Things Fall Apart*. Heinemann, 1958.

Alatas, S.F. *Alternative Discourses in Asian Social Science: Responses to Eurocentrism*. Delhi: Sage, 2006.

Alatas, S.H. "The Captive Mind in Development Studies." *International Social Science Journal*, xxiv (1) (1972): 9–25.

Alatas, S.H. "The Captive Mind and Creative Development." *International Social Science Journal*, 36 (1974): 691–699.

Alatas, S.H. "The Autonomous, the Universal and the Future of Sociology." *Current Sociology*, 54 (1) (2006): 7–23.

Ashcroft, B., Griffiths, G. and Tiffin, H. *The Empire Writes Back: Theory and Practice in Postcolonial Literatures*. New York and London: Routledge, 1989.

Bernstein, R.J. *Beyond Objectivism and Relativism: Science, Hermeneutics, and Praxis*. Philadelphia: University of Pennsylvania Press, 1983.

Boym, S. "Nostalgia and Its Discontents." *The Hedgehog Review*, (2007): 7–18.

Brontë, C. *Jane Eyre*. Oxford: Oxford University Press, [1847] 1975.

Carey, D. & Festa, L. *The Postcolonial Enlightenment: Eighteenth-century Colonialism and Postcolonial Theory*. New York: Oxford University Press, 2009.

Coetzee, J.M. *Foe*. London: Seeker and Warburg, 1986.

Cole, T. *Open City*. New York: Random House, 2012.

Conrad, J. *Heart of Darkness*. New York: Columbia University Press, [1902] 1999.

Dabashi, H. *Can Non-Europeans Think?* London: Zed Books, 2015.

Defoe, D. *Robinson Crusoe*. William Taylor, 1719.

Ferguson, N. *Civilization: The West and the Rest*. New York: The Penguin Press, 2011.

Grosfoguel, R. "The Epistemic Decolonial Turn: Beyond Political-Economy Paradigms." *Cultural Studies,* 21 (2–3) (2007): 211–223.

Kerr, J. "Western Epistemic Dominance and Colonial Structures: Considerations for Thought and Practice in Programs of Teacher Education." *Decolonization: Indigeneity, Education & Society*, 3 (2) (2014): 83–104.

Mahbubani, K. *Can Asians Think? Understanding the Divide between East and West*. Hanover NH: Steerforth Press, [1998] 2001.

Maldonado-Torres, N. "On Coloniality of Being: Contributions to the Development of a Concept." *Cultural Studies*, 21 (2–3) (2007): 240–270.

Marquez, G.G. *One Hundred Years of Solitude*. New York, NY: Harper & Row, 2004.

Mignolo, W.D. *The Idea of Latin America*. Malden, MA: Blackwell Publishing, 2005.

Mignolo, W.D. "Introduction: Coloniality of Power and De-Colonial Thinking." *Cultural Studies*, 21 (2–3) (2007): 155–167.

Mignolo, W.D. "Delinking: The rhetoric of modernity, the logic of coloniality and the grammar of de-coloniality." In *Globalization and the Decolonial Option*, edited by Walter D. Mignolo & Arturo Escobar. Routledge, 2010.

Mignolo, W.D. *The Darker Side of Western Modernity: Global Futures, Decolonial Options*. Durham: Duke University Press, 2011.

Mufti, A. "Global Comparativism." *Critical Inquiry,* 31 (2) (2005): 472–89.

Ndlovu-Gatsheni, S.J. "Why Decoloniality in the 21st Century?" *The Thinker*, February (48) (2013): 10–15.

Ndlovu-Gatsheni, S.J. *Epistemic Freedom in Africa: Deprovincialization and Decolonization*. Routledge, 2018.

Ndongo-Bidyogo, D. *Shadows of your Black Memory*. (M. Ugarte, Trans.). Chicago, Swan Isle Press, (1987), 2007.

Quijano, A. "Colonialidad y Modernidad/Racionalidad." *Peru Indigena*, 13 (1992): 11–20.

Quijano, A. "Coloniality and modernity/rationality." *Cultural Studies*, 21(2–3) (2007): 168–178.

Rhys, Jean. *Wide Sargasso Sea*. London: Deutsch, 1966.

Salih, T. *Season of Migration to the North*. (Denys Johnson-Davies, Trans.). New York: New York Review of Books, [1969], 2009.

Schmidt-Haberkamp, B. "The Writing-Back Paradigm Revisited: Peter Carey, Jack Maggs, and Charles Dickens, Great Expectations." In *Fabulating Beauty: Perspectives on the Fiction of Peter Carey,* edited by Andreas Gaile. (Rodopi: Amsterdam-New York, 2005), 245–263.

Smith, A. "Heteropatriarchy and the Three Pillars of White Supremacy." In *The Color of Violence: The Incite! Anthology*, ed. Incite! Cambridge, Mass.: South End Press, (2006).

Spivak, G.C. 1988. "Can the Subaltern Speak?" In *Marxism and Interpretations of Culture*, edited by Nelson, C. & Grossberg, L. (Basingstoke: Macmillan Education, 1988), 271–313.

Terdiman, R. *Discourse/Counter-Discourse: The Theory and Practice of Symbolic Resistance in Nineteenth-Century France*. Ithaca and London: Cornell University Press, 1985.

Tiffin, H. "Post-colonial Literatures and Counter-Discourse." *Kunapip*, 9 (13) (1987): 17–34.

Toulmin, S. *Cosmopolis: The Hidden Agenda of Modernity*. New York: The Free Press, 1990.

PART 1

Positioning New Paradigms

∴

CHAPTER 1

Must Non-Europeans Think Like Us?
A Critique of Modern Thoughtlessness in Western and Resten Societies

Dustin J. Byrd

1   Introduction

Some years ago while visiting a conservative scholar/friend in Frankfurt, Germany, he told me of a phrase that had recently become in vogue in German academic circles. It states, "philosophy is made in Germany, corrected in Britain, and corrupted in America." As an American philosopher, educated in German philosophy, and perpetually bemoaning the state of philosophy in my native land, I was spontaneously sympathetic with the statement. Nevertheless, upon greater reflection, the insidious nature of the presupposition that the statement rested upon occurred to me: the total disregard not only for the legacy of philosophy in the non-Western world (Resten), but also the tacit assumption that nothing of philosophical importance happens outside of the modern West. Philosophy, it is assumed, is merely an intellectual affair of over-educated Westerners, as if the winds of philosophical knowledge, located with the ancient Greeks, who certainly did not see themselves as "Westerners," only ever blew in one direction. While I'll admit I may be reading more into this sardonic phrase than is originally intended, I contend that its mere existence – as an informing statement of essentialized truth – betrays a tacit yet pervasive Western assumption: non-Europeans cannot think.

In his 2015 book, Hamid Dabashi tackles this assumption, and rhetorically asks, "Can non-Europeans Think?"[1] On the face of it, it is hard to imagine that any intelligent person would argue that non-Europeans lack the human ability to cognitively process information, but it is *not* hard to imagine, especially in the era of xenophobic populism, most acute in Donald J. Trump, Geert Wilders, Marine Le Pen, 5 Star, PEGIDA, Golden Dawn, etc., that someone would argue that non-Europeans are incapable of thinking at the level of an average European or even Euro-American. Indeed, the newest forms of *palingenetic ultra-nationalism,* which has plagued much of the multicultural West in recent

---

1   Hamid Dabashi, *Can Non-Europeans Think?* London: Zed Books, 2015.

years, demonstrates that many Westerners still believe that non-Europeans are not only racially and culturally inferior, but also intellectually inferior.[2] In their view, the non-European is inherently unable to rise to the intellectual and cultural achievement levels of Western civilization, with its liberal values, secular-democracy, and scientific-materialist way-of-being in the world. For example, in 2010, Thilo Sarrazin, a German politician and member of the Social Democratic Party of Germany (SPD), proclaimed that Muslim immigrants in Germany were lowering the intelligence level of the entire country. In his best-selling book, *Germany Abolishes Itself* (*Deutschland schafft sich ab*), Sarrazin argued against Germany's overly generous immigration policy and the failure of multiculturalism, believing that it was destroying the basis of a superior civilization.[3] This sentiment also animated Anders Behring Breivik's far-right and Islamophobic 1,500 page manifesto, *2083: A European Declaration of Independence,* which was made publically available on the same day he bombed Oslo's government district and subsequently gunned down 69 individuals (mostly teenagers) on Utøya island on July 22, 2011.[4] As striking as they are, the sentiments that Sarrazin and Breivik gave voice to are no longer outside of the mainstream public discourse in Europe, as recent elections have demonstrated that many in the West not only sympathize with such xenophobic and neo-fascist sentiments, but are ready to support them politically. For many in the West, the failed policies of integration and assimilation, coupled with religious extremism and terrorism, have proved a reality that was once only spoken in private, at least since World War II: non-European immigrants cannot think, and as non-thinking things, they do not belong to the West, no matter how "assimilated" they are. If they could think, such critics say, they would become westerners beyond mere citizenship. Likewise, they would not demand special privileges and exemptions for their "pre-modern" religious and foreign cultural practices.

Because the question of the non-European's non-ability to think has been raised to a *civilizational problem* by the reemergence of palingenetic ultra-nationalist movements throughout the West, which is not merely a problem of philosophy, as is addressed in Hamid Dabashi's and Walter Mignolo's biting critique of Slavoj Žižek's Leftist-yet-Eurocentric philosophy, this chapter will broaden the inquiry begun by Žižek's critics.[5] From my perspective, it is not merely a problem of thinking *philosophically*, but rather is a problem

2 Roger Griffin, *The Nature of Fascism.* (London: Routledge, 1993), 1–55.
3 Thilo Sarrazin, *Deutschland Schafft sich ab.* München: Deutsche Verlags-Anstalt, 2010.
4 Åsne Seierstad, *One of Us: The Story of Anders Breivik and the Massacred in Norway.* Trans. Sarah Death. New York: Farrar, Straus, and Giroux, 2013.
5 Dabashi, *Can Non-Europeans Think?* iii–xiii.

of thinking itself, especially within the realm of political-economy, culture (broadly construed), and religion (in particular).

In this chapter, I will argue for a different reality than is implied in the Žižek-Dabashi argument, which located the problem of thinking within a discourse of philosophy. As such, I will first critique the trend towards non-thinking in the Western world, which I see as the precondition for palingenetic ultra-nationalism, i.e. new forms of fascism: the apex of *thoughtlessness*. In exploring this, I reformulate the localized question about non-Europeans being unable to think philosophically. The problem, from my perspective, is not that the non-European cannot think, in the conventional sense, but rather the problem is that much of modern Resten "thought" mimics patterns of western thoughtlessness, and thus perpetuates a western epistemological disease: the colonization of the lifeworld by a peculiar way-of-being in the world that reflects Western civilizational presumptions, unarticulated biases and neoliberal interests. In other words, Western forms of calculative thought continue to tacitly colonize non-Western minds at such a rate that a Western "not-thinking worldview" has become dominated within the public spheres of many parts of the non-Western world. This is the case even at times when those Resten nations perceive themselves as being post-colonial, politically independent, and free of Western cultural control. After listing the essential characteristics of modern thoughtlessness, I continue to ask about the possibility of an inter-civilizational discourse, especially in light of the totalizing schema of thoughtlessness in the West and its continuing exportation of thoughtlessness to the Resten world. Here, I'm hopeful, but only if the Resten world can translate its concerns, grievances, values, and principles into a secular language that is accessible to Western civilization. Additionally, if the West, not only its thinkers, but as a civilization, can open itself up to the Resten other, and have a substantive change of consciousness, it may begin to relearn from the other its own communicative resources which were deleted within the encompassing conditions of thoughtlessness. When this symmetrical burden can be achieved, the geographical space for the renunciation of thoughtlessness, the basis of world peace, may prove possible. If not, the world will continue on towards a future saturated with economic exploitation, political totalitarianism, environmental degradation, inter-civilizational tensions, and never-ending war.

2   Was heißt Denken?

In the winter and summer semesters of 1951 and 1952, in the University of Freiburg, Germany, the fascist philosopher Martin Heidegger delivered a series of lectures entitled *Was heißt Denken* (What is called thinking?). In those lectures, he informed his students of a peculiar condition that he saw as being prevalent within moderns. He wrote,

> Especially we moderns can learn only if we always unlearn at the same time. Applied to the matter before us: we can learn thinking only if we radically unlearn what thinking has been traditionally. To do that, we must at the same time come to know it.[6]

By now every reader of Heidegger is aware that his philosophy is thoroughly saturated with his peculiar form of philosophical fascism. The recent release of his "black books," his private ponderings that openly display his vile anti-Semitism, appeals to reactionary romanticism, anti-modernism, and national-istic "authenticity" (*eigentlichkeit*), where there is no need to prove his fascist proclivities. Adorno's 1964 *Jargon der Eigenlichkeit* (Jargon of Authenticity) had already demonstrated that Heidegger's philosophy could not be separated from his fascist thought and politics: they were infused. Nevertheless, Heidegger's romantic suspicion of modern patterns of thought led him to make an insightful point on the rhetorical question of what is *called* "thinking," as ex-pressed in his demand that the "moderns" – and by that term he solely meant "Westerners" – must "unlearn" in order to learn to think.

When Heidegger says "thinking," it is clear that he does not mean mere cognitive processing of information, for even non-humans, let alone non-Westerners, have cognitive processing. Nor does Heidegger mean by the term "thinking," a fleeting interest (*interesse*) in philosophy or other so-called "thought-provoking" material. This temporary concern for a morsel of provoc-ative thought is still under the level of what he would describe as "thinking." What he means by "thinking" is precisely the labor of philosophers, as they are the "thinkers par excellence." In other words, what can truly be called "think-ing" "properly takes place in philosophy," outside of the mere instrumentality of modern cognitive processing.[7] Thus, thinking, in its purest form, gets itself done via philosophy, and as philosophizing-things, philosophers are the true thinking-things, and are the *most human of humans* – as thinking beyond mere cognition is a unique trait of what it means to be human.

This sentiment, I have concluded, is one of the most important veins of thought within Heidegger's Eurocentric framework as it pertains to the thought (or non-thought) of non-Westerners (the Rest), even though Heidegger himself may not have understood the ramifications of his point. Because

---

6   Martin Heidegger, *What is Called Thinking?* (New York: Harper & Row Publishers, 1968), 8.
7   Ibid., 4–5.

the non-Westerner is prejudicially denied the capacity of engaging in philosophy, as it is so understood by western philosophers such as Heidegger (and even assumed by many non-fascist western philosophers), it follows that non-Westerners cannot truly be philosophers, as they cannot think beyond the given and the immediate; they cannot think in universal terms; they cannot separate fact and value, and they cannot think beyond their cultural and/or religious provincialism. If philosophical thinking is the precondition to learning, then the Rest cannot learn either, and thus, at least from a western prejudicial mind, the Rest cannot be a part of western civilization, the society of thought: the society of philosophy.

As a non-thinking thing, the non-Westerner can only relate to the West through their "use value," as a tool, a subordinate, in service to western interests. This is clearly seen in much of the West's "merit" immigration policies: "If you are useful to us, you are welcome. If you are not useful, you may not enter." The immigrants' potentiality – their *entelechy* – counts for little, as it is not already fully realized. Thus, the "usefulness" of the individual is the immediate concern. In such a way, the denial of the "other's" ability to think is a way of integrating the "other" into the *needs system* of the West without allowing the non-identical other to become identical to "the Westerner." As non-thinking-things (since they cannot think philosophically), the non-Westerner is conveniently denied "westernality," which, in the minds of the Eurocentric, is understood as a *particularity* that is nevertheless *universally valid,* while at the same time being inherently prohibited to the universal. Thus, the prejudicial Westerner hypocritically denies that same universality to the "other," no matter how integrated and assimilated they are in western ways-of-being. Thus, the Resten other always remains ensnared in their ontological "otherness," regardless of liberal-enlightenment values and principles that were once declared universal.

Additionally, since philosophical thinking is the work of the philosopher, the *most human of humans,* and the non-Westerner cannot think philosophically (so it is presumed), the full humanity of the "other" is denied, for they cannot appropriate that which makes them fully-human. Thus, the denial of the non-Western other's capacity to fully enter into the abstract discourse of philosophy, is an underhanded way of dehumanizing the Resten "other." Philosophy, once meant to liberate the universal, perversely becomes an ideological tool of the particular to exclude the universal.

In light of this, the underlying anxiety of the West is exposed by the denial of "westernality" to the integrated and assimilated other. Setting aside pre-political foundations, it is possible that the "non-Westerner" becomes more western – with their embrace and identification with essential western norms – than the native Westerners themselves, especially in political thought and philosophy.[8] In other words, the Rest come to embody the thought tradition of the West (as it so defines it, i.e. the philosophical society from Christendom to secular liberal democracy) in such a way that it exposes Westerners' own abandonment of their self-proclaimed universals, especially its Christian-turned-Enlightenment values, principles and ideals. In other words, the West's, but especially Europe's, current identity crisis, includes the destabilizing questions of not only *Was ist der Westen* (What is the West?), and *Was ist denken* (what is thinking?), but also *Was ist westliche denken* (what is western thinking?), and how can the non-Westerner think and embody so-called western "universals" more completely than Westerners themselves. The answers to these questions determine the condition for the possibility of "westernality" of the Resten "other" residing in the West. Thus, the very possibility of a fully "westernized other" induces severe cases of *unbehagen* (uneasiness) in the western world, especially if those who are radically westernized are also devout Muslims, who have found an overlapping consensus between the humanistic universals of Islam and the humanistic universals of the Enlightenment. The fact that many Westerners distrust Resteners, even when they thoroughly embrace and embody so-called "western values," demonstrates that those same values may truly have universality – and as such those universal values are fundamentally separable from an ethnic and national western identity (with its pre-political foundations of race, language, *blut und boden*, etc.). This possibility of a fully realized universality of the Enlightenment causes acute civilizational *anfechtung* (doubt, terror, panic, despair) that such an ethnically-ecumenical Enlightenment could spell the end of European cultural and racial particularity. In other words, Europe could become much "darker" (ethnically), much more diverse (intellectually and religiously), as it embraces the essential universality of its own Enlightenment.

This brings us back to Heidegger's contention about "unlearning," which we must redirect towards the post-secular western society. It appears that the West must now "unlearn" its prejudicial anti-philosophical stance towards the "other" in order to think philosophically about what it means to be "western" in a post-secular modern society, with its own multiculturalism, and its interconnectedness to the rest of the world. "Unlearning" is the painful practice of thinking philosophically – especially dialectically – about western modernity, especially since modernity has flattened both the culture and intellectual heritage of the West while at the same time exporting the West's vilest and

---

8   "Pre-political foundations" are non-political elements that in a matrix serve as the basis for the unique identity of "nations," or a homogeneous people (*Volk*). Such pre-political foundations are race, language, shared history, and religion.

most hypocritical ideologies and political-economic structures to the rest of the world, resulting in the flattening of their particularity with the uncritical adoption of neo-liberalism.

With this in mind, it often appears that the West, as a neo-liberal capitalist post-secular society, which still struggles with the implications of the universal values of the Enlightenment, seems comfortable with resten societies only when they embody the same *abandonment* of critical philosophy and dialectical religion (or at least its *neutralization*) as a determining factor in their societies. In other words, the civilizational anxiety produced by the Rest's appropriation of the so-called "western values," pales in comparison to the pervasive *anxiety* produced by knowing that the Rest may out westernize the West in their appropriation of the West's current economic system: neo-liberal capitalism. For example, in the 20th century, the West waged many wars against those in the non-Western world (and their allies in the West) who were committed to the Marxist Enlightenment, which was the inner-critique of the Bourgeois Enlightenment. Those disillusioned liberals-turned-Marxists who fought to decolonize nations, i.e., to gain independence, justice, liberty, human rights, self-determination, etc., were decimated by the ruling classes in many nations. However, never did the capitalist West fight against those who willingly integrated themselves into the neo-liberal side of the bipolar Cold War. No matter how murderous and destructive they were, they were preferable to the anti-capitalist policies of the Soviet Marxists, Third-World revolutionaries, and Liberation Theologians. Now that the "heir of Marx" is no more, it is not the geopolitical ramifications of revolutionary humanistic solidarity, compassion, mercy, and altruism that the West fears from the Rest, but rather the competition of the resten societies in the realm of merciless private accumulation of collective surplus value, i.e. neo-liberal capitalism, especially the growing economic strength of China and other "emerging" economies. Since the triumph of neo-liberalism in the Cold War, western geopolitical hegemony has prevailed over the globe in a unipolar reality. However, the Rest learned the logic of predatory political-economics from their neo-liberal masters, and thus much of the geographically decolonized Rest have come full circle; they too – by and large – have abandoned (or at least neutralized) their own universal humanistic, solidaristic, and altruistic values – so articulated in traditional religion and culture – in favor of the Western commodity utopia, and have thus joined the western world in its descent into metaphysical positivism, ontological nihilism, and its camouflage: the ever-pervasive and intellectually-slumber-inducing consumer society.

With the reality of neo-liberalism's globalization, we must ask a series of questions: What was the price for liberalism's development in the West? Can the West's experience with this descent into the metaphysical nihilism be predictive of what will happen to the Rest if they so choose to continue to uncritically mimic this colonizing way-of-being? If so, where does that leave inter-civilizational relations in the future?

3   The High Price Paid for Western Modernity

The British historian, Niall Ferguson, argues in his 2011 book *Civilization: The West and the Rest,* that Europe came to dominate the rest of the world in a period beginning around the year 1500, precisely because of a confluence of developments within its own history.[9] These inner-developments allowed Europeans to project their growing power far beyond the geographical boundaries of Europe, and in doing so grew even more powerful. As physical and commercial control of much of the world eventually fell into the hands of various European empires, so too did their cultural, economic and political markers begin to saturate other parts of the world, displacing traditional ways-of-life that had been, in many cases, the dominant modes of existence for millennia. In much of the non-European world, direct colonial control of territory meant a near wholesale displacement of native culture, including religion, traditional arts, traditional social relations, and language, etc. As the Iranian Islamo-Marxist Jalal Al-e Ahmad explained in his book *Occidentosis: A Plague from the West,* when a resten people were afflicted with "Occidentosis," everything *occidental* was valued above all things native. The radical decolonization theorist Frantz Fanon, in his book *Black Skin, White Masks*, discovered the psychological destructiveness that results from the negative valuation of all things "black" (non-European) and the blind valuation of all things "white."[10] This was especially true among the ruling classes in these traditional societies, who, if not directly replaced by the colonial masters, uncritically adopted their way-of-being and often served as their collaborators. What was brought to these parts of the world was a foreign culture predicated on social developments that were unique to Europe (at least in their temporal conflagration), which solely addressed the needs of Europe and reflected their values and cultural norms.

---

9   Niall Ferguson, *Civilization: The West and the Rest.* (New York: The Penguin Press, 2011), 304.

10   Jalal Al-e Ahmad, *Occidentosis: A Plague from the West.* Trans. R. Campbell, ed. Hamid Algar. Berkeley: Mizan Press, 1984; Frantz Fanon, *Black Skin, White Masks.* New York: Grove Press, 2008.

In his historical analysis, Ferguson identified "six killer applications" that were unique to the West, and allowed them to emerge as a global power.[11] These were as follows:

(1) "Competition, in that Europe itself was politically fragmented and that within each monarchy or republic there were multiple competing corporate entities."

(2) "The Scientific Revolution, in that all the major seventeenth-century breakthroughs in mathematics, astronomy, physics, chemistry and biology happen in Western Europe."

(3) "The rule of law and representative government, in that an optimal system of social and political order emerged in the English-speaking world, based on private property rights and the representation of property-owners in elected legislatures."

(4) "Modern medicine, in that nearly all the major nineteenth- and twentieth-century breakthroughs in healthcare, including the control of tropical diseases, were made by Western Europeans and North Americans."

(5) "The consumer society, in that the Industrial Revolution took place where there was both a supply of productivity-enhancing technologies and a demand for more, better and cheaper goods, beginning with cotton garments."

(6) "The work ethic, in that Westerners were the first people in the world to combine more extensive and intensive labor with higher savings rates, permitting sustained capital accumulation."[12]

From a Hegelian perspective, the dialectic of history resulted in the necessary conditions for Europe to expand beyond its borders, ushering in the age of European empires, both industrial and pre-industrial. Without such historical developments, Western Europe would have remained provincial at best. What Ferguson spells out with his "six killer applications" is none other than the basic foundations of western modernity, but Ferguson reads such developments merely through the prism of a *positivist historian*, which systematically neglects the underside of such developments. Modernity, like all other periods in history, is *dialectical*; just as it constructs, so too does it destruct, often via sublation (*aufheben*) and at other times through *abstract negation*. Ferguson, being rooted in the methodologies of positivist historicism, buries the dialectical nature of modernity within his *mere-appearance-ideology* of liberal "progress." This is in contrast to the historical materialist historian and the Critical Theorist, who, like Walter Benjamin, viewed history as the unbroken

11   Ferguson, *Civilization*, 305.
12   Ibid., 305–306.

continuation of a "single catastrophe": history as wreckage piled upon wreckage.[13] It is clear what Europe *gained* by the developments Ferguson identifies. What it lost is less clear amidst the triumphalism of positivist historicism. As not to make that same mistake, we must investigate the night-side of history, for the West's loses are indicative of what *may* be lost if such developments are globalized, or in Ferguson's language, if such "killer applications" continue to be "downloaded" uncritically by the "Rest."[14]

4   The Death of God and Western Freedom

Although it is hard to imagine a modern world without the "six killer applications" that Ferguson identified, it would have been equally difficult to imagine a Europe determined by such monumental developments from the perspective of the theologically saturated medieval European worldview, wherein the basic coordinates of the lifeworld were structured not by that which determines modern life – man as *homo consumens* – but rather by a much more organic set of conditions: the liturgical calendar, the seasons of nature, communal life, and unalienated *habitus factivus* (human productivity). The medieval man, although living in a state of soteriological fear and existential anxiety, nevertheless lived within a reality infused with inherent meaning. His society was constructed in such a way that the individual could rely on the fact that they had an integral place, no matter how seemingly trivial. Since the Divine determined this place in society, the Divine was not oblivious to their existence, but rather took an active role in their life. The seemingly miniscule nature of this existence was ultimately delusional; God was near and determining their life, and in that they took solace. Additionally, morality was absolute; it was not a self-governing form of moral autonomy, nor was it a society of ethical calculations, neither was morality relative to culture, religion, time, etc. Being such, the inherent heteronomic conditions of the medieval society shielded the individual from the terrorizing alternative: Subjective freedom. Although in the modern period, at least since the Enlightenment in the West, freedom is a value highest among all other values, for the medieval man, freedom, as a metaphysical reality, was ontological terrorism, as it destroyed all

---

13   Walter Benjamin, *Illuminations: Essays and Reflections,* ed. Hannah Arendt. (New York: Schocken Books, 2007), 257–258.

14   For Ferguson, it is not a question of whether or not the Rest *will* download the "six killer applications," it is a core assertion in his thesis they have already downloaded such applications, and thus are on their way to catch up to the West in its "progress."

that made life, including suffering, meaningful. The Enlightenment was aimed at "liberating human beings from fear and installing them as masters," but the Enlightenment itself reverted to a totalizing and dominating myth, which only intensified man's existential anxiety – his "being troubled" by his own existence.[15] Post-Enlightenment, disenchantment with the world led the western man to search for that which would slay the chaos and calamity of his metaphysical freedom: a return to unfreedom.

Nietzsche's parable of the *Madman,* and its proclamation of the "death of God," was not a theological statement at its core; it was an existential warning and invitation to freedom camouflaged within an ironic statement meant to shock the reader into contemplating their own ontology and the metaphysical conditions of western modernity.[16] In many ways, Nietzsche's proclamation that the impossible had been made possible, that the immortal – and absolute – had been murdered, is a reflective statement on the very conditions of western society in the mid-to-late 19th century, a time when society, predicated on the "downloading" of the "six killer applications," killed the civilization's ontological foundations: religion, and behind religion, the "totally-other" – the *Absolute* that guaranteed "Truth," be it moral, epistemological, theological, etc. Although religion was not always a source of solidarity in western society, it did maintain the possibility of an inherent meaning within history even amidst the agony of historical catastrophe. Thus, Nietzsche's claim can be read in light of Ferguson's "six killer applications"; competition, the Scientific Revolution, the rule of law and representative government, modern medicine, the consumer society, and the work ethic, were all contributors to the "Death of God"; they were the poison pills from which the traditional medieval holistic religious worldview was destroyed, forever collapsing the West into severe atomism, spiritual vacuousness, moral relativism, and the terror of unbridled freedom.

The murder of God, at least for Nietzsche, meant the death of metaphysical and theological heteronomy. Man was *condemned to freedom* in a world without God; he was finally free to choose his fate within the confines of his time, space and society. He could either choose to continue to follow the heteronomic dictates of a dying religion, and thus submit himself to other-worldly powers beyond his control (which he secretly doubted), or he could seize his

---

15   Max Horkheimer and Theodor W. Adorno, *Dialectic of Enlightenment: Philosophical Fragments,* ed. Gunzelin Schmid Noerr. Trans. Edmund Jephcott. (Stanford: Stanford University Press, 2002), 1.

16   Friedrich Nietzsche, *The Gay Science.* Trans. Thomas Common. (New York: Barnes & Noble, 2008), 103–104.

freedom, emancipate himself from "slave morality," the morality of altruism, meekness, humility, and compassion, and proclaim his autonomy. For the first time, he could truly emancipate himself from the chains of religion and in fact be free, embracing the freedom to transcend the herd's repressive construction of "good and evil."[17] With such an understanding, we can see that the preconditions for the Europeans' so-called intellectual emancipation, including their emancipation from traditional Christian morality, was precisely those conditions that Ferguson identifies as the "six killer applications." Why?

(1)   The ontological destructiveness of political competition, with each monarch and republic claiming the side of God, bred cynicism about the certainty of God's absolutivity. How could God be equally on the side of the believers when the believers are equally against each other? If God was on all sides, then he was on no sides. *Theodicy*, or the question of evil and God's justice, and the inability to answer such a question without degenerating into mere partisanship and intellectual absurdities furthered the demise of the divine and the traditional pre-modern society.

(2)   The scientific revolution furthered the wholesale dismantling of a holistically integrated worldview in Europe precisely because it challenged the church with another epistemological authority; science could provide an alternate understanding of the physical world, its origins, and its formation, without referencing the creative powers of the divine. Against scientific discoveries, religion looked impotent and irrationally recalcitrant. Despite the fact that many of the greatest scientific discoveries to come out of Europe were themselves discovered by faithful men of religion, they nevertheless did not need religious legitimation for those scientific findings. This epistemological shift in regards to the physical world would eventually cause pervasive "disenchantment" (*Entzauberung*) among the once religious masses. The world was Godless and God was worldless.

(3)   The development of secular "rule of law and representative government" meant the decoupling of morality from law. Law became the production of rules predicated on man's reason, not God's commands. As such, man's laws were mutable, often fickle and self-serving. They were temporal, easily replaced, and held no universal consent or legitimation. They lacked the *absolutivity* of divine command. Thus, man, as a self-governor, could craft law in his own image, reflecting his own desires, especially his financial (property) interests. Additionally, what the Divine made illegal, man deemed legal. What the Divine made legal, man deemed illegal, except

---

17   Friedrich Nietzsche, *On the Genealogy of Morals.* Trans. Horace B. Samuel. (New York: Barnes & Noble, 2006), 1–27.

when it served the ruling classes. Thus, *Lex Divina* was dethroned for the benefit of *Lex Humana*. In effect, this kind of human law replaced the Divine in his role as law-giver with the new law-givers: The Bourgeoisie. Consequently, the residue of religiously rooted morality would be forcibly privatized or pushed into civil society, made impotent by its consequent relativity.

(4) Modern medicine also signified a shift in metaphysics. Before modernity, Christians believed that the active agent within "natural medicine" (as opposed to supernatural intervention via saints, relics, etc.) was the Divine. Thus, the Divine healed through medicine. Theologically, medicine itself lacked the inherent properties to heal. Yet, post-Enlightenment, God is unknowable, and therefore his healing qualities are unknowable. As such, it was so discerned that it was ultimately the physical properties of the medicine itself that heals, not the unknowable Divine. The healing power of the divine is thus excommunicated from the notion of healing. Additionally, modern medicine showed concrete results, whereas prayer and other religious rituals invoked as an avenue for healing, remained relatively unsuccessful, thus leading to a shift in faith: the faith in modern materialist medicine.

(5) The result of industrial capitalism and the collapse of a world infused with inherent meaning, the "consumer society" became the new panacea for which to anesthetize the pain of the West's creeping existential nihilism. Life in the West replaced the ontological importance of "being," whether that was rooted in a religious or philosophical worldview, with the trivial yet temporarily satisfying "having" mode of existence: *homo consumens*. No longer was salvation a driving factor in the *sittlichkeit* (ethical life) of the individual; success was this-worldly, and such success meant the maximum accumulation of commodities, an essential component in the West's drift towards societal *necrophilia*.[18] The icy logic of capitalism desacralizes all that was once sacred, undermines all that once bound mankind to itself, and dissolved the hope for something other than what-is-the-case in the cold world of the given. Additionally, as Ferguson infers, the market replaced the divine as fulfiller of needs. In his *Minima Moralia: Reflections on a Damaged Life*, the philosopher Theodor W. Adorno makes an insightful remark on this issue, writing that, "The existence of bread factories, turning the prayer that we be given our daily bread into a mere metaphor and an avowal of desperation, argues more strongly against the possibility of Christianity than all the enlightened

---

18   Erich Fromm, *To Have or to Be?* (New York: Harper & Row Publishers, 1976), 65–80.

critique of the life of Jesus."[19] It is no coincidence that Nietzsche's madman is addressing the men of the market when he proclaims the death of
God; they know they were partially responsible for the excommunication
of faith in the now totally-marketized West.

(6)   Ferguson's sixth "killer application" is the work ethic, which was rooted
       in the 16th century Protestant understanding of work as *beruf* (divine
       calling), and subsequent obedience to the "divine calling" as an act of
       devotion. With the secularization of the western lifeworld, the religious
       aspects of the Protestant work ethic evaporated, leaving behind the now-
       secularized practices of saving, reinvesting, and most importantly, the
       private accumulation of collective surplus value, the *heiliger geist* (holy
       spirit) of capitalism. In other words, the West was on a religious *sonder-
       weg* (deviant path); they elevated monetary profit to that of the "utmost
       concern" in the life of the individual, over all that was once sacred. The
       pursuit of earthly gain, no matter if the means were once considered
       "sinful," drove a society to engage in a form of work that deemphasized
       the family life, the health of the state, and the interconnectedness of the
       community. What became most important was the ever-increasing pro-
       duction of capital, which, through the help of the state, concentrated *not*
       amongst those who worked the hardest, but amongst those who already
       had the most capital. Wealth begets wealth, allowing those who did not
       work to accumulate the wealth of those who did work. In this way, Fer-
       guson is wrong; it was not simply the change in the work ethic that pro-
       duced this pillar of western society, but rather that the surplus value that
       was created by the masses concentrated within a specific part of the pop-
       ulation: The Bourgeois ruling class. It was specifically *their* "capital accu-
       mulation," as Ferguson states, that determined the trajectory of the West.
       For the masses, there was no "capital accumulation," just lives of relative
       poverty, alienated labor, existential misery, and exploitation, which were
       the universal elements of the class struggle that survived the transition
       from the feudal period to the early capitalist period in the West.

As we can see, this great transition from the medieval West to the modern West
meant the loss of a worldview that, while not perfect, sustained the utopian
possibility of a world beyond the world-of-the-given, both in this world and in
the next. The *qualitative* "longing for the totally other," as Horkheimer defines
religion, was replaced with the *quantitative* "longing for the mere here-and-
now," the consumer society that continues to engulf the world in greed, wars,

---

19   Theodor W. Adorno, *Minima Moralia: Reflections on a Damaged Life*. Trans. E.F.N. Jeph-
      cott. (New York: Verso, 2005), 110.

mechanized murder, ecological destruction, and ethical vacuousness. While Ferguson chose to focus upon the benefits of modernity, of which there are many, such as international human rights, international law, modern communications and modern medicine, we cannot forget that modernity brought with it the very possibility of the destruction of the planet and all that it contains: A really-existing apocalyptic possibility, either through nuclear destruction or environmental degradation.[20] *Communicative reason*, that which animates and defines the family, the community, altruism, and the desire to create a world liberated from unnecessary suffering, has been nearly eliminated in the West under the dominant economic and epistemic structures rooted in *instrumental reason*, the calculative logic of *scientism* (science as ideology, not a tool of man's true development), *totalen krieg* (total war), mathematization of human-relations, technification of the lifeworld, and man as means as opposed to ends, etc. This frigid calculating form of reason has become the dominant mode-of-thinking in western civilization since "downloading" the "six killer applications" and the ending of *virtue* as a telos within this life. As Ian Buruma and Avishai Margalit described it,

> To be equipped with the mind of the West is like being an idiot savant, mentally defective but with a special gift for making arithmetic calculations. It is a mind without a soul, efficient, like a calculator, but hopeless at doing what is humanly important. The mind of the West is capable of great economic success, to be sure, and of developing and promoting advanced technology, but cannot grasp the higher things in life, for it lacks spirituality and understanding of human suffering.[21]

While it certainly is not the case that some forms of instrumental reasoning were not present before the West abandoned its religious worldview, it was not the case that such forms of cold calculation were the *dominant schema* of medieval society. As long as the Divine was real, other considerations beyond the advancement of material self-interest had to be considered, for eschatological expectations were a reality even for those who were morally askance.

Yet for critics of western modernity, like the Critical Theorist and psychologist Erich Fromm, it was clear that the Christian values of mercy, charity,

---

20   Jürgen Habermas and Cardinal Joseph Ratzinger, later Pope Benedict XVI, debated this very issue in 2005. The results of their discourse were later published. Jürgen Habermas and Joseph Ratzinger, *Dialektik der Säkularisierung: Über Vernunft und Religion*. Freiburg im Breisgau, Basel, and Vienna: Herder Verlag, 2005.

21   Ian Buruma and Avishai Margalit, *Occidentalism: The West in the Eyes of its Enemies*. (New York: Penguins Books, 2004), 75.

compassion, agape, etc., were ideals that served as powerful interrogators of the really-existing-world, but were in fact never allowed to become the guiding principles of a society, at least not for the ruling classes: Feudal lords, aristocrats, and later the Bourgeoisie. Thus, "Europe's conversion to Christianity," says Erich Fromm, "was largely a sham." He writes,

> At most one could speak of a limited conversion to Christianity from the twelfth to the sixteenth centuries and that for the centuries before and after this period the conversion was, for the most part, one to an ideology and more or less serious submission to the church; it did not mean a change of heart, i.e., of the character structure, except for numerous genuinely Christian movements.[22]

What is implicit in Fromm's argument is the dialectical tension between what Christianity proclaimed *ought* to be the case in the world and what Christians made of the world, which, for Fromm, is inherently hypocritical: religion struggles against its own hypocritical praxis. Because Europe was badly Christianized, it continued to embody the brutality of pre-Christian Greco-Roman values, what Nietzsche called "master morality," which Christianity was never able to fully eradicate in the name of the "Crucified."[23] Despite the Christian veneer, the Aristocratic law of nature, i.e. the natural right of the powerful to dominate and destroy the powerless, the glorification of war, brutishness, selfishness, self-aggrandizement, at the expense of peace, humility, altruism – what Nietzsche called "slave morality," continued unabated throughout Christendom. Western modernity, especially industrial capitalism, put a nail in the coffin of this hypocrisy. Secularized Christian values became a matter of the welfare-state, but even there they were overcome by the imperatives of capitalism, especially in western nations' foreign policies (primarily the United States). Today, the majority of western nations no longer even hold up the façade of Christian *values*, at least not when it comes to the Rest.[24] While politicians in the United States still explicitly invoke the Divine – a practice most Europeans find abhorrent – the resten societies know well the hollowness of

---

22   Fromm, *To Have or to Be?*, 129.
23   Alistar Kee, *Nietzsche Against the Crucified.* (London, SCM Press, 1999), 144–159.
24   One should not confuse the resurgence of Christian "identity" politics in Europe with Christian "values." Indeed, most of those insisting on the Christian identity of Europe have never set foot in a cathedral and would reject the majority of Christianity's traditional "slave morality" (as understood by Nietzsche). Thus, such Christian-identity groups embrace the pagan ethics of Nietzsche's übermensch but disguise it in Christian semantics and symbols.

such religious appeals from their past experiences with Western empires and neo-colonial policies. The moral imperatives of Jesus of Nazareth cannot be found in the weaponized drones, the bombs, the embargos, and the American sponsored *coup d'etats*, not even the imperialistic blond-hair blue-eyed Jesus of past European colonialism can be found in the hegemonic power of the United States and the neo-Czarist Russia of Vladimir Putin.

5   Thoughtlessness in Modernity

So far in this essay, I have referred to "thoughtlessness" (*gedankenlosigkeit*) without giving it a concrete definition. An understanding of what it means to think is already a near-impotent practice in thinking, as it rarely gets us to an understanding of what it means to think within an increasingly thoughtless globalized society. Even Heidegger, in his *Was heißt Denken*, never comes to a satisfactory answer about what it is to think, rather he identifies that which is *called* thinking but cannot, via an ontological analysis, be properly understood rightly as thinking. However, "thoughtlessness," or the absence of true thinking, is much easier to identify, as thoughtlessness appears before us naked as a child on the day of its birth.

At a point in western history, thoughtlessness was a problem of choice. Due to the dialectics of modernity, the individual found himself with the choice to follow its enlightened path, rooted in the communicative reason of prophetic religion, sometimes secularized into revolutionary philosophy and praxis, or they could succumb to the temptation of modernity's night-side, and follow a selfishly deviant path untethered from communicative reason, prophetic solidarity and Socratic non-conformity. However, as the totalizing conditions of modernity's night-side continued to colonize the lifeworld, it became identical with the conditions of western life, within which individuals became less aware of their fading choice, as the condition of thoughtlessness became societally normative. Rooted in the unintended dialectic of Enlightenment, thoughtlessness is in essence, the technocratic, calculative, profit-driven, tyranny of cold instrumental reason, which stealthily invades all levels of society: familial, civil society, and state. Such thoughtlessness reifies the "other," thus reducing human-relations into exercises of strategy, manipulative communication, and distorted discourse, through which the other can be conquered and/or exploited.

"Thoughtlessness," as envisioned above, displays the following characteristics: (1) the systemic *willful abandonment of self-reflexivity* – the refusal to interrogate the self by any meaningful norms and values. It is (2) *amblyopia* to the effects of the actions done by the self and society, especially if such actions call into question the validity of the action itself. Thoughtlessness is (3) the *willful refusal to grant full consideration* to norms and values that have gained universal consent via rational deliberation and discourse. Thoughtlessness is (4) the *abandonment of inter-subjectivity*, which leads to the narcissistic inability to see the self in the other. Thoughtlessness is (5) the lack of *inter-subjective passiology*, the inability to suffer with the suffering other (*compassion*). Thoughtlessness is (6) the inability to see through *mere appearances*, so that the essential nature of things always remains undisclosed, hidden behind a veil of superficiality. Thoughtlessness is (7) the *willful devaluation* of all that is meaningful, transcendent, and other-than-what-is-the-case, as it is episte-mologically beholden to a metaphysical positivist worldview. Thoughtlessness is (8) the *abandonment of the utopian impulse*, the "not yet" and "that which could be" for "that which is" and "must be." Thus, thoughtlessness brooks "no alternative" to what-is-the-case. Above all else, thoughtlessness is (9) the *pervasive unawareness of all that thoughtlessness is*. This pervasive non-awareness of the condition of thoughtlessness is the very condition in which the masses of the West find themselves today, and it is also the precondition for the West's continual domination of the globe, for those who are somnambulant muster no protests against the creeping villainy of exported thoughtlessness, even when such thoughtlessness becomes a threat to their own existence.

The very act of thinking, or at minimum an awareness of the condition of thoughtlessness, is a sign of non-conformity in the thoughtless condition. This is especially acute in the United States of America, where it continues to publicly support the universal fruits of liberal-progressive thought, albeit in a superficial fashion, while actively undermining them at home and abroad through the slumber-inducing culture industry.[25] This thoughtlessness, which is deeply embedded within instrumental reason universalized as the absolute form of reason and knowledge, is precisely what is aggressively exported as modern "progress" throughout the world. As such, thoughtlessness is the most dangerous commodity that the Rest have purchased in their race towards modernization.

As the awareness of what's missing becomes more clear in the desacralized West, many Westerners have turned to anything that will fill the existentially painful void. This "awareness" is also dialectical, and therefore both a positive advancement towards a future reconciliation of the sacred and the profane and a great temptation towards evil, for both can fulfill the void of thoughtlessness.

---

25   Theodor W. Adorno, *The Culture Industry: Selected Essays on Mass Culture*. New York: Routledge, 2001.

6   The Dangers of Thoughtlessness: The Precondition for Palingenetic Ultra-Nationalism

The pervasive absence of meaningful thought, which accompanies modernity's metaphysical-materialism, positivist epistemology, and the preeminence of instrumental reason, creates the conditions wherein the modern western man, having so downloaded the six killer applications, searches for something transcendental by which to fill the void brought about by the evaporation of meaning-producing religion and metaphysics. Such a pervasive void is painful, unbearable, and depressing. The systemic meaninglessness that defines the conditions of industrial and technocratic modernity leave many without any sense of purpose, connectedness, or intrinsic value. Things just "are as they are," and there is no purpose beyond epicurean gratification. For many, the awareness of this stale existence leads them to find meaning in *altruism* (otherism) – the dedication of the self to the wellbeing of others. However, this too is inherently *dialectical*, for the means by which the wellbeing of others is achieved can either be anchored in traditional care ethics, rooted in *agape/ solidarity*, or such wellbeing of the other can be found through much more sinister means. Among the alternatives is *Palingenetic Ultra-Nationalism* and its identification of the enemy – "diabolical otherism."

Wherein Judaism, Christianity and Islam's altruism emphasizes care for the *universal other*, nationalism centers the "natio" (nation) – however it is so defined – as the sole *particular* subject of care. This often comes at the expense of those who find themselves excluded from the nation. These are the "diabolical others," who confront the nation as an existential threat. Nationalism, in this sense, being the deification and idolization of the nation, becomes itself a meaning-producing phenomenon, as it skillfully provides a sacred myth of origin, gives reasons for existing as a nation, and convincingly furnishes an "oceanic feeling" in regards to the nation.[26] As such, the nationalists, so dedicated to the wellbeing of the nation, transcends the meaning-void of modernity, as it provides a prepackaged *interpretation of reality* and decisive *orientation of action*, much like religion before its deflation in modernity. The psychologically once-diminished and isolated modern individual becomes an integral part of the world-historical process, as the advancement of his nation becomes his utmost-concern – his personal means of transcending the ubiquitous nihilism of secular modernity. The once weak and atomized individual becomes powerful once his individuality is subsumed within the collective

---

26   Sigmund Freud, *Civilization and its Discontents.* (New York: W.W. Norton & Co. Inc., 1961), 11.

identity of the nation. The earthly nation becomes the *Novum Deus* (New God) which must be praised and obeyed like the old gods. In the total submission to the will of the New God, the anxiety caused by individual freedom, which accompanied the metaphysical "death of God," allows the nationalist to escape the *anfechtung* of their freedom.[27] He happily abandons his freedom for certainty, security, and a purpose for living. In addition, when such purpose for living is accompanied by a threat from the "diabolical other," the nationalist inevitably develops a siege mentality, a sense that his New God will be defamed and attacked: nationalist blasphemy. And if the nation is destroyed, so too will his sense of purpose, meaning, and identity be destroyed. In his abandonment of individual identity to the collectivity of the nation, he has become psychologically synonymous with the nation, and is prepared to kill and die for that nation without hesitation. Ultimately, for the nationalist, who is no longer an autonomous individual, the nation is not an abstraction. Rather, he experiences the nation simultaneously as he experiences himself. What troubles the nation troubles him; what threatens the nation threatens him; whom the nation fights, so too does he fight. Opposition to the nation is no more a thought for him than is his own suicide, for survival of the nation is his utmost concern. He *is* the nation and the nation *is* him, regardless of what the nation says and does, even if it is against him. Thus, the nationalist abandons autonomous thought, and submerges himself in the singularity of the thoughtlessness of nationalism.

7   Anastasia

What is the power of nationalism? As a way of overcoming the flattened existentiality of modernity, predicated on the night-side of the "six killer applications," nationalism advances a religious-like narrative: A resurrection myth (*anastasia*), which makes it attractive to the powerless. This resurrection of the nation, or *palingenetic myth,* congers the images of Lazarus, raised from the dead, or even Jesus of Nazareth, who was resurrected post-execution; it is the avenging phoenix that rises from the ashes of unjust destruction. Contextually, it is in the chaos of the death of the old order that the power of the palingenetic myth finds itself. In essence, the myth declares the ultimate inability of the "diabolical other" to destroy the preyed upon entity, whether that be death's inability to destroy Lazarus, Rome's inability to destroy Jesus of Nazareth, or one nation's inability to destroy another; the palingenetic sacred story of triumph

---

27   Erich Fromm, *Escape from Freedom.* New York: Henry Holt and Company, 1994.

over adversity – the "rebirth" of that which ought to be permanently dead – gives the nationalist a sense that he himself is reborn within the resurrected nation. Thus, in the face of modernity's thoughtlessness, the rebirth of the nation is the rebirth of the nationalist's *lebensphilosophy* (life philosophy): The unrelenting affirmation of life lived in opposition to that which would deflate the life of the nation.

Here, thoughtlessness shows itself as the precondition for a return to reactionary identity politics. Palingenetic nationalism is an extreme form of thoughtlessness, but a form of thoughtlessness that is attempting to overcome the pain and misery of being powerless within the pervasive conditions of thoughtlessness. In other words, the thoughtlessness of palingenetic ultranationalism is both a symptom of modernity and an attempt to transcend modernity, just as religious fundamentalism is a product of modernity and an attempt to overcome modernity. In that sense, such nationalism, rooted in the palingenetic myth, is the romantic and reactionary fundamentalism of the West – it is its failed attempt to overcome the destructive and life-flattening nature of so-called liberal "progress," as declared by Ferguson's six killer applications.

8   Abandonment of Thoughtlessness and the Conditions of Discourse

This brings us back to the question of the future. Will the Rest, where it uncritically mimics the thoughtlessness of the West, follow the same path of relegating its moral and ethical systems to the dustbin of history in favor of ill-gotten prosperity, or will the "Rest" choose another and more rational path? Will it commit cultural suicide in its own pursuit of western-style modernity, or will the Rest discover *alternative modernities*? The way I see it, the Rest have three options: First, resten societies can choose to retreat from secular modernity, and take comfort in various forms of cultural and/or religious fundamentalism. Fundamentalism, as Jürgen Habermas defines, is the "political imposition of their own particular convictions and reasons, even when they are far from being rationally acceptable."[28] Although this definition of fundamentalism principally concerns religion, it is just as applicable to secular ways-of-being, as it is a "belief attitude" – the *form* of the belief as opposed to its substance – and therefore can be applied to non-religious beliefs as well. In light of the recent terror attacks in Europe, as well as the refugee crisis, both of which have

---

28   Jürgen Habermas in Giovanna Borradori, *Philosophy in a Time of Terror: Dialogues with Jürgen Habermas and Jacques Derrida.* (Chicago: University of Chicago Press, 2003), 31.

highlighted the presence of Islam in post-secular Western Europe, there has been an increase in the claim that Islam and "enlightened" Europe are incompatible by liberal voices, echoing the claims of their neo-fascist counterparts. This liberal "Enlightenment fundamentalism" centers the *particularity* of the European Enlightenment – its outward *western form* – above the *universal substance* that animates the Enlightenment itself. In other words, that which makes the Enlightenment available to all of humanity, has fallen behind European particularity.[29] This option, if resten societies choose to follow it, ends the possibility of the discourse between civilizations, as those who would otherwise enter into a friendly discourse find no discourse partner who will negotiate and/or compromise.

Second, resten societies can proactively engage secular modernity via their own cultural and religious resources – their own semantic and semiotic vocabulary. Yet, this option is accompanied by its own peculiar problems. While preserving authenticity (if I may use that loaded term), and by insisting on equal entrance in an unequal political-economic reality (the West holds most of the determining power), it risks not allowing the "other" into the closed semantic universe of the Rest's culture and/or religion. In other words, if there is no shared vocabulary, no reservoir of shared legitimations and presupposition, then the discourse partners talk past each other. As critics of the West, we could insist that the West "learn" the semantic and semiotic vocabulary of the "Rest," in the hopes that they could come into a discourse with the other through the other's language and cultural signifiers. However, resten political, economic, and moral vocabulary does not animate the current hegemonic neo-liberal world order, and thus discourse within that closed semantic universe – no matter how much it could increase understanding between peoples – would nevertheless remain relatively ineffective in bringing about the necessary changes needed by resten societies. This is the strategy of many conventional Islamists, engaged in the Islamization of their nations via parliamentary politics. While they reject Islamic extremism, their insistence on language rooted within the Islamic tradition effectively bars them from the universal discourse since much of the world cannot find entrance into their particular moral, theological, and juridical lexicon. Thus, they are admired for resisting the fundamentalist temptation, as well as remaining faithful to their cultural roots, but they nevertheless remain on the periphery in international discourse.

---

29   I argue for this claim in my book *Unfashionable Objections to Islamophobic Cartoons: L'affaire Charlie Hebdo.* Newcastle upon Tyne: Cambridge Scholars Publishing, 2017.

Third, resten societies, already familiar with the language and vocabulary of the West, having been colonized by their empires, and later neo-colonized by the neo-liberal world order, have the option of translating their cultural and/or religious semantic and semiotic universes into secular language, i.e. language with non-religious and/or culturally specific legitimation that both the West and the Rest have access to. In this way, the closed semantic universe of the Rest's endangered culture becomes available via shared vocabulary in the discourse between the Rest and the West. In other words, the basis for discourse between those who are not accustomed to listening to the other, can be produced if (1) the power centers in the West (Washington D.C., London, Paris, Brussels, Berlin, Rome), choose to listen, and (2) the Rest choose to translate their closed semantic universe into shared secular vocabulary. This is what Jürgen Habermas calls a "complimentary learning process."[30]

On the face of it, these two demands appear unequal, with the burden predominately laying upon the Rest to desacralize their moral-political language so as to communicate in a "universal" reason-restricted idiom. It is true; if all the responsibilities required to enter into a meaningful discourse laid at the feet of the Rest, then there would be an *asymmetrical burden*. This would be fundamentally unjust, as the asymmetry prioritizes the privileges of the more powerful discourse partner. What then could the burden on the West be? It appears to me that the West's most powerful impediment to discourse with resten societies is its tendency to close itself off from the cultural, political, and economic possibilities emanating from resten societies, including values rooted in communicative reason and religion. In demanding authentic openness from the West, when it is not accustomed to being truly open to the concerns and grievances of the other, requires it to engage in more of a burdensome practice that first realized: *The modern West must begin to learn beyond learning for manipulative reasons*. In essence, it must *unlearn*, as Heidegger said, the way of thinking most associated with night-side of modernity: the domination of instrumental reason and neo-liberal political economics. It must *will* a change in civilizational consciousness, and in doing so abandon the systemic thoughtlessness that has determined its culture, economy, and politics since the triumph of colonialism, capitalism, mechanized mass murder, and the demise of its Abrahamic *sittlichkeit* (ethical order). Before modernity, no matter how badly Europe was Christianized, the core values, principles, and ideals of the non-conformist Jesus of Nazareth, remained ever-present as a potential grand inquisitor to the world-as-it-is. Without such a utopian "other" – or at

---

30   Jürgen Habermas, *An Awareness of What's Missing: Faith and Reason in a Post-Secular Age.* Trans. Ciaran Cronin. (Malden, MA: Polity Press, 2011), 21.

least an impulse towards utopia – against which the already existing society can be critiqued with its own self-professed values – the West merely "is-as-it-is": *There is no alternative* (TINA). Thoughtlessness survives only in the absence of the alternative: dialectical thought rooted in humanistic solidarity. Therefore, in order to enter into this inter-civilizational discourse, predicated on a shared vocabulary, the West's burden is significant: it is a *civilizational shift in consciousness*. It is an awareness of the condition of thoughtlessness and the determination to overcome such a determining condition, before globalized thoughtlessness permanently forecloses upon inter-civilizational discourse, and thus cementing the world in antagonistic relationships.

9   Recovery of the Lost

Outside of the possibility of a real discourse between the West and the Rest, the translation of the Rest's essential ethical, moral, cultural, and religious norms, may, in effect, allow the West to recover that which it had abandoned when it sacrificed its own Christian and secular humanist ethical worldviews for the "six killer applications." In other words, by confronting the West with cultural and religious values translated into humanistic terms that are inherent within traditional religion and culture, the West may – self-reflectively – come to appropriate that which was "irretrievably" lost with the triumph of cold instrumental reason, or what Theodor W. Adorno called the "technification of thought," which was an unintended consequence of the dialectic of the Enlightenment and the "six killer applications."[31] As stated before, there is a growing *awareness of what's missing* in the West, and such awareness is troubling.[32] It is a painful embarrassment to the West that the Enlightenment has yet to answer the ontological and existential questions that have plagued humankind since humankind began to be uneasy with its own existence. Could it be that resten societies, still preserving their core religious and cultural values, principles, and ideals, in the face of pervasive thoughtlessness, may become the conduits of the West's rescue, as it once was when the Muslim world rescued civilization while Europe languished in the Dark Ages, thus laying down the foundations of Europe's own later renaissance (rebirth)? Could the Rest, especially Muslim societies, still in contact with certain prophetic and Socratic values, rooted in its traditional cultures and religions, make a gift to the West of what it once lost? In other words, can the communicative reason of religion,

---

31   Ibid., 15; Adorno, *Negative Dialectics*, 55.
32   Habermas, *An Awareness of What's Missing*, 15–23.

philosophy, family, community, and humanistic solidarity, be translated from the *particular* language of resten societies to *universally accessible* language and be gifted back to the West, so that the West itself can rediscover that which it abandoned in amidst the "progress" of Ferguson's "six killer applications"? True modern "thinking," according to Theodor W. Adorno, "secularizes the irretrievable archetype of sacred texts," thus bringing them into a language accessible to moderns, thus creating the geography for discourse between the West and the Rest.[33] If this is true, we must ask: can such resten societies reanimate the West with the West's own meaning-producing values, not in such a way that the Rest "conquers" or "Islamizes" (as it pertains to Muslims) the West, but rather through inter-civilizational discourse the West rediscovers its own long-evaporated humanistic resources, which are, in essence, identical with that of other societies. In other words, can the West overcome its occidental "idiot-savant" status as a merely machine-making civilization, and come into contact with its own now-forgotten humanistic universals, wherein it can become inclined towards universal human solidarity, self-reflexivity, and inter-subjectivity with the Rest?[34]

10   Conclusion

I claim that the very future of the West depends on whether it can rediscover its own prophetic, Socratic, and humanistic resources via a discourse with the resten other. If it cannot, it will continue down the road towards the destructive romanticism of palingenetic ultra-nationalism, which will lead to its own demise. On the other hand, the Rest have to remain critical of the import of modern western thoughtlessness, for such a plague of occidental instrumental-rationality as metaphysics will eventually undermine resten societies much more thoroughly than the old colonial masters, for such instrumental reason is stealthy, systemic, and hidden behind the ideology of liberal "progress." Its success is predicated on the resten societies own belief that such instrumental reason is unquestionably desirable, since it is a hallmark of modern "progress." But history teaches us that the West has paid an unbearable price for its adoption of instrumental reason, capitalism, and positivism (as metaphysics of what-is-the-case), it has put itself on a *sonderweg* that has cut itself off from much of the world, including its own civilizational roots in ancient Jerusalem, Athens and Rome. It would be a global catastrophe if such thoughtlessness

33   Adorno, *Negative Dialectics*, 55.
34   Buruma and Margalit, *Occidentalism*, 75.

becomes universalized, as its distorted features would serve as the basis of international relations; the approach towards ecology; the framework of economic relations, and the productive force behind cultural norms. Neither the West nor the Rest can afford such thoughtlessness.

Bibliography

Adorno, Theodor W. *The Culture Industry: Selected Essays on Mass Culture.* New York: Routledge, 2001.

Adorno, Theodor W. *Minima Moralia: Reflections on a Damaged Life.* (E.F.N. Jephcott, Trans.). New York: Verso, 2005.

Al-e Ahmad, Jalal. *Occidentosis: A Plague from the West.* (R. Campbell, Trans). Edited by Hamid Algar. Berkeley: Mizan Press, 1984.

Benjamin, Walter. *Illuminations: Essays and Reflections.* Edited by Hannah Arendt. New York: Schocken Books, 2007.

Buruma, Ian and Avishai Margalit. *Occidentalism: The West in the Eyes of its Enemies.* New York: Penguins Books, 2004.

Byrd, Dustin J. *Unfashionable Objections to Islamophobic Cartoons: L'affaire Charlie Hebdo.* Newcastle upon Tyne: Cambridge Scholars Publishing, 2017.

Dabashi, Hamid. *Can Non-Europeans Think?* London: Zed Books, 2015.

Habermas, Jürgen. *An Awareness of What's Missing: Faith and Reason in a Post-Secular Age.* (Ciaran Cronin, Trans.). Malden, MA: Polity Press, 2011.

Habermas, Jürgen & Giovanna Borradori. *Philosophy in a Time of Terror: Dialogues with Jürgen Habermas and Jacques Derrida.* Chicago: University of Chicago Press, 2003.

Habermas, Jürgen & Joseph Ratzinger. *Dialektik der Säkularisierung: Über Vernunft und Religion.* Freiburg im Breisgau, Basel, and Vienna: Herder Verlag, 2005.

Horkheimer, Max & Theodor W. Adorno. *Dialectic of Enlightenment: Philosophical Fragments.* Edited by Gunzelin Schmid Noerr. (Edmund Jephcott, Trans). Stanford: Stanford University Press, 2002.

Fanon, Frantz. *Black Skin, White Masks.* New York: Grove Press, 2008.

Ferguson, Niall. *Civilization: The West and the Rest.* New York: The Penguin Press, 2011.

Freud, Sigmund. *Civilization and its Discontents.* New York: W.W. Norton & Co. Inc., 1961.

Fromm, Erich. *Escape from Freedom.* New York: Henry Holt and Company, 1994.

Fromm, Erich. *To Have or to Be?* New York: Harper & Row Publishers, 1976.

Griffin, Roger. *The Nature of Fascism.* London: Routledge, 1993.

Heidegger, Martin. *What is Called Thinking?* New York: Harper & Row Publishers, 1968.

Kee, Alistar. *Nietzsche Against the Crucified.* London, SCM Press, 1999.

Nietzsche, Friedrich. *The Gay Science*. (Thomas Common, Trans.). New York: Barnes & Noble, 2008.

Nietzsche, Friedrich. *On the Genealogy of Morals*. (Horace B. Samuel, Trans.). New York: Barnes & Noble, 2006.

Sarrazin, Thilo. *Deutschland Schafft sich ab*. München: Deutsche Verlags-Anstalt, 2010.

Seierstad, Åsne, *One of Us: The Story of Anders Breivik and the Massacred in Norway*. (Sarah Death, Trans). New York: Farrar, Straus, and Giroux, 2013.

CHAPTER 2

End or Continuation of World History: The European, Slavic and American World – A New Paradigm?

Rudolf J. Siebert

1 Introduction

In terms of a dialectical religiology, that world history has not come to the end with the modern bourgeoisie, the last man, but that the European World, is being superseded by the American World and the Slavic World, as steps toward a post-modern World Federation and Civil Society, in which the separation between the West and the Rest is overcome, this chapter illustrates that the enlightenment movements and revolutions in the West, from Oliver Cromwell to the American Civil War, were all particularistic in nature. Freedom, Equality, Brotherhood, and Justice were meant for the bourgeoisie of the West, but were denied to the excluded Rest, not only to the clergy and the nobility, but also to the slaves, the wage laborers, the women, the people without property, the Africans, the Asians, the Near Easterners, the American natives, etc. While Europe fought for its own freedom, it brought slavery, colonialism and imperialism to the Rest of the world. The imperialist philosophy of capitalism and free markets for the bourgeoisie prevailed. This essay aims at the universal revolution, which is all-embracing, and includes all people, independent of their race, nationality, gender, or class, and their interests: at post-modern, alternative Future III – the reconciled society, rejecting and opposing post-modern. The Post-European Slavic and American World, the presently leading forces in history, as once were the Egyptians, the Indians, the Chinese, the Persians, the Greeks, the Romans, and the Europeans, must cooperate with each other in the accomplishment of the universal, all-inclusive revolution toward alternative Future III – a world society, in which personal autonomy and universal, i.e. anamnestic, present and proleptic solidarity will be reconciled. This makes a new paradigm within which the Slavic World and the American World can be flexible, can make compromises, and can be creative, and can practice a cooperative and associative model and methodology to solve problems for the common good of humanity, for Mir and Peace, for the West and the Rest, for all people from all continents.

2   Europe

In the perspective of the critical theory of society and religion, or dialectical religiology, around 1800, a system of European equilibrium had formed after Europe experienced a long fluctuation between barbarism and culture. In world history, there has never been a civilization devoid of barbarism.

Europe had been both the center and the geographical limits of the Old World, before the New American and Slavic World appeared at the world-historical horizon. For a millennium, the European World had been the focal point of world history. The *fall of the West* in the 19th, 20th, and 21st centuries, was not the end of world history; there was no return to the past, the Middle Ages, or the Roman, or the Greek, or the Germanic World. World history continues despite the decline of the West and the fall of its empires. There is no need for Muslim fundamentalists to remind the world of this fall; it is self-evident. Contrary to Francis Fukuyama's claim, the European bourgeois is not the last man of history.[1] A new post-European paradigm arises out of the retired European World and its problems: The post-modern, American and Slavic World, which is preparing alternative Future III – a more reconciled and peaceful World Federation and civil society, if alternative Future I – total administration, or alternative Future II – nuclear war, can be avoided.[2] Throughout modernity, Europe had colonized Africa, Asia, the Near East, and America: the West against the Rest! The Europeans gave up their Gothic *Religion of Blood and Soil* and tried to accept the Semitic Christian *Religion of Becoming and Freedom*, and fought the Semitic Jewish *Religion of Sublimity*, and the Semitic Islamic *Religion of Law*.[3] Badly Christened and hardly converted, Europe continually vacillated between the Christ-like and Satanic, with a strong inclination toward the latter up to Auschwitz and Treblinka, Hiroshima and Nagasaki. A common interest bound the European states together, especially after the 7th century: The Muslims and their growing empires, which conquered and absorbed the southern half of Christendom in North Africa and the Middle East for Islam. Millions of Europeans migrated to the American World and to the Slavic World, and brought their culture with them. Thus, world history moved from Asian free universality, through the European particularity, to the

---

1   Francis Fukuyama, *The End of History and the Last Man.* New York: Avon Books, Inc., 1992.
2   Rudolf J. Siebert, *Manifesto of the Critical Theory of Society and Religion: The Wholly Other, Liberation, Happiness, and the Rescue of the Hopeless.* Leiden: Brill, 2010.
3   G.W.F. Hegel, *Lectures on the Philosophy of Religion: Determinate Religion,* ed. Peter C. Hodgson. Oxford: Oxford University Press, 2007.

American and Slavic singularity: the reconciliation of Oriental and Occidental elements.

Eighty years ago, European fascism wanted to make Europe "great again" by colonizing the Slavic World up to the Volga and the borders of Siberia, the Ural, and to leave Africa and Asia to the British Empire. However, the most passionate, fanatical, and extreme fascist, Adolf Hitler, was defeated by the mainly Slavic armies of the Soviet Union (1945CE) like the Crusaders were in Novgorod (1242CE), and like Napoleon was in Moscow (1812CE). Instead of rescuing the European World, Hitler brought the armies of the liberal American World and the communist Slavic World into Thüringia, the very center of Europe: *Point Alpha*. The *cunning of Reason* prevailed.[4] From then on, the Slavic and American World moved into the forefront of the world-historical process, where African, Asian, and Near Eastern states and empires had once ruled, before they moved into historical "retirement," as today European states locate themselves in the quiet niches of history.

In America, the Europeans colonized, and annihilated one race, and enslaved another, as they transformed themselves into Americans. European Protestants settled in North America, and European Catholics colonized Latin and Central America. America became a *land of longing* for all who were bored by the declining armament chamber of old Europe. America became the *land of the future,* in which the world-historical process, and its importance and significance, would reveal itself. The European World declined to the extent that the American and Slavic World developed. In America, the Europeans discovered not only its treasures and its nations, but also nature, and themselves, as well as their destiny. Up into the 19th century, the Slavic World had still masses of serfs, who did the work, and masses of nobility, who ruled. In the 21st century, through the Cold War, the American and the Slavic World were competing, and in some cases cooperating, with each other in all areas of human development and in all parts of the world. However, an Atomic, Biological, and Chemical (ABC) war between the two world-historical powers could mean the end of world history, as both pursued the capacity to annihilate the entire human species. However, such animosity need not had been the only form of competition: Both Worlds could have competed in their struggles to end neo-colonialism, racism, predatory capitalism, urban and rural slums, the class struggle, the battle of the sexes, Eurocentrism, Orientalism, imperialism, cultural superiority, economic exploitation, poverty, epidemics, personal and national inequality, and most of all the exclusion of the Rest by the West.

---

4   G.W.F. Hegel, *Lectures on the Philosophy of History.* Trans. Ruben Alvarado. Aalten, Netherlands: Wordbridge Publishing, 2011.

Both Worlds could learn from each other: The Americans could learn universal, anamnestic, present, and proleptic solidarity from the Russians; and the Russians could learn personal autonomy from the Americans. Together, both Worlds could prepare the world for alternative Future III – a more peaceful, democratic world republic and civil society, with one supreme court, and one international law, and one army, characterized by equality of individuals and nations, as well as by autonomy and solidarity and subsidiarity, as envisioned by the greatest enlightener, Immanuel Kant, and according to the structural models of the United Nations and the European Union.[5] In this way, the negativity of the particular nation-states, the source of all wars of thievery and revenge, which Hegel emphasized against Kant, is to be and can be concretely negated and superseded.[6]

3   Dialectic

According to Hegel, in the expression, *a son of the tribe Koresh,* (bin Quraysh), which is how the Arabs signified an individual of the tribe, lay the idea that this individual was not merely a part of the whole, and that the whole was, therefore, not something outside of him, but that he himself was the whole, which was the entire tribe.[7] It was also clear from the consequence, which it had with such a natural, undivided nation, to make war in its own way, as every individual was slaughtered in the cruelest way.[8] In contrast, in the modern, so-called Christian, or enlightened European World, individuals no longer carried the whole of the state in himself, or herself, as the whole, the tribe. This is precisely because the atomistic and individualistic civil society, including need-system, administration of justice, professional organizations, and police, had moved into the family, including marriage, familial property, the education of children, and the state, including internal state law, or constitution, external state law, and history. Thus the "bourgeois" had stepped over the *citoyen* (citizen). Consequently, instrumental, or functional rationality, as well as functionalist

5   Immanuel Kant, "Perpetual Peace: A Philosophical Sketch," in *Kant: Political Writings,* ed. Hans. S. Reiss. Trans. H.B. Nisbet. (Cambridge: Cambridge University Press, 2001), 93–130.
6   G.W.F. Hegel, *Elements of the Philosophy of Right,* ed. Allen W. Wood. Trans. H.B. Nisbet. (Cambridge: Cambridge University Press, 2010), 360–366.
7   G.W.F. Hegel, *Early Theological Writings.* Trans. T.M. Knox. (Philadelphia: University of Pennsylvania Press, 1971), 260.
8   Ibid.

behavior, overwhelmed mimetic or communicative rationality and action.[9]
In modern European states, it was rather so that the bond among individuals
was a thought, an idea, the constitution. In the European World, there was the
same right for all individuals in the same state, based on *law*, rather than on
love as the family, or on *needs* as in civil society.[10] Therefore, in Europe, war
was made not against the individual, but against the whole, the state, which
lay outside of the individual, located in civil society.[11] Hegel thinks that just
as every other genuinely free nation, it was so with the Islamic Arabs; every
individual was a part, but at the same time also the whole, the tribe, the state.[12]
Only of objects, of something dead, like a machine, was it valid to say that
the whole was something other than its parts. In contrast, in the living organ-
ism, including the spheres of form, assimilation, and species process, the part
was likewise the same as the whole.[13] Only living organisms, subjects, families,
civil societies, states, and nations, not dead machines, could be trinitarian, or
dialectical. When the particular objects as substances, yet retaining its individual quality, were summarized and united in numbers, then their common
denominator, their unity, was only a *notion*, not an *essence*. However, the living
organisms were essences even in their separation from the whole, and their
unity was likewise an essence, its substance.[14] What in the realm of the dead,
the machines, was a contradiction, was not a contradiction in the sphere of
the living. Hegel explains this logic by utilizing the image of a tree: A tree has
three branches, constituted with them together *one* tree, one dialectical process, one trinitarian dynamic, one notion as the unity of universal, particular,
and singular, and one idea as unity of notion, judgement, and conclusion.[15]
But every *son* of the tree, every branch, it leaves and blossoms, was each itself
a tree. The fibers, which lead to the branch, the sap, and the trunk, were of the
same material as the roots. A tree placed upside down into the earth, Hegel
surmises, would drive leaves out of its roots, and likewise the branches would
root themselves into the earth.[16] It was also true that here was only *one* tree,

---

9   Jürgen Habermas, *The Theory of Communicative Action: Reason and the Rationalization
      of Society.* Trans. Thomas McCarthy. Boston: Beacon Press, 1984; Jürgen Habermas, *The
      Theory of Communicative Action: Lifeworld and System: A Critique of Functionalist Reason.*
      Trans. Thomas McCarthy. Boston: Beacon Press, 1989.
10   Ibid.
11   Hegel, *Early Theological Writings,* 260.
12   Ibid.
13   Ibid.
14   Ibid.
15   Ibid.; G.W.F. Hegel, *Hegel's Science of Logic,* ed. H.D. Lewis. Trans. A.V. Miller. (Atlantic
      Highlands, NJ: Humanities Press International, Inc., 1993), 600–704.
16   Hegel, *Early Theological Writings,* 261.

although there appears to be three trees. According to dialectical logic, life has a trinitarian structure. The dialectic is then not an external action of subjective thinking, but rather it is the essence of the content. Thinking, as a subjective action, merely watched the development of the *Notion*, the *Idea*, the tree, the nation, as the latter's own active reasoning, without thinking about its own possible influence on the development. Rationally watching something meant not to bring to the object something from outside a reason, and thereby to work on it, but the object was rational in-and-for-itself.

4   Determinate Negation

"Dialectic" meant the *determinate negation (aufhaben)* of the earlier life form by the later one: The Greek World was determinately negated by the Roman World, the Roman World by the Germanic World, the European World by the American World and the Slavic World, the American and Slavic World by a future World Federation and World Civil Society.[17] Such negation was not abstract, but concrete. It did not only annihilate, but also preserve, and elevate, and fulfill.[18] The negative was also positive. The negativity, the injustices accumulating in the old social system, drove the latter beyond itself, into a new macro-paradigm, which then concretely negated the previous one. Today, for Europeans, the relationship between the two leading regional powers in Asia, China and India, to each other, and their role in Asia, and in the global arena will certainty co-determine decisively the fate of the future world. It is, however, a world in which the formerly embracing power of order, the USA, is right now departing from its world-historical responsibility. But Trumpism, which the dialectical religiology has predicted for decades, may not be America's last word.

After Europe went into retirement, there arose beside America another power of order in the world: The Slavic World. If world history does not move in cycles, but in a more or less linear fashion from Africa, through Asia, to the Middle East, and from there to Europe and eventually to the American and Slavic World and finally a World Federation, then India or China, can as little return to the front of the historical process as Egypt, Greece, or Rome, or Great Britain, or Europe.[19] Quantity alone, populations over one billion persons, like in China and India, do not decide who is at the front of world history. Quality

---

17   Hegel, *Hegel's Science of Logic*, 53.
18   Ibid.
19   Hegel, *Philosophy of History.*

is valid as well. From now on, the Slavic and American World may have to compete for who will deal most adequately with poverty, the position of women in society, the environment, and the economic development, rather than who has more than 4,000 atomic bombs. They will have to compete to demonstrate who can best produce personal autonomy, as well as anamnestic, present, and proleptic solidarity. Whoever will produce the best society will win the loyalty of the *Rest* of the world rather than the *West*. The World, for which solidarity or subsidiarity belong to an obsolete idealism, and for which bourgeois materialism, egoism, selfishness, and narcissism are alone realistic, will fall behind, and will be isolated. The universalistic social state of the Scandinavian type, which admittedly presupposed a high level of solidarity – in the public goods of which all citizens participate on a high *niveau* – renews and strengthens the citizenry's disposition of solidarity, which carries it forward. In contrast to this, the libertarian, the mere residual social state of the Anglo-Saxon type, which only offers meager support for the poor, while the social security of the normal citizens is organized on an individual basis (depending on their given means), initiates a downward spiral of solidarity and readiness to engage in the praxis of social solidarity. It seems that the Slavic World has more solidarity and less autonomy, while the American World has more autonomy and less solidarity.

It is clear that if the world will avoid Alternative Future No. 1 and 2, that both world-historical frontrunners must learn from Europe as well as from each other.[20] That comes to the mind of the dialectical religiologist, after 50 years of travel and work between the American and the Slavic World, through Europe. The European World is the tree from which the American World and Slavic World have branched out and particularized. The pressure of the accumulating injustices of history, has driven millions of Europeans into the Slavic World and American World. Now they determinately negate the old European World, and thus supersede it, destroying as well as preserving and elevating that which could be rescued from the ashes of history. These two leading post-European powers are more than the West, and able to include and promote the Rest, as they move beyond themselves and their antagonism to a higher, more perfect union: a world federation.

5   Trinitarian Dynamic

Immanuel Kant, the subjective idealist and greatest bourgeois enlightener, had been fully aware of the many trinitarian religions in world history, and

---

20   Siebert, *Manifesto*.

he explained them from the trinitarian structure of the human mind. He took from them, and rediscovered, and sublated from the religious to the philosophical level, the principle, category, schema of *triplicity* or *trinitarian dialectic and dynamic.*[21] Kant's student, the greatest idealist, Georg W.F. Hegel, transformed with the help of the idealist, Friedrich W.J. von Schelling, their teacher's still spiritless category and schema of *triplicity*, into his own trinitarian, dialectical notion, as the unity of the universal, the particular, and the singular, and into his own dialectical Idea, as the unity of the notion, the judgement and the conclusion, on which his whole dialectical philosophy was built, and which he also applied to world history.[22] Here, the particular determinately negates the universal, the singular, and the particular. Here the judgement concretely negates the notion, the conclusion and the judgement. Hegel's materialistic disciples and followers from Ludwig Feuerbach, Karl Marx, and Vladimir Lenin, to Max Horkheimer and Theodor W. Adorno, separated the dialectical method from the idealistic content, the notion, Idea, and system; and interpreted and rejected them as mere magic and mythology, and thus became dialectical or historical materialists, who were, nevertheless, willing to retrieve idealistic elements: in terms of an idealistic materialism.[23] They moved from *idealistic notion-dialectic* to *materialistic reality-dialectic*. In this essay, I follow the idealist-materialistic as well as the materialistic-idealistic dialectical methodology, combining notion-dialectic and reality-dialectic. I do this on the presumption that the German materialists, Feuerbach, Marx, and Engels, as well as their followers, negated too abstractly the German idealists, from Kant through Fichte, and from Schelling to Hegel, and their disciples. This lack of dialectics leads to deficiencies in socialist theories and their revolutions of the 19th and 20th centuries, particularly in Lenin's theory and in the October Revolution of 1917, which lead to Stalinism, and *red fascism*, and the victorious neoliberal counter-revolution of 1989, after astonishing victories over the liberal counter-revolution of twelve Western armies against the Soviet Republic in the 1920's and over *Operation Barbarossa*, the fascist counter-revolution of four million Western and Central Europeans (most of them baptized Catholic and Protestant Christians), who killed twenty-six million Russians and six million

---

21   Ibid. Also see Cyril O'Regan, "The Trinity in Kant, Hegel, and Schelling," in *The Oxford Handbook of the Trinity,* ed. Gilles Emery and Matthew Levering. (New York: Oxford University Press, 2014), 254–266.

22   Ibid.; G.W.F. Hegel, *Hegel's Phenomenology of Spirit.* Trans. A.V. Miller. (Oxford: Oxford University Press, 1977), 29–30; Hegel, *Lectures on the Philosophy of History.*

23   Max Horkheimer and Theodor W. Adorno. *Dialectic of Enlightenment: Philosophical Fragments,* ed. Gunzelin Schmid Noerr. Trans. Edmund Jephcott. Stanford, CA: Stanford University Press, 2002.

Jews. Future, humanistic, democratic revolutions need, in order to be more successful, a new paradigm, which will supersede in itself more concretely the German idealism and the German materialism, in order to show a new way toward a future post-European American and Slavic World, as moments in the process toward Alternative Future No. 3: a more peaceful world federation and global civil society.[24]

6   European Equilibrium

Since the reign of the Holy Roman Emperor Charles V, approximately 500 years ago, the Spanish and Austrian monarchies have been disunited. Since 1700 both monarchies were ruled by completely different families. Austria lost large provinces. France and England elevated themselves to the same height and greatness of power. Prussia and Russia had just formed themselves. Thus, around 1800, a system of European equilibrium had formed itself.[25] Europe had become a system, because of which European powers almost always took an interest in war, and every power was prevented from harvesting the fruits of their wars, either alone or in relationship with other nation-states, or in proportion with its achieved advantages. The wars had already in themselves changed their nature to such an extent that the conquest of a few islands, or provinces, cost years of effort and enormous amounts of money, not to speak of the always growing loss of human life. The idea of a European "universal monarchy" (*Dominus Mundi*), or "universal imperium," had always been an empty phrase in Europe. That such a global rule, when a plan for it had been made, was not realized, showed only too clearly the impossibility of its execution, and thus the emptiness and abstractness of this thought. In the 19th century, there could no longer be any talk about such a universal monarchy. Despite this, Austria remained still over-powerful in Germany, i.e. more powerful than any German estate, more powerful even than many of those German estates combined. However, at the same time, Prussia came into this relationship. Austria and Prussia stood in reference to a danger for the German estates on the same level. That what was otherwise called "German freedom," had to be careful in regards to both Austria and Prussia. The Russian and American Worlds were still out of sight for the European super-powers.

---

24   Siebert, *Manifesto.*
25   Hegel, *Lectures on the Philosophy of History,* 372–410.

7 Vacillation

The European World went through a long vacillation between barbarism and culture.[26] In any case, the German state did not accomplish the transition from barbarism to culture, it was rather defeated by the convulsions of this transition from barbarism to culture. The member states tore themselves loose into complete independence. The German state dissolved. The Germans were not able to find the means between repression, or oppression, and despotism, what they called universal monarchy, on one hand, and the complete dissolving on the other. The very Catholic Charles v, the last so-called "universal monarch," resigned from power and withdrew to Valladolid in Spain, and regretted that he had not killed the Protestant reformer Martin Luther, for he had destroyed Charles's Empire and his Church![27] The struggle for German freedom meant negatively the striving against the universal monarchy. Positively, it became the gaining of the complete independence of the member states. These member states stood by their princes. They were one with them. But they had to realize that in the sovereignty of their princes, German freedom was not achieved. In modernity, since the beginning of the Reformation in 1517, more than 500 years ago, the princes triumphed over the universal monarchy, and the unity of the European World remained in jeopardy.

8 Spirit

The spirit of the European World, and later of humanity, *acted* essentially, and it made itself into what it was in-itself, into its deed, into its work, and thus it became object for-itself, and it had itself as an existence before itself.[28] Thus, the spirit of the European World was a determinate spirit, which built itself up into a present world, which stood now and existed, in its religion, in its *cultus*, in its customs, in its constitution, and in its political laws, in the whole extent of its institutions, in its events and in its deeds.[29] That was its work: that *was* this particular European World. What their deeds were, were also understood to be the people. For example, Hegel writes, *Every* Englishman would say: *we*

---

26 Rudolf J. Siebert, *Die Anthropologie Michael Heldings, eines Humanisten und Theologen im Umkreis der Geistigen Neuordnung des 16. Jahrhunderts* (1506–1561). Sigmaringen: Hohenzollernsche Jahreshefte 1965.

27 Eric Metaxas, *The Man Who Rediscovered God and Changed the World.* (New York: Viking, 2017), 433.

28 Hegel, *Philosophy of History,* 68.

29 Ibid.

are those who navigate the oceans and own the world commerce, to whom belongs East India and its wealth, who have parliament and juries, etc.[30] The relationship of the individual to the spirit of the nation, Hegel claims, was that it appropriated to itself this substantial being, that this may become its mental disposition and skill, so that it may be something substantive in the world.[31] The individual found the being of the nation as an already complete, firm world before himself or herself, into which he or she had to integrate himself or herself.[32] Now, in this its work, its world, the spirit of the European World enjoyed itself, and was satisfied in-itself.[33] There was the West, and there was the Rest, the latter being exploited by the former. Thus, the European World grew as it assimilated the Rest: Africa, Asia, Near East, America, and Russia.

9   Contradiction

Seen in the light of Hegel's dialectical philosophy of history, the European World was once moral, virtuous, strong, while it consequently produced what it willed, and it defended its work against external powers in the work of its self-objectification.[34] Hegel argued that the conflict between that, what the European World was itself, subjectively, in its internal purpose and being, and what it really was, was superseded: It was with-itself.[35] It had itself objectively before itself. But later, this activity of the spirit of the European World was no longer necessary; Europe had what it wanted.[36] Europe, Hegel thought, could still do much in war and peace, in the internal and the external, but it was as if the living substantial soul itself of the European World was no longer in action.[37] Therefore, the thorough, highest interest of Europe had lost itself and its life, for interest is present only where there are contrast and contradiction.[38] The European World lived in such a way as the individual, who moves over from the manhood to the old age, in the enjoyment of himself, to be merely what he wanted and could achieve on the strength of his own will and praxis.[39]

---

30   Ibid.
31   Ibid.
32   Ibid.
33   Ibid.
34   Ibid.
35   Ibid.
36   Ibid.
37   Ibid.
38   Ibid., 69.
39   Ibid.

When a man's imagination went beyond this, he had to give up his wants as purpose, because reality did not offer itself to such a purpose; reality was a thus limiting factor upon his purpose.[40] According to Hegel, this *habit – the clock is wound up and moves on by itself –* is what brings about the natural death of the individual.[41] The *habit* is an action without contrast, to which it can be left over to its formal duration, and in which the fullness and depth of the purpose no longer needed to be mentioned; it was merely an external sensual existence, which no longer immersed itself into the thing itself.[42] Thus, individuals and nations die a natural death; when the latter continued for some time, it was only a lifeless existence without interest, which was without the need of their institutions, precisely because the need was fulfilled: a political nullity and boredom.[43] Thus, Hegel argues, if a truly *universal interest (Vorstellung)* should arise, then the spirit of the European World would have to come to the point of willing something new: A *Novum*.[44] But where should this *Novum* come from? It would be a higher, more universal idea of spirit, having transcended beyond its original self.[45] Thereby, a further determined principle, a new spirit, is present, which determinately negates the previous ones. The American World and the Slavic World concretely negated the European Word: first against Napoleon, and then against Hitler.

10   Novum

According to Hegel's dialectical philosophy of history, such a *Novum* comes then into the spirit of a nation, which has come to its completion and realization; It dies not merely a natural death, for it is not merely a singular individual, but a spiritual, universal life.[46] Rather, in it appears the natural death as killing of itself by itself.[47] The reason why this is different from the singular, natural individual, is because the spirit of the nation exists as a *genus (gattung)*.[48] Therefore, the negative of itself comes into existence in itself, in

---

40   Ibid.
41   Ibid.
42   Ibid.
43   Ibid.
44   Ibid.
45   Ibid.
46   Ibid.
47   Ibid.
48   Ibid.

its universality.[49] Thus, for Hegel, a nation can die a violent death only when it has become naturally dead in itself already, as e.g. the old German Empire Cities, or the old German Empire constitution around the year 1800.[50]

The universal spirit dies in general, not merely a natural death; It goes not only into the habit of its life, but insofar as it is a peoples' spirit, which belongs to world-history, so it comes also to the point, to know, what was its work, and to that, to think itself.[51] It is in general only world-historical insofar as in its fundamental element, in its basic purpose, lay a *universal* principle: only insofar is the work, which such spirit produces, a social-moral, political organization.[52] If particular desires, or passions, drive nations to actions, then those deeds pass by without any trace, or their traces are rather only ruin and destruction.[53] Thus, in ancient Greece, first of all *Chronos* (Time) ruled the *Golden Age,* without social-moral works, and what was generated, the children of this Time, were consumed by it itself.[54] First of all *Jupiter* (Heaven), the Atmosphere – in Latin *sub Jove frigido,* the "thundering Father of Gods and men" – the political God, the right and the social morality of the state, the highest power on earth, the God of hospitality, the first Person of the Greek Trinity, who out of his head gave birth to Minerva, or Athena, the third Person of the Greek Trinity, the socio-moral right, the state, to whose circle belonged *Apollo* (Light), together with the Muses, has conquered Chronos, and has put a goal to its passing away.[55] Apollo was the political God, who produced a social-moral work, the state.[56]

11   Protestant States

The Protestant European states, which presupposed the original harmony and unity of religion and state, with its mere formality and lack of content, were thus given room, because of such arbitrariness, to engage in tyranny and oppression. In England, this was particularly true under the last kings from the House of Stuart, where passive obedience was demanded of the population. The Regent was accountable only to God. Besides this, there was the

---

49   Ibid.
50   Ibid.
51   Ibid.
52   Ibid.
53   Ibid., 69–70.
54   Ibid., 70.
55   Ibid.
56   Ibid.

presupposition, that only the Regent knew what was essential and necessary for the state: for in his will lays a more detailed determination, that he was an *immediate revelation* of God. With even further consequences, this principle was developed in such a way that it transformed into its opposite; for the difference of the priest and the layman was not present among the Protestants, and the priests were not privileged to possess the divine revelation. Against the principle of divine authorization of the Regent, there has been posited the principle of the same authorization, that was also fitting for the layman in general: the "priesthood of all believers."[57] Thus, in England, the Puritans, a Protestant sect, asserted that they had been inspired through *revelation* on how to govern. After such inspiration from the Lord, the Puritans, excited by indignation, beheaded King Charles I from the House of Stuart in 1649CE.[58] If in general it was certain that the laws reflected divine Will (*Deus Vult*), then it was just as important to know for certain this divine Will. Knowledge of the divine will was not only for the privileged, but was fitting for all.

12   Enlightenment

In Europe, religion, through the Church, could, concerning the modern antagonism between the religious and the secular, admittedly be prudent and externally accommodating, but then would enter inconsequentially into the spirits of the people and the communities. The European World held onto a particular religion, Christianity, what Hegel called the "Religion of Becoming and Freedom," and hung at the same time on opposite principles, namely principles of the secular, modern, bourgeois, and later socialist, and psychoanalytical enlightenment movements and revolutions. Insofar as Europeans carried out these secular enlightenment principles, and wanted simultaneously to still remain Christian, this was of no consequence, as it lacked dialectics. Thus, the Frenchmen, who held onto the principle of secular freedom rooted in the bourgeois enlightenment and revolution, had indeed ceased to belong to the Roman Catholic paradigm of Christianity, because the latter could not abandon any element of its faith substance, but it demanded in all things

---

57   Alister McGrath, *Christianity's Dangerous Idea.* New York: HarperOne, 2007.
58   The Puritan movement was led by Oliver Cromwell, who was an English military and political leader. He served as Lord Protector of the Commonwealth of England, Scotland and Ireland from 1653 until his death, acting simultaneously as head of state and head of government of the new republic after the execution of King Henry from the House of Stuart.

unconditional submission to the Church and its *Magisterium*.[59] Thus, religion and the secular state stood in contradiction. As such, the state relegated religion to the sidelines of the society. It was forcibly privatized, being only a concern for the individual, family, and civil society, about which the state did not have to concern itself. Additionally, the state banned religion from interfering in matter of the state's constitution, as well as politics and policies in general. Those positing the enlightenment principle of freedom pretended that such principles were the true ones, because they hung together with the innermost self-consciousness of modern man. If it was indeed the reason that founded these enlightenment principles, then it has the verification of reason, insofar as such principles were true and did not remain merely formal (without content), only in that they led them back to the knowledge of absolute Truth, and this was the intended object of their philosophy. This philosophy, however, had to be complete and comprehensive. This was so because when the philosophical knowledge does not fully-realize and complete itself, then it is abandoned to the one-sidedness of *formalism*, the absence of content. In philosophy's full-realization and completion, it came to that what is recognized as most High: God. Thus, philosophy became theology. Therefore, it could well be said, that the state constitution ought to be separated from religion. Nevertheless, because of their contentlessness, the ever-present danger remained that those enlightenment principles remained afflicted by one-sidedness by abstraction, and by untruth. Thus, at present, the Europeans see the world through the prism of the principle of freedom and human rights, as well as for state constitutions: these enlightenment principles were right and true, but they were nevertheless afflicted by the bourgeois formalism; they were mere prejudices. Additionally, philosophical knowledge has not grounded itself in theology – the philosophy of the ultimate ground: there alone was present the reconciliation of the Substantial, Essential, Objective, Idea, Spirit, totally Other than finitude, the horror and terror of nature and history, absolute Justice, and unconditional Love.

13   Republican Constitution

If the historical idealist compared North America with Europe in the 18th, and 19th centuries, then he found there the perennial example of a *republican*

---

59   The *Magisterium* of the Catholic Church refers to its ultimate authority as the sole interpreter of sacred scripture, whether it be in the form of written analyses or manifested in tradition. Thus, the task of such interpretation falls upon the authority of the Pope and his bishops.

constitution. The subjective unity was present in the American Republic, because there stood a President at the peak of the federal state, who in the beginning was elected only for four years as a safety against monarchical ambition and regression. Universal protection of property and almost tax-freedom were facts continually extolled all over Europe, which consequently attracted millions of immigrants. Through this was given the fundamental American character, which existed for the private person, the bourgeois, rather than the *citoyen* (citizen); civil society rather than the political state; toward acquisition and profit; the private appropriation of collective labor; of the predominance of the particular interest, which turns toward the universal only for the sake of its own pleasure. There took place admittedly lawful conditions, a formal positive law of right, but this legality was without moral uprightness. Thus, the American businessmen's reputation was that of a cheat, fraud, and swindler, protected by the positive laws of right, which they, of course, made themselves. This bad reputation survives today, in 2018, in the image of the *ugly American*, which has been revived again by the Trump Administration, and Trumpism, which brings out the worst in the American character and disposition, very much in contrast to the constitution.

14   Trust

When on one hand the Protestant Church in North America gave rise to the faith essential, i.e. *trust*, it rested upon an emotional basis, which was allowed to migrate into the most manifold arbitrariness.[60] According to this American standpoint, Hegel points out that everybody could adopt their own worldview, their own religion, and therefore their own God; the result was the disintegration of the church into innumerable denominations, sects, and cults, each growing deeper in madness and lunacy.[61] This complete arbitrariness is so developed that the different religious communities accept and reject clergymen on a whim.[62] This is so because the Church does not exist as something in-and-for-itself.[63] If it did, it would have a substantial spiritual and external institution, but rather such forms of religion are constituted by individuals' "particular good pleasure."[64] In North America, there dominates the most untamed wildness of imaginations, and all religious unity is missing.[65] Today,

---

60   Hegel, *Philosophy of History*, 78.
61   Ibid.
62   Ibid., 79.
63   Ibid.
64   Ibid.
65   Ibid.

in 2018, over 1,200 Protestant churches, denominations, sects, and cults, have maintained themselves, while in the European states, where the deviations limit themselves only to a few confessions: Catholics, Lutherans, Calvinists. All this diversity has developed in utter contrast to the teaching of the initiator of Christianity, Rabbi Jesus of Nazareth:

> I am not in the world any longer,
> but they are in the world.
> And I am coming to you.
> Holy Father,
> keep those you have given me true to your name,
> so that they may be one like us...
> While I was with them,
> I kept those you had given me true to your name.
> I have watched over them and not one is lost
> except the one who chose to be lost: the son of perdition,
> and this was to fulfill the scripture...
> May they all be one,
> Father, may they be one in us,
> as you are in me and I am in you,
> so that the world may believe it was you who sent me.
> I have given them the glory you gave to me,
> that they may be one as we are one,
> With me in them and you in me,
> may they be so completely one
> that the world will realize that it was you who sent me
> and that I have loved them as much as you loved me.[66]

It is hard to speak about this *Una Sancta* – efforts to unite the churches – in the American World, harder even than in the European World, or in the Slavic World.

15   Universal Purpose

For Hegel, what the political dimension is concerned in North America, so for a long time the universal purpose was not yet posited as something firm for itself, and the need for a firm holding together was not yet present.[67] Such a need for

---

66   Gospel of John 17:11–23.
67   Hegel, *Philosophy of History*, 79.

a real state and a real state government would come into existence only when there was already a difference of social classes in American civil society, when wealth and poverty had become extremely exaggerated, and when a large mass of people could no longer satisfy their needs in ways they had been used to.[68] However, because of its westward expansion, America for a long time did not develop such deep tensions between the social classes, as the masses continually streamed beyond the Mississippi river all the way to California.[69] Through this, the main source of the masses' dissatisfaction disappeared, and the continuation of the present bourgeois condition was guaranteed.[70] Therefore, for a long time, a meaningful comparison of North American free states with European countries was impossible, because in Europe such a natural outlet for the population was not present, despite emigration to America and Russia.[71] If the forests of *Germania* had still existed, the French Revolution would not have happened.[72] North America could only be compared to Europe when the infinite space, which this state offers, was filled, and when civil society would be pushed back into itself.[73] This geographical factor prevents a socialist revolution in bourgeois America in spite of all the urban and rural slums. Thus, the many urban and rural slums continue to prevail.

16   Future

America has been the *land of the future*.[74] Hegel reminds us that its history, perhaps in the many disputes between the North, Central, and South America, or between the American and the Slavic World, reveals its world-historical purpose.[75] America has been, and often still is a *land of longing* for all those people, like Hegel, Goethe, or Napoleon, who were bored by the historical armaments chamber of the old Europe.[76] Napoleon was supposed to have said: '*Cette vieille Europe m'ennuie*' (This old Europe bores me).[77] After the American World, like the Slavic World, had been built from the ground up, world history could take place from the 20th century, through World War I and II, to the present.

---

68   Ibid.
69   Ibid.
70   Ibid.
71   Ibid.
72   Ibid.
73   Ibid.
74   Ibid., 80.
75   Ibid.
76   Ibid.
77   Ibid.

For Hegel, what until then took place in the American or the Slavic Word, was only the echo of the Old World, Europe, and as the expression of a foreign liveliness.[78] As a *land of the future*, it had not been the concern of historians, who are interested in what-has-been, and with what-is.[79] Nor was it of interest for the philosophers, who are concerned with what has neither been, nor will be, but rather with what *is* and what is eternal: With the Reason and Providence of history.[80]

17   Bourgeois Revolutions

In human history, each life form dialectically accumulated its own negativity, out of which developed a new paradigm, which then determinately negated the old one, uniting in-itself the old as well as new elements.[81] The *Glorious Revolution* of Oliver Cromwell and the Puritans in 1688, fed on the injustices of the English feudal system, and initiated the new bourgeois, or capitalist system, which negated concretely the previous one.[82] In 1687, one year before the first bourgeois revolution in England, there was not one house in colonial Boston, however small were its means, that had not one or two enslaved Africans, and even some that had five or six; that was part of the cruelty of the pre-revolutionary 17th century Europe and America.[83] To be sure, this first bourgeois revolution in England was *glorious* only to the slave-trading merchants of England, and their colonial cohorts. For the indigenous people and the slaves, who were victimized throughout the 17th century and beyond, there was no glory in being caught, or enslaved, or shot down by a musket. There was the West, and there was the Rest: its victim.

18   Glorious Revolution

The *Glorious Revolution* of 1688 was indeed a revolution, in that it decapitated King James II of England, and removed the nobility from power, and replaced the first estate, the Anglican clergy, and the second estate, the nobility,

---

78   Ibid.

79   Ibid.

80   Ibid.

81   Hegel, *Hegel's Science of Logic*; Hegel, *Philosophy of History*.

82   Louis Proyect, "Slavery and the Origins of Capitalism." August 23, 2018. https://www.counter punch.org/2018/08/24/slavery-and-the-origins-of-capitalism/.

83   Ibid.

by the third estate, the bourgeoisie.[84] Even when the kings returned after the first bourgeois revolution, they were merely constitutional monarchs, without power, living by the grace of the bourgeois parliament in London. Thus, the revolution was made in the interest of the low, middle, and the high bourgeoisie, and not in the interest of the fourth estate, the workers, or the farmers, or the natives, or the women, not to speak of the slaves. The first bourgeois revolution was, indeed, progressive, in that it produced a new social paradigm, which did away with royal abuse. But the negation of the old order was too concrete, or not abstract enough, in that it preserved not only elements of the old feudal society, but even moments of the older, pre-feudal slaveholder society, the Egyptian, Greek, and Roman Empires, together with their own colonialism. The first bourgeois revolution was progressive as well as regressive; it was a revolution as well as a counter-revolution. The abolishment of slavery, which already had been made under feudalism, was restored again before and after the bourgeois revolutions. Slavery was finally abolished only in the last bourgeois revolution, the American Civil War, in which the Northern capitalist ruling class, annihilated Southern slaveholder ruling class in order to rescue the Union, and thus emancipate the slaves. The Southern prerevolutionary deal – "Give us the Niggers and we'll give you the Quakers" – did not work. The American Union could not endure two ruling classes. The last bourgeois revolution did not only bring the *legal* liberation of the African slaves in the West, at least in theory, but it also initiated the emancipation of the Rest.

19   American Revolution

The so-called "American Revolution" of 1776 was more an emancipation movement of the American colonial bourgeoisie from the British home bourgeoisie, than a real revolution.[85] A revolution means that the ruling class is overthrown by the ruled class. One cannot have a revolution in the same social class: The Boston bourgeoisie against the London bourgeoisie is not a revolutionary struggle. Also, one cannot make a revolution against a king of England, who had already been demoted to a constitutional monarch for over a century. In antiquity, the people living in the colonies had the same rights as the people in the homeland: e.g. the people living in Dubrovnik were the bearers of the same rights as those in Athens. This was not the case in modernity. Colonialism

---

84   Ibid.
85   Please see Howard Zinn, *A People's History of the United States.* New York: Harperperennial, 2003.

and slavery may have been worse in modernity than in antiquity. In any case, in 1776, the American colonial bourgeoisie wanted to sit in Parliament in London, like the English bourgeoisie: "No taxation without representation!" Also, the "Founding Fathers" of the so-called "American Revolution," which acquired this name only in the 1800s, wrote the Constitution in Philadelphia in the interests of the American bourgeoisie, and not for the American workers, farmers, indigenous people, slaves, indentured servants, or women.[86] It was progressive, in that it established a bourgeois republic, but it was too concrete and not abstract enough, and too regressive, in that it preserved too many elements not only from Medieval feudalism, but even from the slave states of antiquity, which remained a problem through the Middle Ages and modernity, up to the approaching end of modernity. Leftwing historians, taking the side of the slaves, the workers, native Americans, women, and the indentured servants, may even call the American Revolution of 1776, a "counter-revolution," taking into consideration the connection between slave resistance and the origins of the United States of America, and thus engage in the debunking of the myths of the American "Founding Fathers" in Philadelphia. These leftist historians engage in *ideology critique*: the myths, or untrue ideology of "democracy," e.g. an accountable and legitimate voting system, of independent media, of an independent judiciary, of a protecting and friendly police, of the happiness of buying, of improvement through hard work, of freedom, equality, brotherhood, social justice, etc.[87] According to Lee Camp, America would collapse if it were not for these myths or ideologies: critically understood as "false consciousness," the masking of bourgeois interests, shortly: the *untruth*. The bourgeois revolutions were not universal, but rather they were particular. There was the West, and there was the Rest, and for the Rest these revolutions did not apply. Yet, particular revolutions produce new ones sooner or later. There will be Thomas Jefferson's particular revolution until the universal revolution is accomplished, which does not only include the West, but also the Rest: the slaves, the workers, the farmers, the women, the dwellers of the global urban and rural slums.

20   Socialist Revolutions

This debunking of the bourgeois-democratic revolutions in the West went against the grain of bourgeois theorists, who were 'overly influenced by the

---

86   Ibid., 77–102.
87   Lee Camp, "American Society Would Collapse If It Weren't for These 8 Myths." July 26, 2018. http://www.informationclearinghouse.info/49928.htm.

bourgeois historians that preceded Marx and Engels,' and who followed the non-dialectical *stagist* conceptions, that 'saw human history as a [mechanical] *escalator* leading upward to advanced civilizations.'[88] The liberal Georg W.F. Hegel, the teacher of Karl Marx, did not, as his bourgeois (and some Marxists, including Louis Proyect) distractors charge, have a non-dialectic, mechanical, "stagist," or escalator theory of history, for which the Prussian state was the most advanced civilization. If Hegel had such a theory, he would not have been posthumously charged with high treason against the Prussian state. Also, for Marx, who did not only read Darwin, but who replaced Hegel's *idealistic* notion-dialectic with his own *materialistic* reality-dialectic, the stages of past history did not always give way automatically to a more enlightened society: with hunters and gatherers mechanically giving way to slavery, and slavery automatically giving way to feudalism, and feudalism mechanically giving way to capitalism, and capitalism automatically giving way to socialism, and socialism mechanically giving way to communism, etc. Dialectics does only fit organisms and living processes, it does not fit dead machines and mechanical processes. For Hegel and Marx, dialectics were not simply a mechanical *giving way*, but rather the organic, determinate, concrete, or specific negation of one historical period by the next.[89] It was rather that the negativity of the old society, its injustices, produced a new social paradigm, which then concretely superseded the previous one, retaining, however, old elements, and adding new ones. The negation of the old order by the new one could be too abstract, and thus preserve too little. Or such negation could be too concrete, and consequently preserve too much, and was therefore no negation at all. In any case, the determinate negation could fail. Regression could always happen. The dialectic contained its tragedies. Revolutionaries could make their hands bloody as they initiated the new and supposedly more moral order. While the bourgeois revolutionaries, who had promised *liberté, égalité*, and *fraternité*, guillotined Louis XVI in Paris, and his Austrian wife, Marie Antoinette and their child; the Soviets in Moscow, who had promised justice, shot Czar Nicholas II and the German Czarina, as well as their five children, in Yekaterinburg. Nothing shows clearer man's tragic condition. Marx knew that capitalism could possibly be followed by socialism or communism, but also by cruelest barbarism. Lenin, the socialist revolutionary, could indeed, as Trotsky wrote, be juxtaposed to the bourgeois revolutionaries Cromwell and Robespierre: 'Lenin is the proletarian 20th century Cromwell.'[90] For Proyect, 'such a definition would be the highest

---

88   Proyect, "Slavery and the Origins of Capitalism"

89   Hegel, *Hegel's Science of Logic,* 711.

90   Louis Proyect, "Slavery and the Origins of Capitalism."

compliment for the petite-bourgeois 17th century Cromwell.'[91] The socialist revolutions followed the bourgeois revolutions, as soon as the fourth estate, the proletarians, noticed that the latter's program of *liberté, égalité, and fraternité* was not universal, it was not meant for them, but rather only for the bourgeoisie. The proletariat suffered the whole of the negativity and injustice of the new bourgeois society, and thus developed their own new paradigm against it, socialism, which would determinately negate it. As such, socialism was the "inner-critique" of the Bourgeois Revolutions. The materialistic dialecticians of the *Frankfurt School* knew that the most desirable alternative Future III – the totally reconciled society, may not happen, and that the undesirable alternative Future I – the entirely administered society, or the even more undesirable, alternative Future II – the totally militarized society, may possibly come about instead.[92] Neither for Hegel, nor for Marx, or the Marxists, was there inevitable and unimpeded progress.

Unfortunately, like the Bourgeois revolutions, the socialist revolutions so far have not been universal. There was socialism in one country, or several countries, and there was the Rest: feudal and bourgeois residuals, nationalities, religious groups, forced labor, etc. The future humanist, democratic, socialist revolutions must not only go beyond the West, but they must also fully include the Rest. They must be truly universal.

21   Destruction

The Post-European American and Slavic World may lead history to alternative Future III – a peaceful world federation and global civil society, or they may lead to alternative Future I – the totally administered, computerized, bureaucratized, nine-lane highway and skyscrapers signal society, based on instrumental rationality, steered through the medium of money and power without any personal or social ethics and morality. They may lead the world with their over 4,000 atomic weapons each, to alternative Future II – ABC wars and mutual, or even global, destruction.[93] The American Senator John McCain, who after he had died from brain cancer in August of 2018, was canonized and made into a national saint by the American media and political establishment, stated in April of 2001 that he hated his enemies, the Vietnamese communists, even before they held him captive in Hanoi Hilton, because hate sustained him

---

91   Ibid.
92   Siebert, *Manifesto.*
93   Siebert, *Manifesto.*

in his devotion to their complete destruction. Such hate helped him overcome the virtuous human impulse to recoil in disgust from what had to be done as bomber pilot over Hanoi during the Vietnam War, which cost the lives of two million Asians, and 58,000 American soldiers, not to count those who committed suicide after coming home.[94] McCain stated in October of 2001, that, however heady the appeal of a call to arms against Islamic terrorists, however just the cause, we should still shed a tear for all that will be lost when war claims its wages from us: shed a tear, and then get on with the business of killing our enemies as quickly as we can, and as ruthlessly as we must.[95] Such statements did not prevent a Christian memorial service for McCain, who had lived a secular life, in the Episcopalian Cathedral in Washington D.C., with all the images of the founder of Christianity, Rabbi Jesus of Nazareth, who had taught:

> You have learned how it was said: you must love your neighbor and hate your enemy. But I say this to you: love your enemies and pray for those who persecute you; in this way you will be sons of your Father in heaven, for he causes his sun to rise on bad men as well as good, and his rain to fall on honest and dishonest men alike. For if you love those who love you what right have you to claim any credit? Even the tax collectors do as much, do they not? And if you save your greetings for your brothers, are you doing anything exceptional? Even the pagans do as much, do they not? You must therefore be perfect just as your heavenly Father is perfect.[96]

The Post-European American and Slavic World must indeed be *exceptional*, if they were to lead humanity toward Post-Modern Alternative Future III – a free and reconciled World Federation, following the model of the UN and the European Union, but having only one army.[97]

22   The Cry of the People

Through the first bourgeois Revolution of 1688 in England, and through the last bourgeois revolution, the American Civil War from 1861–1865, and through

---

94   Joseph Kishore, "The Canonization of John McCain: Media, Political Establishment turn Warmonger into a Saint." September 1, 2018. https://www.wsws.org/en/articles/2018/09/01/pers-so1.html.

95   Ibid.

96   Matthew 5: 43–48.

97   Siebert, *Manifesto*.

the first socialist revolutions in France and Europe in the 19th and 20th century, spreading from here to China, as well as Central and South America, especially Cuba, Nicaragua, Venezuela, and El Salvador, sounds the cry of the oppressed and exploited people: The Rest besides the West.[98] In Latin America and elsewhere, the United States was involved in the rise of fascism. There took place torture, murder, and the persecution of the Catholic Church, in so far as it took sides in the struggle of the poor classes against the capitalist owners of the coffee plantations, etc., and the fascist *Alianza Republicana Nacionalista* (ARENA) Party, who defended their interests. In 1980, Archbishop Romero was murdered by the fascist *ARENA Party* in the *Providence Hospital* of San Salvador.[99] In the meantime, Pope Francis has initiated his canonization process.[100] Six Jesuit priests and teachers, who enlightened the under-paid workers on the coffee plantations about their economic situation, especially the unjust expropriation of their surplus- and labor-value, were murdered by members of the ARENA party. Their housekeeper and her 15-year-old daughter, were likewise murdered by the same men. Nuns, whom I had taught about Christianity, socialism, and fascism at Maryknoll in New York, were raped and murdered in El Salvador by members of the ARENA militia. Liberation theologians died together with 70,000 members of the *Basic Christian Communities*, in the El Salvadoran Civil War. Christians joined socialists in the struggle for justice and freedom. Christians took the *Cross of the Present* upon themselves, not only in order to recognize theoretically the *Rose of Reason and Providence* in it, and to know what was right, as Hegel had suggested, but also in order to break their chains, and practically pluck the flowers of liberation and redemption, and initiate a new paradigm out of the terrible injustices of the old system, in order to determinately negate it, as Marx had demanded.[101] For Hegel and Marx, the negative, the injustices, and all their suffering was also the positive, the beginning of alternative Future III: a free and just society.[102]

---

98   Clara Nieto, *Masters of War: Latin America and U.S. Aggression – From the Cuban Revolution through the Clinton Years*. New York: Seven Stories Press, 2003.

99   James R. Brockman, *Romero: A Life. The Essential Biography of a Modern Martyr and Christian Hero*. (Maryknoll, NY: Orbis Books, 2005), 227–248.

100   Jon Lee Anderson, *Archbishop Óscar Romero Becomes a Saint, but his Death Still Haunts El Salvador*. October 22, 2018. https://www.newyorker.com/news/daily-comment/arch bishop-oscar-romero-becomes-a-saint-but-his-death-still-haunts-el-salvador.

101   Karl Marx, *The Communist Manifesto*, ed. Frederic L. Bender. New York: W.W. Norton & Co., 1988.

102   Siebert, *Manifesto*.

In El Salvador and other Latin American countries, the *apocalypse* of settler colonialism commenced.[103] In all its naked violence, the white supremacy of Europe and America appeared in full force, just as it did in Africa and Asia.[104]

23   Slavery and Colonialism

According to materialist historians, in overthrowing the English Crown through the first bourgeois revolution in 1688, Oliver Cromwell helped at the same time to foster the growth of bourgeois slavery and colonialism.[105] What was good for the West was a disaster for the Rest. As the Marxist Louis Proyect points out, while many bourgeois 'historians have pointed out the scorched earth attack on Catholic Ireland carried out by Cromwell's [Protestant] *Roundheads*, the apocalypse of settler colonialism shines a light on the depravities visited on African slaves, who were never entitled to *whiteness*.'[106] 'This was a gift to the Irish in a world where race would replace religion as a dividing line between the blessed and the damned': the West and the Rest. Proyect argues that under the petite bourgeois revolutionary Cromwell, 'England engaged in one war after another to dislodge the Spanish and Dutch from the Caribbean.'[107] 'If Barbados and Jamaica,' he writes, 'evoke ocean cruise commercials today, these islands were sources of capital in the 17th century, especially through the sugar plantations that had a symbiotic relationship to English colonies in the North,' some of which turned into the United States of America a century later.[108] Proyect continues, 'like cotton's role in the industrial revolution' of the 18th century,

> sugar was essential to the mercantile capitalism of the 17th century.' In the Cromwellian era, lasting from 1640 to 1660, British ships poured into the ports of Barbados and Jamaica to deliver [African] slaves while the sugar cane they harvested was turned into other commodities, including rum, being so marketable in Boston, New York, and London. To exploit

---

103   Gerald Horne, *The Apocalypse of Settler Colonialism: The Roots of Slavery, White Supremacy, and Capitalism in the 17th Century North America and Caribbean.* New York: Monthly Press Review, 2017.
104   Louis Proyect, "Slavery and the Origins of Capitalism." Proyect article is in response to Horne's book, cited in the footnote above.
105   Ibid.
106   Ibid.
107   Ibid.
108   Ibid.

the riches of the sugar colonies and the slave trade that made it possible, a trading monopoly called... *The Royal Adventurers of England* was
formed. As the East India Company was to the plunder of Asia, so was
this intended to pick Africa apart like a vulture. Despite the Roundhead
"revolution" against the English Crown, royalist merchants were eager to
rely on Cromwell's military to dispose of Dutch and Spanish rivals in the
Caribbean.[109]

The historical materialists were skeptical toward the *Roundhead revolution.* It
was a revolution, nevertheless, but not a socialistic one, or a bourgeois one.
In the 20th century, the European fascist states, tried to colonize and enslave
Russia, as the British, the Dutch, and the Spanish had done to Asia, Africa, and
America, just being several centuries too late, and therefore failing. Russia was
rescued from European fascism by its socialist revolution of the 20th century.
The revolutionary class struggles in the West had no advantage for the Rest of
the world. Rather their success was for the Rest a tragedy.

24   Restoration

According to Proyect, after the death of Oliver Cromwell in 1658, the English
monarchy was "restored" and consequently fully committed to the "mercantile capitalist agenda" of the bourgeois politicians, whom it had previously
considered "mortal enemies."[110] 'In a partnership with the Royal Adventurers,'
Proyect writes, 'King Charles II promised 30 acres to any aspiring colonist to
help "settle" Barbados and Jamaica.'[111] Of course, that same sort of promise
was never kept for the freed slaves in the Southern United States, some two
hundred years later. Proyect reminds us that 'New Englanders flocked to Barbados and Jamaica to take advantage of the offer. Between the two islands,
Jamaica was much more attractive since Barbados had been wracked by slave
upheavals, small and large, for decades,' which made it unattractive for white
investment.[112] The Rest were not always passive and silent as it was plundered
by the West; often, as was known about Barbados, slaves attempted to emancipate themselves through violent attacks on white colonists, who consequently
lived in a perpetual state of fear of such events. 'Some [bourgeois] whites fled

---

109   Ibid.
110   Ibid.
111   Ibid.
112   Ibid.

Barbados for the more tightly garrisoned Jamaica, while others went to the mainland, especially to South Carolina.'[113] While King and bourgeoisie cooperated in the West, the Rest, the slaves, freed or unfreed, in Barbados, Jamaica, South Carolina, and wherever else colonialization planted itself, had to pay the price. In Barbados at least, the Rest, the slave revolutions, pushed back against the West: The King and the bourgeoisie alike.

25   Philosophy of Capitalism

The Marxist historian Louis Proyect reminds us that the American state of South Carolina exemplified the acute antagonisms between the West and the Rest in the 17th century, in which the "exemplars of the capitalist," and so-called "democratic" English republic 'regarded slavery as a property right won through Cromwell's [petite] bourgeois revolution.'[114]

> The Royal Adventurers of England had been transformed into the Royal African Company that retained its worst features. It was led by the Duke of York, whose name was bequeathed to the Island called New Amsterdam, seized from the Dutch earlier in the century. Among the chief investors in this trade monopoly was John Locke who served as the secretary to the board of governors in South Carolina.[115]

Locke expressed the purpose of his philosophical enterprise in words, which could also be found in the philosophical work of Immanuel Kant, the subjective idealist, and greatest bourgeois enlightener.[116] The bourgeois, Kantian philosophy can be seen as an extension of the Lockean philosophy of liberalism. Locke and Hume have as the primordial and fundamental empiricists immersed the philosophizing into material finitude and subjectivity. They tried to explain the world from the standpoint of the material, sensuous subject. They tried to derive materialistically the thought out of the immediately given of the world of appearances. For Locke, as for all empiricists, thinking had only the meaning of abstraction and formal identity. Locke's thought, that we abstract the true from experience, was a most trivial one. Locke, Spinoza, and Leibniz constituted the metaphysics of the time. Locke and Leibniz disputed

---

113 Ibid.
114 Ibid.
115 Ibid.
116 Ibid.

over the inborn ideas. According to Locke, the singular was the first, out of which the universal was formed. Locke and Leibniz, both standing for themselves and opposed to each other, made the singular into the principle. Locke carried further the thought of Francis Bacon, who also started from experience and induction. Locke elevated against the stiff and rigid unity of the Spinozistic Substance the singularities of the perception into the Universal.[117] For Locke, finite knowledge was the first. Locke was concerned with knowing the universal, the general ideas, the representations in general. For Locke, the truth only had meaning when there was an agreement between human perceptions and the perceived things.[118] Locke's philosophy was highly honored in bourgeois, capitalistic Europe. Being the philosophy of the English, the French, and the Germans, it was still honored in the 19th and 20th century. Locke taught that universal representation, truth and knowledge, rested on experience; the dialectical representation was left behind: the truth in general. Locke's philosophy was particularly directed against René Descartes. Locke held on, against Aristotle, to the representation of the soul as a contentless *tabula rasa*.[119] All knowledge was grounded in experiences, which were first of all sensations. Locke held on to appearances, and in doing so abandoned completely the primary purpose of philosophy. There could be nothing more superficial than Locke's derivation of the ideas from experience, sensations, and appearances. The ideology of the Frenchmen contained nothing else. Locke was far back in the history of knowledge: behind even Plato. Locke has no idea of the speculative, the dialectical. Thus, Locke's empiricism is the metaphysics of the representations in his time. It is the philosophy of the West against the Rest: the colonized, the slaves, and the workers.

26   Negro Slaves

Locke, the father of liberalism, and the possible author of the South Carolina Constitution, stipulated that 'Every freeman of Carolina shall have absolute power and authority over his negro slaves, of what opinion or religion so ever.'[120] Very few doubt that the eminent philosopher 'considered chattel slavery to be permissible despite the case he made against slavery in his Second

117   G.W.F. Hegel, "Metaphysics of Understanding: Locke" https://www.marxists.org/reference/archive/hegel/works/hp/hplocke.htm.

118   Ibid.

119   Ibid.

120   Proyect, "Slavery and the Origins of Capitalism."

Treatise on Government, which was likely directed against the Ottoman Turks' who often enslaved white people.[121] According to Proyect, following the thought of Ellen Meiksins Wood, the liberal Locke was the 'quintessential philosopher of capitalism,' an economic system ideologically defined as being 'based on free wage labor rather than forced labor.'[122] The evidence gathered in Gerald Horne's book, *The Apocalypse of Settler Colonialism,* 'indicates that the 17th century was not exactly the great leap forward an [liberal] escalator theory of history was predicated on.'[123] In any case, a leap for the West, was not yet a leap for the Rest.[124]

27   Consolidation

Following Horne's research, Proyect argues that the "glorious revolution of 1688" was 'nothing less than the consolidation of a mercantile capitalism that allowed the United Kingdom to rule the world': the Rest in the name of the West.[125] 'Even if [a bourgeois] Parliament was preferable to absolutist rule by family dynasties,' the price imposed on the Rest, particularly Africa, Asia, Near East and America, 'made the notion of "unqualified progress" sound hollow.'

According to Proyect, from the glorious revolution of 1688, 'conflicts grew between the British slave-owners in Parliament and the [English] counterparts in the new American World until 1776 erupted.'[126] 'The slave traders in the [American] colonies resented the power of the Royal African Company to dictate the terms of trade.'[127] Thus, as the West grew, it swallowed, assimilated, and consumed the Rest, as much as possible.

According to Proyect, whoever takes seriously the connection between settler colonialism, the roots of slavery, white supremacy and capitalism in the 17th century, North America and the Caribbean, 'will be guaranteed to treat the term "bourgeois-democratic revolution"' with great skepticism.[128] He will identify the bamboozled radicals as those members of civil society, who have believed for generations, that the values of the bourgeois revolution, freedom, equality and brotherhood for all had never been intended for all people in the

---

121   Ibid.
122   Ibid.
123   Ibid.
124   Ibid.
125   Ibid.
126   Ibid.
127   Ibid.
128   Ibid.

West, not to speak of the Rest. *It was not a universal revolution.* It did not liberate the West *and the Rest.* In the name of universal emancipation, it liberated only a few in the West.

Today the West continues down its death-spiral of monopoly- and oligopoly-capitalism. Before it is determinately negated by a new post-modern macro paradigm, it does become clear, that the only meaningful revolution in human history will have to be a *universal* one, which is carried out in order to abolish the class society, and to create a new global society based not only on the redistribution of wealth but also on genuine recognition and respect for all human beings, whatever their differences. Without such a universal revolution, barbarism and the threat of global mutual annihilation will continue unabated.

28   Global System

According to Vladislav Krasnov, a Russian, who emigrated from the Slavic World to the American World, the present *Global System of the United Nations* is not equipped, to deal with today's risks in 2018.[129] It is no longer fit to deal with 21st century problems and risks. We urgently need fresh new thinking. According to Vladislav Krasnov, other aspects of culture are also cooperative and global. For example, Japanese woodblock printers influenced French Impressionists. The nonviolent tradition of Henry David Thoreau, Leo Tolstoy, Mahatma Gandhi, Martin Luther King Jr., and Nelson Mandela, is international. Culture is cooperative; it need not be competitive. Global cultural cooperation can lead us to alternative Future III – a sustainable and peaceful world society.[130] Our modern communication systems, if properly used, can give us a more stable, prosperous, and cooperative future society, instead of barbarism *a la* Adolf Hitler. Such barbarity is indelible, as Alan Bullock stated: 'Je mehr ich über Hitler lerne, desto schwerer fällt es mir, ihn zu erklären.'[131] Emil Fackenheim stated, 'Es wird niemals eine angemessene Erklärung geben... Je näher man der Erklärbarkeit kommt, desto mehr merkt man, dass nichts Hitler erklärbar machen kann.'[132] However, Yehuda Bauer argued to the contrary. He stated, 'Hitler ist

---

129   Vladislav Krasnov. "The Folly of the New Cold War." www.raga.org/resources.html.
130   Siebert, *Manifesto*.
131   'The more I learn about Hitler, the more difficult it is for me to explain him.' Wolfgang Bialas and Lothar Fritze (ed.) *Ideologie und Moral im Nationalsozialismus.* Göttingen: Vandenhoeck & Ruprecht Gmbh & Co., 2014.
132   'There will never be an adequate explanation. The closer one comes to the explainability, the more one notices, that nothing can make Hitler explainable.' Ibid.

im Prinzip erklärbar; das bedeutet aber nicht, dass er erklärt worden ist.'[133] In 1985, a Holocaust survivor from Auschwitz remembered: "Er [Hitler], ist mir auf viele Fragen eine Antwort schuldig."[134]

Albert Einstein, who provided the scientific presupposition for Hiroshima and Nagasaki, wrote a letter to Fritz Haber's son, the Jewish Noble Laureate, who launched the Age of Chemical Warfare, and inventor of Zyklon B, the insecticide with which many Jews were gassed by the fascists. In the letter, Einstein wrote that,

> he [Fritz Haber] was forced to experience all the bitterness of being abandoned by the people of his German circle, a circle that mattered very much to him, even though he recognized its dubious acts of violence. It was the tragedy of the German Jew: the tragedy of unrequited love.[135]

For the historian Heinrich August Winkler, 'how it happened that Hitler came into power was still in 2000 the most important question of nineteenth-and twentieth-century German history, if not of all German history.'[136] According to the journalist and publisher Gabor Steingart, "Auschwitz was a German wound that never heals."[137]

In the view of the dialectical religiology, with Adolf Hitler, the alienation of the West from the Rest reached its utmost extreme. Fascism must never return – not in the West, nor in Resten societies. The West and the Rest must become reconciled.

29 Conclusion: The American and Slavic Worlds: Interdependence and Cooperation

According to René Wadlow, and the *Association of World Citizens*, 'our time will be remembered someday as the strange epoch during which the economic, ecological and scientific interdependence of our planet burst into the open

---

133 'Hitler is explainable in principle; that however does not mean that he has been explained.' Ibid., 110.
134 'He [Hitler] owes me an answer to many questions.' Ibid.
135 Patrick Coffey, *Cathedrals of Science: The Personalities and Rivalries that Made Modern Chemistry.* (New York: Oxford University Press, 2008), 169.
136 Peter Ross Range, *1924: The Year that Made Hitler.* New York: Back Bay Books, 2016.
137 Ibid.

and yet there are new political divisions being made.'[138] The world, according to Wadlow, is constituted by two conflicting trends:

1. 'a potent, deep-seated tidal wave toward interdependence,' and
2. 'the final carving out of the planet into new States.'[139]

As such, the world must adequately address the vexing problem of new emerging States rising of the ashes of the former Yugoslavia and Soviet Union: Abkhazia, Kosovo, Nagrono-Karabakh, South Ossetia, and Transnistra.[140] Thus, Wadlow and *The Association of World Citizens* has proposed forms of "asymmetrical federalism," or "con-federal forms of administration."[141] At one time, Rene Wadlow believed that it was possible to create a "pan-Albanian cultural union," coalescing 'Albanians in Albania, Kosovo, and Macedonia while at the same time having an autonomous Kosovo still within Serbia.'[142] Although Wadlow proposed this model in the Kosovo negotiations, the idea failed to garnish support.[143] Governments avoid complexities, and opt for 'simple solutions.'[144]

Heraclitus stated long ago not only *panta rei* (everything flows) but also *polemos pater panton,* (war is the father of all things). Hegel agreed in his dialectical *Science of Logic,* and *Philosophy of Law,* and *Philosophy of History.* The states' sizes, their shapes, their ethnic makeup are the results of wars. There are virtually no frontiers today that are not the result of wars: world wars, anti-colonial struggles, annexations by victors, wars against indigenous populations, etc. However, modern weapons technology, the most advanced murder weapons, Atomic-Biological-Chemical (ABC) bombs, and global rocket delivery, have made Heraclitus's and Hegel's war theory highly problematic, and even obsolete. Flexibility, compromise, and cooperation are necessary to find mutually acceptable forms of government. There is a need for political creativity. These virtues are admittedly often in short supply. Thus, we need to encourage cooperative and associative methods of problem-solving, ways of thinking about new institutions and practices. Wadlow and his Association, as well as Vladislav Krasnov, work particularly for peaceful cooperation between the Slavic World and the American World, even as world history continues.

---

138   René Wadlow, *The Guns of August: Question of Autonomy Remain.* August 24, 2018. http://www.ovimagazine.com/art/16121.
139   Ibid.
140   Ibid.
141   Ibid.
142   Ibid.
143   Ibid.
144   Ibid.

According to the dialectical religiology, the Slavic and the American World can, with the help of cooperative and associative methods of problem-solving, create a non-violent, universal *re-volution*, or better still, *pro-volution*, and a new macro-paradigm, in which the West and the Rest are reconciled in direction of alternative Future III – a peaceful and productive world federation, rooted in solidary: a global civil society, if they are able to prevent together Future I – the totally administered, bureaucratic, computerized, technocratic, signal society, rehearsed already by Adolf Hitler and Josef Stalin, and Future II – ABC wars, prepared already by World War I with its 10 million casualties, and World War II with its 70 million victims.[145] A *re-ligion*, or better still *pro-ligion*, which understands and defines itself as *the longing for the totally Other than the horror and terror of nature and history, for perfect justice, and for unconditional love, coupled with the hope that the murderer shall not triumph over the innocent victim, at least not ultimately,* could be the very foundation of such a non-violent, universal *re-volution,* or *pro-volution,* carried out by the American and Slavic World with the consent and help of the Resten world.

Acknowledgements

The author would like to thank Dustin J. Byrd for editing the initial draft of this essay.

Bibliography

Anderson, Jon Lee. *Archbishop Óscar Romero Becomes a Saint, but his Death Still Haunts El Salvador.* October 22, 2018. https://www.newyorker.com/news/daily-comment/archbishop-oscar-romero-becomes-a-saint-but-his-death-still-haunts-el-salvador.

Brockman, James R. *Romero: A Life. The Essential Biography of a Modern Martyr and Christian Hero.* Maryknoll, NY: Orbis Books, 2005.

Camp, Lee. "American Society Would Collapse If It Weren't for These 8 Myths." July 26, 2018. http://www.informationclearinghouse.info/49928.htm.

Coffey, Patrick. *Cathedrals of Science: The Personalities and Rivalries that Made Modern Chemistry.* New York: Oxford University Press, 2008.

Fukuyama, Francis. *The End of History and the Last Man.* New York: Avon Books, Inc., 1992.

---

145   Siebert, *Manifesto.*

Habermas, Jürgen. *The Theory of Communicative Action: Lifeworld and System: A Critique of Functionalist Reason.* (Thomas McCarthy, Trans.). Boston: Beacon Press, 1989.

Habermas, Jürgen. *The Theory of Communicative Action: Reason and the Rationalization of Society.* (Thomas McCarthy, Trans.). Boston: Beacon Press, 1984.

Hegel, Georg. W.F. *Early Theological Writings.* (T.M. Knox, Trans.). Philadelphia: University of Pennsylvania Press, 1971.

Hegel, Georg. *Elements of the Philosophy of Right.* Edited by Allen W. Wood. (H.B. Nisbet, Trans.). Cambridge: Cambridge University Press, 2010.

Hegel, Georg. *Hegel's Phenomenology of Spirit.* (A.V. Miller, Trans.). Oxford: Oxford University Press, 1977.

Hegel, Georg. *Hegel's Science of Logic.* Ed. H.D. Lewis. (A.V. Miller, Trans.). Atlantic Highlands, NJ: Humanities Press International, Inc., 1993.

Hegel, Georg. *Lectures on the Philosophy of History.* (Ruben Alvarado, Trans.). Aalten, Netherlands: Wordbridge Publishing, 2011.

Hegel, Georg. *Lectures on the Philosophy of Religion: Determinate Religion.* Edited by Peter C. Hodgson. Oxford: Oxford University Press, 2007.

Hegel, Georg. "Metaphysics of Understanding: Locke" https://www.marxists.org/reference/archive/hegel/works/hp/hplocke.htm.

Horkheimer, Max and Theodor W. Adorno. *Dialectic of Enlightenment: Philosophical Fragments.* Edited by Gunzelin Schmid Noerr. (Edmund Jephcott, Trans.). Stanford, CA: Stanford University Press, 2002.

Horne, Gerald. *The Apocalypse of Settler Colonialism: The Roots of Slavery, White Supremacy, and Capitalism in the 17th Century North America and Caribbean.* New York: Monthly Press Review, 2017.

Kant, Immanuel. "Perpetual Peace: A Philosophical Sketch." In *Kant: Political Writings,* edited by Hans. S. Reiss. (H.B. Nisbet, Trans.). Cambridge: Cambridge University Press, 2001.

Kishore, Joseph. "The Canonization of John McCain: Media, Political Establishment turn Warmonger into a Saint." September 1, 2018. https://www.wsws.org/en/articles/2018/09/01/pers-s01.html.

Krasnov, Vladislav. "The Folly of the New Cold War." www.raga.org/resources.html.

Marx, Karl. *The Communist Manifesto.* Edited by Frederic L. Bender. New York: W.W. Norton & Co., 1988.

McGrath, Alister. *Christianity's Dangerous Idea.* New York: HarperOne, 2007.

Metaxas, Eric. *The Man Who Rediscovered God and Changed the World.* New York: Viking, 2017.

Nieto, Clara. *Masters of War: Latin America and U.S. Aggression – From the Cuban Revolution through the Clinton Years.* New York: Seven Stories Press, 2003.

O'Regan, Cyril. "The Trinity in Kant, Hegel, and Schelling." In *The Oxford Handbook of the Trinity,* edited by Gilles Emery and Matthew Levering. New York: Oxford University Press, 2014.

Proyect, Louis. "Slavery and the Origins of Capitalism." August 23, 2018. https://www.counterpunch.org/2018/08/24/slavery-and-the-origins-of-capitalism/.

Ross Range, Peter. *1924: The Year that Made Hitler.* New York: Back Bay Books, 2016.

Siebert, Rudolf J. *Die Anthropologie Michael Heldings, eines Humanisten und Theologen im Umkreis der Geistigen Neuordnung des 16. Jahrhunderts* (1506–1561). Sigmaringen: Hohenzollernsche Jahreshefte 1965.

Siebert, Rudolf J. *Manifesto of the Critical Theory of Society and Religion: The Wholly Other, Liberation, Happiness, and the Rescue of the Hopeless.* Leiden: Brill, 2010.

Wadlow, René. *The Guns of August: Question of Autonomy Remain.* August 24, 2018. http://www.ovimagazine.com/art/16121.

Zinn, Howard. *A People's History of the United States.* New York: Harperperennial, 2003.

CHAPTER 3

Echoes of the Past: Colonial Legacy and Eurocentric Humanitarianism

Mladjo Ivanovic

1 Introduction

Despite the misleading title of this chapter, colonialism is not so much a phenomenon of the past. Insofar we consider values and normative commitments
of Europe (or "the West"), it exists in Eurocentric capitalism and liberal, neo-
colonial and humanitarian guises of Europe's continuous involvement in shaping global conditions and managing lives who must endure pathologies of the
present moral, political, economic, and environmental order. To acknowledge
intertwinement of these different axes of global conditions (i.e. intersection
of militarism, culture, race, gender, ecology, politics and economy) is not the
same as understanding how their collusion results in mechanisms of oppression and subjugation – or why such mechanisms are so persistent. Moreover, it
invites us to foreclose comprehension of the disenfranchisement and suffering
they engender. To this end, the purpose of this chapter is to explore and to interrogate current material and epistemological practices aimed at governance
of the most vulnerable layers of humanity. By reflecting on the struggles of
forcefully displaced people and the challenges of Western humanitarianism
(and contemporary humanitarian agency of Western (privileged) spectators
in general), I hope to show that we are confronted with social processes and
subjectivity which foster inadequate goals in regard to solidarity with distant
others. As we see from the ongoing struggles of millions of people worldwide,
any radical alternative to tragic humanitarian situations needs to take into account the tumultuous dynamics between history and our present reality. A reality which confronts us with the uncomfortable but vital questions of power,
responsibility and justice; and, in doing so, calls us to reflect upon historical
choices that have ultimately designed our global political, social, economic,
and ecological conditions today.

   One reason why Europe is currently in crisis mode is not only because it
is confronted with the largest wave of migration since the World War II, but
because present humanitarian challenges disclose Europe's embroilment in an
intense and often contentious discourse as to what it means to be "European"

and subsequently "Non-European." Against this backdrop, we are confronted with extreme right's claims that immigrant and refugee population (mostly of Muslim religious origin) do not belong to Europe (e.g. their worldviews are incompatible with permissive European cultural norms; their religion is barbaric, backward, and uncivilized, etc.). Thus, a humanitarian victim (e.g. refugee) remains a product of a traumatic origin. From the beginning, her life is defined by discursive negotiations, exclusion and violence, and these inhumane patterns continue through dehumanizing practices of the international community, humanitarian organizations and the Western public in general – all instances that were supposed to safeguard refugees' vulnerabilities. Looking at workings of social media, news outlets, humanitarian NGO, etc., it seems that the identity/image of refugee/migrant falls prey to multiplying centers of power and production of knowledge that reduce human suffering to a seductive simplification of their (and also our) reality without a real commitment to action.

In what follows, this chapter is divided into three main parts. *The first* identifies some of the weaknesses of humanitarian discourse and practices, and it has an analytical dimension in that it attempts to tease out the epistemic forces, cultural habits, forms of knowledge, skills and expertise that were folded into the ontological organization and form of subjectivity that is at the center of humanitarian attention and "solidarity." In terms of today's migration crisis, refugees are deemed as people without history who constitute the new frontier of European civilization, one that is conceptualized through a parade of volunteers, human rights lawyers, activists, and humanitarian organizations. Conceptualized as an empty space, the understanding of refugee becomes an epistemic and ontological landscape which the principles and accomplishments of Western rationality colonize with meaning and inscribe with value. *The second* part focuses on material and epistemological legacy of colonialism manifested in practices and ideological tendencies of Eurocentric humanitarianism. Taking into account that encounters between Western humanitarian agent and Non-Western other takes place amidst values and receptivity of hegemonic culture, humanitarian narratives – based on discriminatory racial, gender, cultural, and economic geographies – exemplify the distorted perspectives on humanitarian victims' structural and symbolic disadvantages. Historically, interactions between dominating and dominated cultures resulted in the repudiation of subaltern others by Western (colonial) hegemony. Constitutive to refugees' material and epistemological quandary is the tendency of dominating Eurocentrism to award complex historical events with antagonistic and oversimplified categories – thus, avoiding raising incriminating questions of responsibility and justice.

Finally, I conclude by hinting at an alternative way of thinking about responsibility and solidarity. I hope that by bringing inconsistencies of humanitarianism into the spotlight, I show how humanitarianism has become an echo of colonial mechanisms that inextricably serve both to define and to justify certain discourses and practices that ultimately govern human beings. By disclosing pathologies internal to humanitarianism, my work at the same time calls attention to practices that an alternative, counterhegemonic humanitarianism needs to avoid.

2   Humanitarian Solidarity and Epistemological Displacement

The question of solidarity cannot be examined separately from the organizational structure that dominates our present moral discourse – *humanitarianism*. Humanitarianism articulates and offers a site wherein different dimensions of moral, economic and political intersect with, and determine one another, in ways that variously come to define what humanism and solidarity are.[1] We can understand humanitarianism to be a project based upon the application of moral sentiments, a project that mobilizes compassion, speaks of human suffering, and seeks to ameliorate global inequalities and injustices, and yet exactly these inequalities and injustices ultimately help humanitarianism self-validate its own existence. The fact that suffering is also a characteristic language of the contemporary world and that compassion has become a significant political force, the western humanitarian subject is exposed to the constant risk of renouncing objectification in her description, and ultimately of reinforcing the social construction to which she unwittingly contributes. The humanitarian discourse has always focused on the impact of its knowledge on the attitudes of the public and the messages such knowledge aims to convey.

---

1   What I understand as humanitarianism in the contemporary conventional liberal context is a definite set of ideas and practices that can be located materially in their institutional and discursive form. As Didier Fassin argues, *humanitarianism* is a system of governance that designates "the deployment of moral sentiments in contemporary politics." Governance here should be understood in a broad sense, as a set of procedures established and actions conducted in order to manage, regulate, and support the existence of human beings and an economy of harm that they are exposed to. On the other hand, "moral sentiments" refer to emotions that direct our attention to the suffering of others and make us want to remedy that suffering. Similarly, "humanitarian" should be understood in meaning, 'as connoting both dimensions encompassed by the concept of humanity: on the one hand the generality of human beings who share a similar condition (mankind), and on the other an affective movement drawing humans toward their fellows (humaneness).' Didier Fassin, *Humanitarian Reason: A Moral History of the Present*, (Berkeley: University of California Press. 2011), 2.

As such, it denotes a certain way of looking at the world. Alongside the technological and practical adjustments in recent years, there is an ongoing shift in discursive formation reflected in increased public presence of humanitarian conundrums in an unjust world. The ongoing translation of social reality into the new language of compassion (and a development of practices that embody such language) seems to mirror the West's epistemological and affective conversion of its moral capacity. Hence, despite the proliferation of literature that deals with suffering and trauma, and the fact that these themes are commonplaces of the social sciences and new political discourse, humanitarianism is ultimately just *politics of inequality*.[2] There is often a form of cynicism at play when one deploys the language of moral sentiments at the same time as implementing policies that increase social inequality, regulations that restrict the rights and liberties of immigrant populations, or military operations with essentially geostrategic goals. From this critical perspective, the language of humanitarianism seems to be nothing more than a deceptive cover for the imposition of unjust and brutal market forces of an equally unjust and brutal world. But even if this is the case, and I think it is, the question still remains: *Why does it work so well?*[3]

In order to answer this question, it is not enough to ask how humanitarianism generates support among its audience. We must instead focus on explaining why people often prefer to invoke the idea of suffering and compassion instead of responsibility and justice. Although at the heart of contemporary humanitarianism lies moral acknowledgment of unfortunate others whose suffering calls for public action, such calls also disclose the moral distance between those who watch and those who suffer. Despite innate optimism of current Western liberal culture, compassion itself is manifested as the personal choice of a Western consumer; it remains a form of public action insofar as it silences vulnerable others by negotiating their humanity as a consumerist practice devoid of genuine solidarity. Even if we are able to transcend the contingent social differences that constitute post-modern individuals, the moral cornerstone of solidarity that we discover today, bears the form of life that has

---

2   More on this theme, please see Mladjo Ivanovic, "The European Grammar of Inclusion: Integrating Epistemic and Social Inclusion of Refugees in Host Societies." *Radical Philosophy Review*, 21, (1) (2018): 103–127.

3   Despite its benign objective of maximizing efficiency in providing aid and increasing accountability to donors, the financial regime of the aid and development field ultimately justifies a neoliberal logic of control that ultimately collapses the cosmopolitan aspirations of humanitarianism into the corporate aspirations of the West. In doing so, it not only fails to serve the ideal of global cosmopolitan solidarity, but delivers harmful effects on vulnerable others by establishing relations of dependence that reinforce already-present inequalities.

an elementary biological character and lacks all the qualities which make it possible to treat it as a life.[4] Evoking images of others who are suffering, such an encounter between a Western spectator and the gruesome scenes of human vulnerability seem to yield only the most basic biological fact: namely that victim feels pain and suffering. Thus, recognition of what we share in common with other individuals leads to the disheartening reduction of the distinctively human to the merely biological. What this reduction does is not only an exhaustion of the concept of humanity but also through this process of exhaustion, it creates conditions for the production of a specific *form* of humanism that enables "Western" civilization to identify and define itself. As Rancière describes this feature of contemporary humanitarianism,

> The predicate "human" and "human rights" are simply attributed, without any phrasing, without any mediation, to their eligible party, the subject "man." The age of the "humanitarian" is one of immediate identity between the ordinary example of suffering humanity and the plenitude of the subject of humanity and of its rights. The eligible party pure and simple is then none other than the wordless victim, the ultimate figure of the one excluded from the logos, armed only with a voice expressing a monotonous moan, the moan of naked suffering, which saturation has made inaudible. More precisely, this person who is merely human then boils down to the couple of the victim, the pathetic figure of a person to whom such humanity is denied, and the executioner, the monstrous figure of a person who denies.[5]

The irony of this "monotonous moan" is that humanitarian solidarity today carries within itself virtually all of the vices of Eurocentric hegemonic order that sustains power relations between the West and the global South. Thus, the convenient fiction of human equality remains just that – a fiction.

These fundamental dependencies and inequalities invoke fear that Western moral sentiments ultimately promote configurations of power that legitimizes the corrupted rationality of capitalism and the inequalities that it engenders. Interfering in the current struggle over the boundaries between humanitarianism, economy, and politics, the explicit invocation of justice is the only morally

---

4 Please see Hannah Arendt, *The Origins of Totalitarianism*. New York: Harcourt Brace Jovanovich, 1998; Giorgio Agamben, *Homo Sacer: Sovereign Power and Bare Life*. Stanford: Stanford University Press, 1998.

5 Jacques Rancière, *Disagreement: Politics and Philosophy*. (Minneapolis: University of Minnesota Press, 1999), 126.

legitimate alternative to the neocolonial imaginary and its dehumanizing processes. And yet, before we can chart the ways in which this shift is possible, there are other problems that demand our attention. One way to think through the challenges of humanitarianism is to conceive the contemporary humanitarian agency of Western spectators as a form of subjectivity that has inadequate conceptions of motivation or inadequate goals in regard to solidarity with vulnerable others. Hence, solidarity as a personal preference not only constitutes the West as a self-assertive, narcissistic public, it also constitutes the vulnerability of the other, often as a semi-fictional figure that inhabits epistemological limbo wherein the Western public negotiates her ontological and moral worth. Thus, just as the solidarity of the Western humanitarian agent belongs to the private realm of personal choices and affections, whereby often these choices appear to be made independently of the configurations of social powers that actually constitute and define them, the Non-Western other is disposed of her vulnerability and thrown into the realm of public negotiations as an image of human suffering that awaits Western acknowledgment.

As a consequence, these images lack historicity and any concrete link to justice. Even if these representations are linked to historical circumstances and sustain an impotent rhetoric of common humanity, their depiction in public imagery does not present those people as historical agents who are part of a world that invokes a sense of solidarity and obligations. Rather, their agonizing experiences are reduced to a process of distributing resources, wherein the relation between the Western spectator and Non-Western victim is negotiated both materially and symbolically. The suffrage of the humanitarian victim, consequently, is manifested as a personal experience of the Western bystander who remains ignorant of the moral and political weight inherently entailed in the inhumane conditions faced by the other. Hence, it is not the case that stories of humanitarian tragedies lack a "vocabulary of justice" but, rather, that such stories lack autonomy in the sense that their experiences and relation to responsibility and justice is subordinated to experiences of the Western humanitarian agent and stories about "the West." Hence, the notion of shared humanity cannot be taken as universal property, devoid of any classifications. Rather, it is often a lethal neocolonial construct of diverse material and discursive practices which selectively humanize certain groups of people rather than others.[6] Closely linked to this notion of "humanitarian" selectivism is

---

6   For origins of this theory, please see Quijano, Anibal. "Coloniality of Power, Eurocentrism, and Latin America," in *Coloniality at Large*, ed. Mabel Moraña, Enriqué Dussel, and Carlos A. Jáuregui. (Durham, NC: Duke University Press, 2008), 181–224; more on this theme in the following section of this chapter.

the complex overdetermination of the subject's cognitive (and subsequently moral and political) dispositions by social forces that ultimately determine our encounter with social and global maladies.

Although an analysis of the discursive engine of the liberal humanitarian present helps us understand the limits of such a discourse, what ultimately renders the moral disposition of Western agents is the entanglement of their epistemic and affective faculties with normative architecture that "frames" the otherness of non-Western subjects according to mechanisms of an ontological formation primarily reinforced by policies, techniques, and ideologies explicitly oriented around the epistemic negotiation, and reduction, of complex and idiosyncratic identities of Non-western people (e.g. refugees, migrants, immigrants, etc.).[7] What is so specific about such epistemic and ontological negotiations is that the experiences of refugees are rendered unintelligible due to the underlying paradox of humanitarian communication that I term here as *epistemic displacement*. I understand this phenomenon as a process wherein knowledge of refugees is constituted by their simultaneous hyper-visibility (i.e. constant representation in media and public discourse), and invisibility (i.e. the limited capacity of such representations and discourse(s) to allow understanding of the complex nature of refugees' conditions and their subsequent subordination to Eurocentric narratives). This paradoxical position has often been explored in decolonial and black feminist thought. Moreover, one of the important lessons of recent developments in social epistemology is understanding of Eurocentrism as a system of discourses and practices that sustain subjugation of historically disenfranchised people through material and epistemological mechanisms. The result of such mechanisms is that our humanitarian present ultimately reflects (and upholds) social, political and cultural supremacy of white, male and Eurocentric domination. As Kristie Dotson has recently argued on a similar theme, subordination and subsequent

---

7   What is so specific about current epistemic and ontological negotiations of refugees is not only that they are rendered unintelligible, but this process of erasure highlights a paradox of what I understand as an *epistemic displacement*; a process wherein hypervisibility in media, public discourse, academic work, etc. result in subsequent erasure and unknowability. In this sense, discursive and ontological formations grow out of actual social experience, which is to be understood in terms of the relations of power, historically speaking, in which such experiences take place. Philosophy, social theory, science, religion, law, and so on, are not autonomous or isolated, either conceptually or practically; however, their current idealization tends to couch them as if they were. At the same time, linked to this (ideological) autonomy, construing these disciplines as idealized rather than immersive allows us to ignore the problems that may give rise to their more problematic formulations – not just the fact that we are, in some respects, always making sense of our world, but also that we are, so to speak, making sense of our making sense of it.

erasure are co-constitutive aspects of the same historical processes that have led to pervasive and systematic accounts of exclusion of people of color, and more specifically subordination of black women.[8] In her analysis, 'subordination may also result in routinely assuring a corresponding failure to understand a range of structural positions present within that population and the nature of subordination that coincide with those positions.'[9] Thus, insofar as acknowledgment of struggles of refugees (as Non-Western others) depend on successful mediation of their experiences and initiation into the dominant culture and epistemic norms that guide political and moral valorization within Western societies, such processes are inevitably 'constituted by material and epistemological compromises' that further negotiate their intelligibility as *the Europe's other*.[10]

The difficulty for our purposes is that in the case of refugees/migrants a common nature of these compromises gestures towards their ultimate *unknowability*.[11] Many of current issues in regard to Western indifference towards struggles of Non-Western people highlight limits of humanitarian discursive representations of human suffering due to their genesis (and sustenance) on epistemic failings. Being a product of social processes that differentiate our "self" from others and condition our capacity for affective attachment and reflexive engagement with the political conditions of human vulnerability, we are confronted with the uncomfortable but vital question of our cultural situatedness, privilege, ontologically unstable alterity, and lastly, with justice in its national and international contexts. As I have argued in more details elsewhere,[12] to the extent that every society is defined by values and institutions that presuppose a capacity for social actors to influence the decisions of others, it is important to keep in mind the ways in which social imaginaries set up the contexts in which the interpretative and symbolic dimensions of social discourses form and guide individual knowledge and action. We are surrounded by forms of knowledge that privilege certain perspectives, and one way to make sense of ways in which humanitarian relation with distant others is plagued by indifference and/or selectivism is to discuss epistemic and ontological grounds of such processes.[13]

---

8   Kristie Dotson, "Theorizing Jane Crow, Theorizing Unknowability." *Social Epistemology*, 31 (5) (2017): 417–430.

9   Ibid., 417.

10   Ibid.

11   This concept of "unknowability" received substantial analysis and articulation in Kristie Dotson's "Theorizing Jane Crow."

12   Ivanovic, "The European Grammar of Inclusion."

13   In other words, such mechanisms of epistemic and ontological formation enable construction of agency, and then draw the contours of a political discourse that often links

The strongest textual evidence for such an epistemological and ontological matrix is found in the poststructuralist tradition, more precisely in Foucault's works on power and genealogy.[14] His critical engagement with power/knowledge regimes offers historically specific analyses of the present conditions designed to lay out contingent conditions of possibility of our subjectivity as historically, socially, and culturally specific/contingent.[15] Foucault uses the notion of a "grid of intelligibility" to describe particular relations of power through which we make sense of ourselves and the world around us. In volume 1 of *The History of Sexuality* he writes,

> Powers condition of possibility, or in any case the viewpoint which permits one to understand its exercise, even in its more "peripheral" effects, and which also makes it possible to use its mechanisms as a grid of intelligibility of the social order, ... it is the moving substrate of force relations which, by virtue of their inequality, constantly engender states of power, but the latter are always local and unstable.[16]

Such "force relations" refer to the ways certain historical and social conditions make possible (i.e. render intelligible) specific landscapes of meaning, through which social agents make sense of cultural, political, economic reality. Foucault characterizes this grid of intelligibility as the organizational sphere wherein 'the multiplicity of force relations' operate and constitute a series of formations that have both epistemic and ontological dimensions which are internally related, according to the 'rule of immanence.'[17]

The idea that our ways of apprehending is determined by the social and cultural conditions in which we find ourselves, involves a highly constraining nature of our epistemic agency. In other words, "grid of intelligibility" creates

---

our articulation and reception of others with historical processes that lead towards unjust conditions and different forms of social exclusions. Only once we have spelled out the regulative structure of such discursive fields (with regard to broader standards that guide moral and political deliberation, but also acknowledging constraining power such standards have), will we be in a position to understand the role that our cognitive dispositions – specifically, the notions of epistemic violence, epistemic agency and epistemic oppression – play in the overall process of humanitarian solidarity and social/global justice.

14   Michel Foucault, *The History of Sexuality Volume 1: An Introduction.* New York: Random House, 1978; Michel Foucault, *Society Must Be Defended. Lectures at the College de France 1975–76.* New York: Picador, 2003.

15   Amy Allen, *The Politics of Our Selves* (New York: Columbia University Press, 2008), 5; 45–71; 75–95.

16   Foucault, *The History of Sexuality Volume 1,* 93.

17   Ibid., 98.

a frame that institutes and maintains relations of coherence and continuity among norms that guide our perception, knowledge, and subsequently our actions (or lack thereof). These relations are not value-neutral; rather, they delimit a range of what can be seen or understood, according to the constitutive and violent work of those norms which guide our articulation and ascription of knowledge. As a result, a coherent and socially intelligible subject is one whose "essential" features accord to certain norms (and relations between them) implicit to the grid which enables "intelligibility" in the first place. The implications of such a dependence of a subject on social conditions and cognitive dispositions that these conditions engender, points at the controlling and violent nature of the processes that constitute social identities. Erin Gilson reiterates this point very clearly when she suggests that the "excess" of objects in regard to discursive and ontological determinations points at the innate reductive character of such a process.[18] To wit: 'What is not contained within the frame remains incomprehensible, unperceivable within its terms, but also, in its unintelligibility, defines as intelligible what is circumscribed by the frame.'[19] Thus, in order to elaborate normative aspects of the construction what (or who) "Non-Western other" is, one has to disclose ways in which their apprehension is grounded in the relation between her and the normative framework that ascribes a certain meaning to her spatial and historical situatedness. These techniques and practices are in themselves mechanisms of subjugation that drag the other into the "Western" context, while at the same time discounting the vital role of cultural differences. Given that the constitution of the non-European other is filtered through Eurocentric colonial logic(s) (as well as historical-cultural biases that continue to dominate the visual culture of the Western world), the question arises whether the differences in specific epistemic and material positions make it possible to comprehend people in a way that would not end in reductive accounts of knowledge – accounts in which possibilities for deeper engagement with their conditions are attenuated or completely disabled.[20]

---

18   Erinn Gilson, *The Ethics of Vulnerability*. New York: Routledge, 2014.

19   Ibid., 44.

20   One way a society creates a specific identity is by endorsing a social imaginary grounded in an evaluative frame which guides moral and political agency. This social imaginary functions as a tether that binds a given sociopolitical culture together, and renders the social conditions that surround its subjects intelligible. As such, social imaginaries are rooted historically in social conditions and relations of social forces which operate by establishing contexts wherein the subject recognizes herself and encounters the other. This encounter is conditioned by interpretative structures that govern the apprehension of others, and, through that apprehension, guide our moral faculties.

As a discursive formation, encountering the other is not only an invitation to either associate or dissociate, but already from the beginning reflects and constitutes social relationships, wherein the participation of Non-Western other is typically involuntary. Hence, as I have pointed out earlier, she is in an ungrateful position, wherein her perceptive (and subsequent normative) pacification not only leads to a diminished moral and political status, but such reduction also stands as a prelude to her subsequent marginalization and subjugation. Not only does such asymmetry of power ultimately make the humanitarian impulse towards suffering of others dependent on the Western subject's capacity to acknowledge or deny her agency, but further, the difference in the said capacity here also represents an exercise of domination over others, because their epistemic marginalization subsequently leads to a material, social one. These processes are interrelated and as such limit our potential to have reciprocal relationships with others because the agency and autonomy are always assumed to fall onto one side, the side of Western (European) agent.

The moral lesson to be taken here is that the figure of the other as a vulnerable entity always remains in discontinuity with the spectator. In this dialectic between exposure, articulation, ascription, and recognition the very subjectivity of the victim emerges in a process of dissimulation. She appears in this discourse as the subject without a choice, a quasi-agent for whom submission and death have already been chosen by others. Such denial of agency is often accomplished through perceptual politics that determine what is worth noticing, what can be acknowledged, foregrounded, deemed valuable, and what is relegated to the background, and rendered invisible. This epistemological and ontological dynamic – wherein the success of an ethical encounter between two different moral perspectives tenuously hovers between an unclear ethical recognition of the claims that the other makes, and an attempted reduction of their complexity to some form of passive appropriation – builds a backdrop of our humanitarian reality. This lack of agency extends to representations of her experiences that usually are coerced and carried out with disrespect.[21] Thus, the call for the inclusion of the other (on her own terms) is not only essential

---

21 For example, when we reflect on images of hurt Syrian children, although the photographs of their tragic conditions serve as a powerful medium to force public attention, its resonance ultimately depends on who wants to see it, and the political contexts that support their interpretation. Perceiving a photograph that depicts such a traumatic moment, thus, does not only raise questions about the ways in which one represents inhumane conditions, but also implicates the viewer in the helplessness and vulnerability of victims. Therefore, such a perception may aestheticize struggles and suffering of others and thereby surrender their images as spectacle, or it can politicize such representations by thinning out the experience of the spectators that may result in co-optable and sterile

for the reevaluation of epistemic and ontological processes that affect the construction of agency but also draws the contours of a moral discourse that would link human vulnerability (and solidarity) with justice. To avoid the trap of trivializing humanitarian appeals in the face of human suffering, current political culture must stage vulnerability not as an object of fleeting compassion, but as a demand for critical reflection and deliberation about historical (and present) processes that lead towards unjust conditions. It is only once we reverse the ways in which the victim becomes the site of her own dehumanization that spectators can begin to perceive her as a moral unit with her own complex and challenging contexts of existence.

3   Colonialism and Eurocentric Humanitarianism

In order to unmask the naïve idealism of Western populistic humanitarian impulses, social critique has to challenge the social contexts that give rise to human suffering, and inspire citizens to acknowledge their own complicity in the web of moral, political and economic conditions that result and sustain global inequalities and injustices. Given the ethical and political dimensions to representing the bodies, suffering and conditions of forcefully displaced people, and particularly because often humanitarian victims themselves have no access to, or input in, those ethical and political discourses that qualify the non-Western place in the epistemological systems of the West, witnessing serves as the most practical (and, perhaps, the *only* practical) empathetic space. The experiences of these people are real, concrete conditions (whether we acknowledge them or not), and the manners in which we articulate global maladies (e.g. poverty, violence, hunger, discrimination, etc.) that seem to be their daily reality also illuminate the too-simple mechanisms for self-reflection by which Western humanitarian systems operate. The moral appeals that these conditions convey – and the empathy gap in the discourse regarding the suffering of others – means that most of the humanitarian capacity to mobilize public support depends on the systems' power to constitute distant others as objects of our attention and concern. For example, what is currently happening within and at the outskirts of European borders is not only failure of humanitarian systems and the binding weakness of international law but also reveals the troubling nature of the cultural, gendered, and racialized nature of our Western moral and humanitarian agency, and its flawed mechanisms

populist agendas and selectivism. And yet, what often remains ignored are questions of responsibility that such exposure to representations of human suffering entail.

of self-evaluation, solidarity and humanitarian inclusion. By questioning how a specific understanding of the other is formed, we draw attention to the inconsistencies associated with the problematic relation between witnessing atrocities and the moral responses that such knowledge entails. In the context of gender, racial, sexual, ethnic, economic or cultural exclusion and subordination, we could see that there are cognitive and affective deficits that amount to specific forms of epistemic insensitivity and impotent notion of solidarity that plagues Western audience today.

In response to the kinds of concerns about difficulties inherent in cross-cultural and intersubjective communication, as we have seen success of such communication will largely depend on what has resulted from an epistemic/ ontological constitution of *alterity*. The traditional notion of *the other* referred to a set of formal and relative differences in relation to the subject, whose formation and agency were determined by historical circumstances and political location (formations that have unfortunately often taken place under reductive, Eurocentric terms). Drawing on work of philosophers Levinas and Kristeva, Ofelia Schutte argues that at a conceptual level 'the breakthrough in constructing the concept of *the other* occurs when one combines the notion of the other as different from the self with the acknowledgment of the self's decentering that results from the experience of such differences.'[22] She further argues that such 'breakthrough involves acknowledgment the positive, potentially ethical dimensions of such decentering for interpersonal relations and form of our ethical and political agency, in contrast to simply taking the decentering one might experience in the light of the other's differences as a deficit in the individual control over the environment.'[23] According to Schutte, acknowledgment of ways in which 'cultural (as well as sexual, racial, gender, and other kinds of difference)' determine interpersonal and social interactions of individuals is necessary if we want 'to reach new ethical, aesthetic, and political ground.'[24] With reference to insights offered by Kristie Dotson and Michel Foucault, the political and epistemological challenges of Western humanism in face of complex processes that constitute otherness seem to be a convenient starting point for elaborating another aspect of the relationship between different forms of injustice (e.g. epistemic, ontological, social, etc.) and material aspects of unjust social conditions.[25]

---

22   Olivia Schutte, "Cultural Alterity: Cross-Cultural Communication and Feminist Theory in North-South Contexts." *Hypatia,* 13 (2) (1998): 54.

23   Ibid.

24   Ibid.

25   We have seen that each society creates a normative fabric that socializes its members into its culture, through a set of discursive norms and material practices that render certain

Looking at work of decolonial thinkers, and Anibal Quijano in particular, one can see that intertwinement of colonialism with present global conditions of capitalism resulted in a form of rationality that has established Western Europe as a predominant global power and its culture as dominant cosmology. Quijano argues that one of the fundamental axes of this model of power is 'the social classification of the world's population around the idea of race, a mental construction that expresses the basic experience of colonial domination and pervades the more important dimensions of global power, including the specific rationality: Eurocentricism.'[26] In other words, Quijano points at colonial origin (and character) of the discursive imaginary of "race" and overarching epistemological system of Eurocentrism that serve as material and epistemic axes of capitalism (and subsequently humanitarianism). Referring to their stability and durability as drivers of present global conditions, Quijano writes,

> Two historical processes associated in the production of that space/time converged and established the two fundamental axes of the new model of power. One was the condition of the differences between conquerors and conquered in the idea of "race," a supposedly different biological structure that placed some in a natural situation of inferiority to the others. The conquistadors assumed this idea as the constitutive, founding element of relations of domination that the conquest imposed. On this basis, the population of America, and later the world, was classified within the new model of power. The second process involved the constitution of a new structure of control of labor and its resources and products. This new structure was an articulation of historically known previous structures of the control of labor – slavery, serfdom, small independent commodity production, and reciprocity – around and on the basis of capital and the world's market.[27]

---

forms of behavior socially acceptable and intelligible. The omnipresence of the normative framework sets a stage wherein social identity of social actors unfolds in relation to their "others" as a continuous negotiation of different epistemic and political perspectives. Retrospectively, one can argue that in order to be socially recognized, it is necessary for a subject to meet the normative criteria that determine her presence within the realm of intelligibility, even if this realm directly or indirectly works to exclude, or attempts to erase, the essential characteristics of diversity and particularity that some cultural milieus and individuals have. Such accounts of *othering* show how ontological determinations constitutive of social reality, ultimately occur against the backdrop of epistemological system whose phenomena cannot be reduced to the mere social manifestation of oppression and violence.

26   Quijano, "Coloniality of Power," 181.
27   Ibid., 182.

This notion of "inferiority," grounded in biological and cultural features of people, has subsequently established social relations that led to the development of new historical social identities (i.e. Indians, Blacks, Mestizos, etc.) and has at the same time redefined Europe in terms of its self-understanding in relation to rest of the world. After all, Europe was not only materially dependent upon the exploitation of its colonies, but racial differentiation proved necessary for the establishment of Europe's identity as a cultural epicenter of the world (often constituted in direct relation to those it deemed culturally and geographically inferior). Insofar these relations with Non-Europeans were relations of exploitation and domination, the creation of such social identities (i.e. Indian, Blacks, Mestizos, etc.) was constitutive of hierarchies that allowed colonial powers to establish control over resources and labor based on social roles and geopolitical locations of people who were forced to endure European false "humanism(s)."

What I find particularly inspirational about this tradition is its emphasis on history and present global conditions as a web of social relations that result from the intertwinement of material and symbolic forces whose workings condition the social circumstances and experiences of social actors. Thus, by understanding our social reality in terms of an interdependence between the individual and the histories of its cultural, economic and political environment, decolonial thinkers help us to conceptualize limits of our moral and political subjectivity saturated by power relations in the wake of capitalism and the aftermath of colonialism. An understanding of political and moral deficits of today's (humanitarian) agency is impossible without focusing on the social pathologies of capitalism and underlying ideological discursive formations of Western epistemology that are co-constitutive of our reality.[28] Philosophically, though, this conviction that cognitive endowments and social factors affect the living conditions of subjects and their agency also poses a farther-reaching meaning for today's increased necessity of including epistemic forms of oppression and violence in theories of social justice. There is an intimate and necessary correspondence between how we conceive of others and how we treat them, and such correspondence is historically an expression of exclusionary and violent processes that colonial history, capitalism, and present humanitarianism share.

Situating colonialism and instrumental logic of capitalism at the foundation of human rationality, decolonial thinkers help us understand repressive tendencies of Western cognitive constitution (e.g. tendencies to contextualize and

---

28   Walter D. Mignolo, "The Geopolitics of Knowledge and the Colonial Difference." *The South Atlantic Quarterly*, 101 (1) (2002): 57–96.

sustain the pathological nature of social relations that results in the humanitarian agent's inability to empathetically appropriate her human and natural surroundings). In Edward Said's *Orientalism,* which unmasked oriental studies as an intellectual side of colonial domination, Said explains with a great historical detail the invention of the Orient as a crucial part of making the identity of the Western world. "Orientalizing" a culture, in this sense, implies a distinctive discursive process of othering wherein Non-European culture is turned into *the other* of the Western world, portraying its members and their practices as alien and exotic. As he highlights this performative instance of colonial discourse,

> [N]either the term Orient nor the concept of the West has any ontological stability; each is made up of human effort, partly affirmation, partly identification of the Other. That these supreme fictions lend themselves easily to manipulation and organization of collective passion has never been more evident than in our time, when the mobilizations of fear, hatred, disgust, and resurgent self-pride and arrogance – much of it having to do with Islam and the Arabs on one side, "we" Westerners on the other – are very large-scale enterprises.[29]

In the context of this dependence on a complex backdrop of political motives and social conditions that inform and necessitate epistemological positions of social agents, one of the most fundamental discursive logics of colonialism was to (mis)understand other cultures as ahistorical – that is, as immutable, exotic, backward traditions that were confining their members in "uncivilized" values, subsequently warranting Western interventions when colonial interests were requesting their enslavement or annihilation.[30] Obsessive focus on cultural differences and unfamiliar aspects of different traditions has often resulted in a numbness in the West for common values and similar ways of living, what has in turn made engaged relationship with Non-Western other difficult, if not impossible.[31]

---

29   Edward Said, *Orientalism* (New York: Vintage Books, 1999), xvii.

30   Said identifies three major mechanisms of othering in regard to other cultures: *totalization of a culture, the erasing of history,* and *exoticizing of cultural traits and practices.* What these attitudes accomplish is an oversimplification of complex historical and political conditions that disregard the diversity of Non-European cultural identities and practices.

31   This can be seen in recent selectivism who is prioritized for immediate and extensive aid among refugees and how is not. It seems obvious that better support is given to refugees who we deem similar to us (Football coach, pet friendly family, etc.)

If Said and Quijano are right in their claims that Europe's ideological and material dependency on its colonies leads to their subsequent erasure, what lessons can we take for current predicaments of *otherizing* world of humanitarianism. If our subjectivity is developed within a web of social relations that constitute the normative background of our epistemic sensibilities and moral/political faculties, this very evaluative framework simultaneously constraints and enables our ability to know ourselves and others. As the preceding pages show, the structure and dynamics of such processes (i.e. formations, negotiations, inclusions, exclusions, humanizations, dehumanization, etc.) compel us to admit that such an acknowledgment of the unavoidable impurity of our cognitive, moral and political faculties necessitates giving away overly-ambitious claims that some philosophers or social activists (especially those in the humanitarian field) make regarding the possibility of mobilizing solidarity independently of addressing its social, epistemic and ontological constraints. Too often such attempts end up as ignorant, illusory or reinforcing the same injustices and inequalities they aim to combat by ignoring the often incommensurable experiences of differently positioned social groups. As Quijano writes in regard to the assimilation of diverse and heterogeneous histories of Non-Europeans into a homogenizing discourse dominated by Europe,

> In effect, all of the experiences, histories, resources, and cultural products ended up in one global cultural order revolving around European or Western hegemony. Europe's hegemony over the new model of global power concentrated all forms of the control of subjectivity, culture, and especially knowledge and the production of knowledge under its hegemony... They repressed as much as possible the colonized forms of knowledge production, models of the production of meaning, symbolic universe and models of expression and of objectification and subjectivity... All of those turbulent processes involved a long period of the colonization of cognitive perspectives, modes of producing and giving meaning, the results of material existence, the imaginary, the universe of intersubjective relations with the world: in short colonization of the culture.[32]

When we connect these insights with current humanitarian challenges, it seems like most of these struggles echo the colonial legacy of European societies in one way or another. The intersection of racism, sexism, human governance, cultural imperialism and other forms of exclusionary practices is one of the main obstacles for humanism and inclusion of those whose lives are

---

32   Quijano, "Coloniality of Power," 189.

affected by historical and present injustices (e.g. inclusion of refugees in Euro-pean societies), and the adamant refusal of the latter in enforcing immediate humanitarian obligations.

In the end, how do we begin to tackle these issues and pave the way for genuine moral and political engagement amid so many injustices and human vulnerabilities? Not only do these epistemological and ontological negotia-tions take place within a power saturated reality but they also circumscribe and define who we are, our sense of self, the way we are perceived by others, what we are able to see and who the Other is. Additionally, they impose a con-dition of "reproducibility," a prerequisite that allows for the perpetuation of social conditions whose history (and longevity) often mistakenly influence us to believe they are "natural" in some way, rather than a product of historical choices that have been made at the cost of conquered, enslaved and oppressed people. Yet, in light of shifting social and cultural contexts, the reproducibility of power relations also entails a possibility to break out of previous oppres-sive contexts. One lesson we can take from this brief excursion into decolonial theory is that only when we detach from reductive accounts of 'knowing' and 'seeing,' when we reconfigure the direction from which power flows, do these hegemonic imaginaries fall apart.

4   Conclusion: *Echoes of Solidarity*

Throughout this chapter, I have argued that by invoking human vulnerability and suffering as the moral cornerstones of solidarity, humanitarianism col-lapses important political questions of responsibility and (global) justice with moralizing discourses, around which the Western public is called to organize a charitable action towards the misfortune of Non-Western others. Ironically enough, compassion and the representation of human suffering – the two structural aspects of the humanitarianism – often failed to mobilize and sus-tain moral dispositions to act on the vulnerability of others. We have seen from the preceding pages that Western humanitarian agent ultimately cultivates a flawed disposition of solidarity, which often ignores the historical injustic-es and contemporary inequalities sustained by a dehumanizing logic of the global market and neoliberalism (this is most evident in the widespread indif-ference and moral selectivism of the Western humanitarian public). Whereas an extensive analysis of compassion would disclose the limits of liberal dis-courses of care and responsibility, the suspicion towards public imagery of hu-man suffering (and knowledge that such imagery forms and articulates) raises another set of problems. In the case of media representations that expose

Western subjects to human vulnerability and gruesome atrocities, the extent to which such portrayals make available the normative discourses that subtly regulate moral and political threshold of the Western spectator, such practices are ultimately instruments of power. Amnesty appeals, celebrity activism, social media activism, journalistic reporting and academic reiterations all set the frame that articulates and enables the encounter with vulnerable others, and yet what these practices actually do is to impose a homogeneous ideology of solidarity that ultimately fails to move Western public beyond narcissistic and increasingly corporate interests.

By analyzing the entanglement of moral impulses with the economy and ways in which such entanglement is manifested through the diverse mechanisms that form what we can understand as our humanitarian present, I sought to demonstrate how humanitarianism has colonialism and capitalism as its necessary conditions of possibility. In other words, humanitarianism manifests all communicative, representational and institutionalized paradoxes and ideological tendencies of neocolonialism and neoliberalism, which ultimately thrives on inequality, suffering, militarism and moral selectivism. As we could see from my reference to recent work in social epistemology and decolonial theory, these paradoxes and ideological tendencies ultimately disclose two intertwined moments of social processes that constitute and sustain humanitarian agency, namely, epistemic and ontological negotiations within a representational structure that systematically differentiates those lives who are worthy of Western concern, from those lives that are silenced and rendered invisible. Thus, rather than directing my analysis at limits of current international law and international institutions, avoiding a naïve denunciation of humanitarian management has helped me focus on the inner mechanisms of the production of "humanity" under inhumane conditions of an unjust global order. This is why reflecting on calls for cultivating compassionate dispositions towards distant others discloses the underlying logic of economic domination of all spheres of social life, wherein solidarity is not only rendered a matter of consumerist choice, but it has also prioritized the pursuit of self-assertion and pleasures of the Western identity over the morality of otherness and justice.

This pervasive instrumentalization (and commodification) of solidarity, however, does not occur in a vacuum. The formation and articulation of knowledge about the suffering of others take place in public sites wherein images, news broadcasts, diverse "artistic" renderings of human deprivation on social media, etc. are entangled with relations of power that deploy epistemic and ontological mechanisms of othering according to the hegemonic logic of Eurocentrism. Thus, attempts to ground normative commitments through public renderings of lives situated in a spiral of historical (and present) injustices not only emerge within a particular discursive and historical context, but they also unavoidably realize exclusionary structures of power that form and sustain identity and existence of the West at the cost of the rest of the world. According to this understanding, when we reflect on humanitarian efforts we can see that processes aimed at helping humanize victims (albeit still selectively), ultimately contribute to the reproduction of global hierarchies that recall the lethal legacy of colonialism and imperialism.

By giving accounts of how such hierarchies form and sustain our agency in a way that prevents us from looking at others without the reductive lens of Eurocentrism, I have tried to go beyond a figure of the humanitarian victim, and problematize the subjectivity of the spectator. Instead of despairing for the inhumanity of perpetrators and social conditions that their agency brings into existence, my intention was to call into question the historically invariable role of bystanders. Similarly entangled in ontological formation and defined by, often, unexamined certainties of "objective" knowledge that aims to vindicate the history of the West (and present choices that West makes), the bystander often becomes arbitrarily collectivized in the hegemonic figure of the Western actor, who remains blind and ignorant about her own role in perpetuating historical inequalities and injustices done to others whose agency is commonly ignored or rendered insignificant.

Bibliography

Agamben, Giorgio. *Homo Sacer: Sovereign Power and Bare Life*. Stanford: Stanford University Press, 1998.

Allen, Amy. *The Politics of Our Selves*. New York: Columbia University Press, 2008.

Allen, Amy. *The End of Progress*. New York: Columbia University Press, 2015.

Arendt, Hannah. *The Origins of Totalitarianism*. New York: Harcourt Brace Jovanovich, 1998.

Dotson, Kristie. "Theorizing Jane Crow, Theorizing Unknowability." *Social Epistemology*, 31 (5) (2017): 417–430.

Fassin, Didier. *Humanitarian Reason: A Moral History of the Present*. Berkeley: University of California Press. 2011.

Foucault, Michel. *The History of Sexuality Volume 1: An Introduction*. New York: Random House, 1978.

Foucault, Michel. *Society Must Be Defended. Lectures at the College de France 1975–76*. New York: Picador, 2003.

Gilson, Erinn. *The Ethics of Vulnerability*. New York: Routledge, 2014.

Ivanovic, Mladjo. "The European Grammar of Inclusion: Integrating Epistemic and Social Inclusion of Refugees in Host Societies." *Radical Philosophy Review*, 21 (1) (2018): 103–127.

Mignolo, Walter D. "The Geopolitics of Knowledge and the Colonial Difference." *The South Atlantic Quarterly*, 101 (1) (2002): 57–96.

Mignolo, Walter D. *The Darker Side of Western Modernity: Global Futures, Decolonial Options*. Durham: Duke University Press, 2011.

Mignolo, Walter D. *Local Histories/Global Designs: Coloniality, Subaltern Knowledges, and Border Thinking*. Princeton: Princeton University Press, 2012.

Morana, Mabel and Jaurequi, Carlos. *Revisiting the Colonial Question in Latin America*. Iberoamericana / Vervuert, 2008.

Quijano, Anibal. "Coloniality of Power, Eurocentrism, and Latin America." In *Coloniality at Large*, edited by Mabel Moraña, Enriqué Dussel,and Carlos A. Jáuregui, 181–224. (Durham, NC: Duke University Press, 2008), 181–224.

Rancière, Jacques. *Disagreement: Politics and Philosophy*. Minneapolis: University of Minnesota Press, 1999.

Said, Edward. *Orientalism*. New York: Vintage Books, 1999.

Schutte, Olivia. "Cultural Alterity: Cross-Cultural Communication and Feminist Theory in North-South Contexts." *Hypatia*, 13 (2) (1998): 53–72.

Smith, Andrea. "Native Studies at the Horizon of Death: Theorizing Ethnographic Entrapment and Settler Self-Reflexivity." In *Theorizing Native Studies*, edited by Audra Simpson and Andrea Smith. (Durham: Duke University Press, 2008), 207–223.

PART 2

Positioning Counter-discourses

∴

CHAPTER 4

Women Refashion Iran: Decolonizing the Rehistoricized Narratives

Esmaeil Zeiny

1 Introduction

After 9/11 and the consequent political aftermath, the world has witnessed an unprecedented proliferation of Muslim writings in autobiographical form. In this, life narratives by and about Muslim women from the Middle East, particularly by Iranian women in diaspora, experienced a greater boom, have garnered a particular interest in the West and have gradually become important to a growing Western readership. What triggered this burgeoning of writings by the Iranian immigrant women is threefold: (a) a genuine interest and inquisitiveness in how "native" Muslim women speak of their own experiences: veiled and not allowed to appear unveiled to men outside the family, Muslim women have always been an ongoing source of fascination and curiosity for many in the West; (b) 9/11, the consequent President Bush's "Axis of Evil" speech and his launching of "war on terror": when liberal newspapers and Democrats supported the "war on terror," reading this emerging literature of Muslim women became an alternative; (c) the feeling of self-authorization that has historically been denied to these Iranian women writers and their pent-up frustration for not being allowed to write: Iranian women's voices and concerns were historically discouraged in the Iranian patriarchal society as the focus was to keep women's voices and concerns within the domain of household. All these triggering points have been working in tandem to provide Iranian immigrant women writers a long-awaited atmosphere to write their thoughts and concerns that have been unheard and unseen.

Iranian women in exile have chosen autobiography as a favorite literary medium to represent their personal and collective past; the past from which they were absent, unseen and unheard in a country where they had played a significant role in refashioning its history. From Pari Khan Khanum (1548–1578), the daughter of the Safavid Shah Tahmasp I (r.1524–1576) through Khayr al-Nisa Begum (1549–1579), the mother of Shah Abbas the Great (r. 1588–1629) to Malek Jahan Khanum (1805–1873), the Persian princess of the Qajar Dynasty,

Iranian women held sway in the country and exerted serious political influence throughout the history. Moving forward to the contemporary era, Iranian women had prominent and often decisive participation in political and social movements such as the 1905–11 Constitutional Revolution and the 1979 Iranian Revolution. Scattered through the different eras of Iranian history, Iranian women's roles changed and their objectives evolved but they have always been involved in refashioning the country. However, their significant roles have fallen victim to disregard not only in their own country but also in the West. Although the Western representations of Iranian Muslim women are gradually changing to that of an articulate and socio-politically active woman with their recent involvement in the 2009 Green Movement, the White Wednesdays and the 2018 Girls of Revolution, the Western depictions of these women have historically been constructed as weak, oppressed, passive, inferior and victims of religious and patriarchal rules.

It is in response to this historical absence of women in Iran and the West's stereotypical depictions of Muslim women that the Iranian women in exile decided to put pen to paper and write their autobiography. Thus, these life narratives are allegedly presenting an alternative history of Iran and Iranian women. However, the effort to address and challenge a Western audience's preconceptions about Iran, Iranian men and women, and Iranian culture seems to be deliberately impuissant as many of these life narratives provide the readers with the Orientalist stereotypical accounts. Written to unfold the lives of Muslim women, these narratives are oftentimes replete with generalizations, exaggerations and they reduce all diversities of Muslims and Muslim women to a single image as if one Iranian woman's account is every Iranian woman's story. Having become a staple of publishing houses in the West, these life narratives have been 'growingly commodified, circulated and consumed uncritically in the hope of journeying 'behind' and 'beyond' the veil of the Muslim world and its women for the unheard and unseen stories.'[1] Receiving universal praise by Western critics, these diasporic feminist-oriented narratives are taken for granted by many readers in the West who fail to understand that this version of reconstructed history is an ideological narrative appropriated for Western imperialism. This calls for the decolonization of their re-historicized narratives and the rethinking of issues that have been commonly raised.

---

1   Esmaeil Zeiny, "Diasporic Muslim Discourses: Re-visiting & Challenging the Stereotypes." *Islamic Perspective*, London Academy of Iranian Studies, 17 (2007): 2.

2   The Rehistoricized Narratives

For over thirty years since the 1979 Revolution and more than a decade after the 9/11, Iranian women writers in diaspora have been creating a literature engaged with what have become the most suitable topics of the day: immigration, exile, religious fundamentalism and women's right. This diasporic literature could be read through a postcolonial lens by tapping into, appropriating and interpolating the master discourse of history both in Iran and abroad.[2] The master discourse, in this context, is generally described as the state-derived story of events, emphasizing the Iranian authorities' perspectives. These women writers are 'deliberately challenging and transforming its elements, to reconstruct and negotiate histories reflective of their own identities, experiences and desired futures.'[3] Iranian women in diaspora have been challenging the dominant homogeneous narratives of Iranian history in which the 'erasure and elision of gender, language and ethnicity'[4] has been insisted upon; a dominant history in which many alternative histories and experiences have not been mentioned. The conspicuous absence of historical acknowledgement and representation in public did not allow the women to be historically legitimized. Since 'what it means to have a history, is the same as what it means to have a legitimate existence: history and legitimization go hand in hand.'[5] This feeling of not being legitimized made the Iranian women in exile grab the opportunity offered by the West to write their own version of history through autobiography. By engaging with history, these diasporic writers are tapping into rewriting, reconstructing and challenging the historical narratives to unveil the untold and unnoticed multifaceted of Iranian experiences and to bring them from the periphery to the center.[6]

Therefore, for these diasporic women writers whose works resist the hegemony of official history, the obsession with history is not necessarily about feeling nostalgic about one's past to retain the sense of identity but more

---

2   For a comprehensive study of Iranian Diasporic Literature, please see Sanaz Fotouhi's *The Literature of Iranian Diaspora: Meaning and Identity since the Islamic Revolution*. London, New York: I.B.Tauris, 2015.

3   Sanaz Fotouhi, *The Literature of Iranian Diaspora: Meaning and Identity since the Islamic Revolution*. (London, New York: I.B.Tauris, 2015), 23.

4   Nasrin Rahimieh, "Marking Gender and Difference in the Myth of the Nation: A Postrevolutionary Iranian Film," in *The New Iranian Cinema: Politics, Representation and Identity*, ed. Tapper R. (New York: I.B. Tauris, 2002), 38.

5   Bill Ashcroft, *Post-colonial Transformation*. (London: Routledge, 2001), 83.

6   Fotouhi, *The Literature of Iranian Diaspora*.

importantly, it is also what Ashcroft (2001) calls "appropriation and interpola-
tion" of master narrative of history. Challenging the grand narrative of history
can function well through 'interpolate[ing] the master discourse of…history,
engaging it on its own terms.'[7] Interpolating history can 'subvert the unques-
tioned status of the "scientific record" by reinscribing the "rhetoric" of events'[8]
formed by the marginal voices and narratives. This sort of interpolating the
"master discourse of history" is manifested in Iranian diasporic women autobiographies in which the authors relate specific events from the perspectives
of previously muted voices. The purpose of many of these authors is to rewrite
history, to interrogate and repossess the culture, to correct misunderstand-
ings, to rectify an injustice whether personal or historical, and to interpret the
events from their own points of view. As Gusdorf beautifully states, 'no one can
better do justice to himself than the interested party, and it is precisely in order to do away with misunderstanding, to restore an incomplete or deformed
truth' that the writers relate their story.[9] For instance, Mehry Reid in her 1995
Snake Marble: A Persian Memoir has a chapter named 'Window to the Past' in
which she says she has written her memoir to leave her descendants a family history and memories of customs, traditions, and way of life.[10] Within the
same line of historicization, the cover page to Shusha Guppy's *The Blindfold
Horse* (1988) describes the book as an 'evocation of a way of life that has been
destroyed forever.'[11] Satrapi argues that she has written *Persepolis* (2003) to
erase some of the misconceptions that Westerners have about Iran, its people,
and its history.[12] In the same vein, Marina Nemat in an interview with Behnood
Mokri, Voice of America argues that she wrote *Prisoner of Tehran* (2007) for the
next Iranian generations to know the true history of Iran and Iranian people.[13]

This personal view becomes political and that 'the personal is political has
always been at the heart of all feminisms, therefore it is not surprising that

7   Bill Ashcroft, "Remembering the Future: Utopianism in African Literature." *Textual Prac-
         tices*, 32 (5) (2009): 709. Fotouhi has also explained how diasporic writers "appropriate and
         interpolate" the master narrative of history in her book.
8   Ashcroft, *Post-colonial Transformation*, 92.
9   Geroge Gusdorf, "Conditions and limits of autobiography," in *Autobiography: Essays Theo-
         retical and Critical*, ed. James Olney (Princeton, NJ: Princeton University Press, 1980), 36.
10   Mehry M. Reid, M. &Thomas R. Reid, *Snake's Marble: A Persian Memoir*. Veradale: Vantage
         Press, 1995.
11   Shusha Guppy, *The Blindfold Horse: Memories of a Persian Childhood*. London: Heine-
         mann, 1988.
12   Marjaneh Satrapi, *Persepolis: The Story of a Childhood*. New York: Pantheon Books, 2003.
13   Marina Nemat, *Prisoner of Tehran*. New York: Simon & Schuster, 2007.

memoirs have become popular with women'[14] in diaspora to interrogate a history and a culture from which they find their experiences of their self and their life excluded. The writers of these autobiographies are not ignorant of their close contact with history. They write their autobiographies to contribute to history, and to win the battles in history that had been lost in their life in Iran. Therefore, behind the impulse to write their life narratives lays the idea that memory becomes history. It is certainly rewarding that Iranian women are finally voicing their concerns through autobiographies and are willing to take agency for their life stories. They realize that their life stories are not only significantly important but also they can be received enthusiastically. However, in their zeal to reconstruct the history of Iran, there lies a great danger. The danger arises when these texts become models for understanding Iran and Iranians, and when they are used to teach history. For example, Satrapi's graphic memoir, *Persepolis* (2003) was one of the reading items in West Point, the United States military academy, and it was on the reading list of some other educational centers in North America and Europe as well. It was accompanied by unit guides and teaching supplements. Reading this memoir to understand Iranian history, Cathryn Clarke writes that as a Canadian with 'limited knowledge of the history or current situation in Iran, Satrapi's book did, indeed, show me a more accurate and more human picture of Iran and of Iranians.'[15] The very popular Nafisi's *Reading Lolita in Tehran* (2003)[16] which topped the *New York Times* bestseller list for more than ninety weeks has been marketed to both book clubs and teachers with the reader's guide at the end of the book and a teacher's guide available online.[17] It is part of a curriculum across North America in the disciplines of international relations, women's studies, English studies and anthropology, with course titles as varied as "Women and Islam," "Understanding Totalitarianism," "Understanding Culture and Cultural Difference" and "Conflict and Gender." The book has been taken as a reflection of women's oppression living under the Islamic republic and a lack of every kind of freedom since the Revolution of 1979.

Unfamiliar with the cultural and religious contexts of Iran, Western readers take the authors' renditions as accurate and authentic due to the authors' nativity and first-hand information. Many Readers are unaware of the fact that these writers can easily distort realities into fiction. Whitlock argues that life

---

14   Helen M. Buss, *Repossessing the World: Reading Memoirs by Contemporary Women.* (Wilfrid Laurier University Press, 2002), 3.

15   Cathryn Clarke, "Fuller Image." *The Iranian.* September 12, 2003.

16   Azar Nafisi, *Reading Lolita in Tehran.* New York: Random House, 2003.

17   Please see Random House, Teacher's Guide for Reading Lolita in Tehran. (2006). http://www.randomhouse.com/catalog/display.pperl?isbn=9780812971064&view=tg.

narratives that come into the West from the East and distributed to form public opinions bolster stereotypes;[18] this signifies their potentialities as propaganda. Arguments on legitimacy and authenticity are always of vital importance in the trajectory of minority life narratives and testimony should be always subjected to cross-examination. By recognizing the hoax or rogue as the "dark side" of life narratives, accusations of chic dissimulation and the questioning of legitimacy and authenticity are always present when a testimonial narrative is able to draw forth empathy and cognizance of human right issues.[19] This holds true with diasporic Iranian women's memoirs; they elicit sympathy through historicizing the oppression of women in post-revolutionary Iran. When the Western readers read the contemporary life narratives written by Iranian women, they feel sympathy for the women living in those societies. The generalization about Iranian Muslim women submission is, in fact, a trope to kindle Western feminist sympathy towards women of the Third World which promotes the idea that women in Iran are in dire need of liberation by the West. Pulling the Western eyes behind the *chador* or under the burka is an effective rhetorical approach that draws out both 'sympathy and advocacy' which can be put to 'various political and strategic uses.'[20] These kinds of life narratives are, in Whitlock's term, 'soft weapons' as the authors employ strategies to elicit sympathy from the Western readers. Many of these autobiographies have assumed center-stage in appropriating the legitimate cause of women's rights and put them in the service of Empire building projects disguised under the rhetoric of 'war on terror. According to Christian Ho,

> Among many other legacies, the September 11 terrorist attacks will be remembered by some for catapulting women's rights to the center stage of global politics, as the United States launched the war on terror in Afghanistan and then Iraq, the liberation of women from barbaric regimes became a powerful rationale for intervention.[21]

Anchored within such discourse, in most of these rehistoricized narratives, Iranian veiled women are depicted as submissive and have no agency at a time when these women, veiled and unveiled, are refashioning the country's politics and culture. Considering that the veil is a significant symbol of Islam for the

---

18 Gillian Whitlock, *Soft Weapons: Autobiography in Transit*. (Chicago: University of Chicago Press, 2007), 112.

19 Ibid.

20 Whitlock, *Soft Weapons*, 47.

21 Christian Ho, "Responding to Orientalist Feminism." *Australian Feminist Studies*, 25 (66) (2010): 433.

West, it should be of no surprise that these narratives, framed in the West for the Western audience, open with the image of the headscarf as a sign of women's oppression. For example, Nafisi, in her *Reading Lolita in Tehran* (2003), uses an Orientalist perspective in respect to the veiled Muslim woman as she believes that a woman with a veil is invisible and in Western dress she is not invisible; rather she becomes robust and conspicuous: '...shed their mandatory veils and robes and bust into color... they took off more than their scarves and robes. Gradually, each one gained an outline and a shape...'[22] Nafisi establishes a binary opposition between the imposed veil, as a homogenizing sign of women's oppression, and the effulgent individuality characterized by various clothing and hairstyles. What she believes is tantamount to the idea that veiled women can have no agency and they cannot retain their individuality. While describing one of her students, Sanaz, when she wears the *chador*, Nafisi takes an Orientalist stand by stating that Sanaz's gait has changed and it is 'in her best interest not to be seen, not to be heard or noticed.'[23] Similarly, Satrapi adopts the same view in portraying veiled women. She describes her mother's photo of the passport with the veil on as 'she sure didn't look very happy. In fact, she was unrecognizable.'[24] Her mother is reduced to invisibility with the veil on suggesting that Muslim women are invisible in the society.

It comes as no surprise that these authors use the issue of the veil right from the beginning to reinforce the West/East dichotomy. They nullify the feasibility of being for the women in Iran by explicitly stating that women can only be present when their robes and scarves are taken off.[25] Veiled women are rehistoricized as submissive and victim of the Iranian patriarchal society. They are disembodied, fragmented and have no visibility. All these negative depictions of veiling make the white and the unveiled body of Western women stands as a global norm; thus, as seen in the instances of veiling, these writers become a voice representative of the interests of imperialism when they make the unveiled body a universal norm. These memoirs advance the aims of imperialism by making the issue of Muslim women as a plight in the Islamic world, which needs immediate attention of the Westerners as the saviors of the brown women, and yet puts this crisis right at the disposal of American warmongering. Whitlock (2007) argues that it would be an extremely difficult job for the Western audiences of the women's autobiography from the Middle East to face a

22   Nafisi, *Reading Lolita,* 3.
23   Nafisi, *Reading Lolita,* 26.
24   Satrapi, *Persepolis,* 126.
25   Esmaeil Zeiny, "Neo-colonialism as an Imperialistic Project: A Critique of Three Iranian Diasporic Memoirs." National University of Malaysia, Dissertation, 2013.

line of veiled women on the covers of multitude life narratives and not get the sense to unveil or "disentangle" and "liberate" the Muslim woman.[26] One feels empowered by their resistance to the imposed dress code and can sympathize with Iranian women as subordinated to enact the male Islamist patriarchal rules; however, there appears a feeling of alienation when these writers, in their attempt to rehistoricize Iran in their own terms, generalize and reduce all the veiled women to submissive women. It is true that mandatory dress code has been imposed on women but this version of reconstructed history lacks the presence of any articulate and powerful veiled women such as women authors, poets and politicians. In their enthusiasm to recapture Iran for their Western readers, many of these authors tend to relate the events of the Hostage Crisis. For instance, when passing by a street near the American Embassy, Nafisi gets to observe the demonstration and writes, 'I could never accept this air of festivity, the jovial arrogance that dominated the crowds in front of the embassy.'[27] This scene is depicted as if the majority of Iranian population were celebrating the hostage-taking. She never mentions that a considerable number of Iranian public also abhorred the hostage-taking. However, it was mentioned in passing in Nemat's text where she asserts that this act of hostage-taking 'sounded like absolute madness to me and to everyone I talked to.'[28]

Failing to mention that the Iranian public also disapproved of this act, the Western readers are presented with descriptions of a gathering of happy throng outside the occupied American Embassy chanting slogans "Death to America." What has been unmentioned in the memoirs is that a host of Iranian public reprimanded the hostage-taking of the American Embassy and believed that those hostage takers did a very wrong act irrespective of America's fault in its foreign affair. This has not been mentioned as the writers need to be selective in their attempt to offer an alternative history.[29] Another historical event which has been copiously cited in the diasporic memoirs is the Iran-Iraq war. In spite of copious references to the 1980 Iran-Iraq war, these writers never mention the courage, devotion, honor, or any other qualities like motivation among the Iranians who gave their lives to defend their country. Rather, they have been portrayed as very young and 'caught up in the government propagandas that offered them a heroic and adventurous life at the front and

26   Whitlock, *Soft Weapons*.

27   Nafisi, *Reading Lolita*, 106.

28   Nemat, *Prisoner of Tehran*, 116.

29   Keshavarz (2007) has also pointed these out and highlighted the element of selectivity in their life narratives. Please see her *Jasmine and Stars: Reading More than Lolita in Tehran*, Chapel Hill: The University of North Carolina Press, 2007.

encouraged them to join the militia, even against their parents' wishes';[30] they were encouraged by the government to become martyrs as 'the government announced, becoming martyrs; after all, guaranteed way to go to heaven.'[31] The authorities encouraged young people to go to war in return for a key to heaven; 'if they went to war and were lucky enough to die, this key would get them to heaven.'[32] According to Keshavarz (2007), obviously, there are people who rush to war in response to a promise of a hero's reward. These kinds of people can arise anytime and anywhere even outside of Iran. Is there any war without propaganda?

For example, the American soldiers fought in Iraq and Afghanistan, thousands of miles away from their home. Can anyone say there is no propaganda involved? After all, Iraqis were the aggressors; they were the one who first began to attack.[33] However, as veterans of the Iran-Iraq war, Marandi and Pirnajmuddin (2009) refute Satrapi's claim about the key to heaven and argue that they would like evidence to support this claim as they have never seen anything like that during the war.[34] They criticize Satrapi for the absurdity of her claim by stating that one of the characteristics of Iranian native Orientalist discourse is the absurdity of such claims.[35] While the diasporic memoirists condemn both the Islamic Republic and Iraq's leader Saddam Hussein, they never criticize the U.S politics in the region, never mention that the United States backed Iraq during its war against Iran and omit the CIA staged coup d'état to topple the democratically elected Prime Minister, Mohammad Mosadeq. Another characteristic of these life narratives, as Dabashi (2011) states, is the "selective memory" of historical incidents that writers apply in their texts.[36] These re-historicized narratives are autobiographies of selective memories; the writers erase the historical facts and situations in favor of imperialism. The principal task of these writers is to fake 'authority, authenticity, and native knowledge'[37] by giving information to the Western public about the outrageous behaviors happening in their birthplace; thence, justifying the imperial projects of the West. The success of these narratives can be attributed to their topicality and the geopolitical climate of the time.

---

30   Nafisi, *Reading Lolita*, 208.

31   Nemat, *Prisoner of Tehran*, 139.

32   Satrapi, *Persepolis*, 99.

33   Keshavarz, *Jasmine and Stars*.

34   Seyed Mohamamd Marandi & Hossein Pirnajmuddin, "Constructing an Axis of Evil: Iranian Memoirs in the "Land of the Free.'" *Ajiss*, 26 (2) (2009).

35   Ibid.

36   Hamid Dabashi, *Brown Skin, White Mask*. New York: Pluto Press, 2011.

37   Ibid., 72.

Nafisi's *Reading Lolita in Tehran* (2003) and Satrapi's *Persepolis* (2003) emerged exactly at the time when President George W. Bush started launching his global project of "war on terror" and after his notorious "Axis of Evil" speech addressed to Iran, Iraq, and North Korea. The other autobiographies published from 2004 onwards are within the series of an influx of Iranian women life narratives portraying the life in the Islamic Republic as the nemesis of the West. These narratives which are just a few examples of disinformation and propaganda are taken as reality and truth by their readers. Although there are some commendable elements in these rehistoricized narratives, one should be intelligent enough to question the accuracy and the marketing strategy of the texts. The stringent rules are imposed upon women in Iran but these authors' life narratives are less to unveil those restrictions than to promote them in a 'manner that best serves the empire they help to sustain.'[38] Their narratives can be seen as a colonizing tool which promotes war against Iran. These memoirs can be manipulated and transformed to be at the disposal of the ideological machinery of the West in order to manufacture consent for imperial projects of war on terror. The writers' claim to write a version of history that dispels the common Western misconceptions about Iran and Iranians have to be refuted as it could be argued that if they had decided to write a true history and eliminate the misconceptions and stereotypes, why do they choose to begin their autobiography by amplifying the veiling as a symbol of oppression and why do they not frame the historical incidents in their proper culture and ideological contexts?

The writers pine to challenge the states 'old organised forgetting and organised remembering'[39] historical patterns but they fall into the same trap of selectivity and attenuate the veracity of their own rehistoricized narratives by representing Iran and Iranians stereotypically through not grounding their portrayals in their proper contexts. In these sorts of writings, the portrayals of "third world" are usually not grounded historically, traditionally and culturally, and therefore misrepresent Iranians and Iranian women's roles, cultural practices, and shared ideologies. The fact that these life narratives are now part of a curriculum at military and academic institutions in the West reinforces Dabashi's claim that such literary pieces in reconstructing history contribute to the justification of the imperial rule and intervention in the Islamic societies.[40] The prevalent post-9/11 rhetoric of "saving Muslim women" to justify war

---

38   Ibid., 73.
39   Paul Connerton, *How Societies Remember*. (Cambridge: Cambridge University Press, 1989), 47.
40   Dabashi, *Brown Skin*.

and military intervention resonates with these diasporic writers where Iranian women are routinely depicted as essentially victims. For instance, Negar Mottahedeh points out that 'it seems undeniable that *Reading Lolita in Tehran* and its author have been promoted, at least in part, to fulfill the ends of total war.'[41] In a similar stand, John Carlos Rowe asserts that *Reading Lolita* 're-legitimates Western Cultural texts as forerunners of the political revolution and regime change in Iran that the Bush administration has openly advocated.'[42] These autobiographies are, therefore, a restaging of Orientalist and imperialist ideologies which have become the "soft weapon" not only because of their ability in lending voices to unheard and unseen stories, but also since they are '...easily co-opted into propaganda... a careful manipulation of opinion and emotion in the public sphere and a management of information in the engineering of consent.'[43] Thus, how the past is remembered, forgotten or silenced in these rehistoricized life narratives deserve a pause for reflection and decolonization.

Decolonization, in this sense, is not the elimination of diasporic memoirs or taking away the authors' agency in its entirety, but rather it is the reassessment and reevaluation of the issues and events commonly raised in their narratives. It is bringing to surface the understanding that contemporary diasporic autobiographies do not adequately represent the diversity and complexity of Iran and Iranians in the time of ever-changing contexts and realities. Decolonization, in this context, is sifting the truth from imaginatively constructed realities. Moreover, it is seeking to 'reimagine and rearticulate power, change, and knowledge through a multiplicity of epistemologies, ontologies and axiologies.'[44] Therefore, decolonization does not simply suggest that we reassess and reevaluate the issues raised in the diasporic narratives and refrain from taking them for granted but it also suggests that we attempt for transformation. As Fanon writes, 'it is no longer a question of knowing the world, but of transforming it.'[45] Transformation occurs through alternative narratives wherein the diasporic often one-sided and out-of-context portrayals of Iran and Iranians are contested, challenged and pushed back. This decolonization will not be

---

41   Negar Mottahedeh, "Off the Grid: Reading Iranian Memoirs in Our Time of Total War." (2004), http://www.merip.org/mero/interventions/mottahedeh interv. html.

42   John Carlos Rowe, "Reading 'Reading Lolita in Tehran' in Idaho." *American Quarterly*, 59 (2) (2007): 271.

43   Whitlock, *Soft Weapons*, 3.

44   Aman Sium, Chandni Desai & Eric Ritskes, "Towards the 'tangible unknown': Decolonization and the Indigenous future." *Decolonization: Indigeneity, Education & Society*, 1 (1) (2012): III.

45   Frantz Fanon, *Black Skin, White Masks*. Trans. Richard Philcox. (New York: Grove Press, 1967), 1.

complete without challenging and contestation put forward through life narratives written by other Iranian women, especially the Iranian women inside
Iran. This sentiment is corroborated by Alfred (2009) who argues that decolonization can only be 'achieved through the resurgence of an Indigenous consciousness channeled into contention with [imperialism].'[46] This "indigenous
consciousness" is manifested through the alternative narratives that rebut the
institutionalized misconceptions about Iran and Iranians. In the spirit of reas-
sessing and reevaluating the commonly raised issues in diasporic narratives,
what follows is a depiction of Iranian women's important role and bravery in
refashioning the country's politics and culture, despite the imposed restrictions and discriminatory regulations.

3   Refashioning Iran

Although Iranian women's legal status has changed during various political
and historical eras and has gone through many ups and downs, they have always played crucial and representative roles in refashioning the country. Their
significant roles in the political and social evolution of the country are undeniable. Yet, the proclivity to trivialize and neglect their roles and movements,
and the subsequent disregarding of women's rights has been rife. For instance,
during the Constitutional Revolution of 1905–1911, Iranian women organized
many clandestine associations and meetings in support of the nationalist and
anti-imperialist movement, initiated street riots and strikes, participated in
fights against foreign forces, boycotted the importation of foreign goods, and
raised funds for the establishment of the National Bank but they were not
included in the definition of "citizen" in the constitution demanding the
'equality of all citizens in law.'[47] The male constitutionalists and the religious
leaders denied these women also the voting rights on the grounds that they
lack political and social insights overlooking their heavy involvement in political activities such as the Tobacco Protest (1891–1892) that culminated in the
Constitutional Revolution and their movements which led to the writing of
the first constitution. Much to the male constitutionalists' chagrin, however,
the outcome of the constitution prompted the female constitutional activists
to organize many more semi-clandestine associations to modify the situation,

---

46   Gerald Taiaiake Alfred, "Colonialism and State Dependency." *Journal de la Sante Autoch-
      tone*, November, (2009): 48.
47   Ali Akbar Mahdi, "The Iranian Women's Movement: A Century Long Struggle." *The Mus-
      lim World*, 94 (2004): 427.

improve their socio-political status and further their goals through publishing and education.

Despite facing *ulama*'s fierce opposition, these women succeeded in opening up schools and associations in major cities such as Tehran, Tabriz, Mashhad, Rasht, Hamadan and many other cities across the country within a short period of time.[48] By 1913, there were some 63 schools for girls and 9 women's societies in Tehran.[49] Targeting education, women published a considerable number of newspapers and magazines including *Danish, Amuzegar, Shekoufah, Bahar, Zanan-e Iran, Nameh Banovan* discussing women's rights and education.[50] The most influential and prominent leading women in the movement of this period included Maryam Amid Mozayyen ol-Saltaneh, Mah Sultan Khaanoum, Sediqeh Dawlatabadi, Khaanoum Azmodeh, Roshanak Nodoust, Shahnaz Azad, Muhtaram Eskandari, Shams ol-Muluk Javahir Kalam, Homa Mahmoudi Afaaq Parsa, and Zandokht Shirazi.[51] All the socio-political movements that these women led and later Reza Shah's (1925–1941) policies of modernization and Westernization tremendously altered the lives of Iranian women for better. For the first time ever, according to Sedghi 2007, a number of women 'entered into the modern sectors of the economy, public and non-sex segregated schools were established, family laws were modified...'[52] and 'women officially entered institutions of higher education and taught.'[53] Women did gain some rights in various social arenas but Reza Shah forcefully closed their independent organizations and developed a state-sponsored women's association of *Kanoon-e Banovan* (The Ladies Center) in 1934, headed by his daughter Ashraf Pahlavi.

Pursuant to Reza Shah's modernization policies was the 1936 Unveiling Act which prohibited women to appear veiled in public. Dressing up for modernity has been fashioned through unveiling women.[54] Whereas this forced unveiling was not well-received amongst a great number of Iranian women, particularly the lower-middle-class women, the dominant feminists of the time celebrated

---

48   Ibid.

49   Massoume Price, (2000). "Women's movement: A brief history 1850–2000." *The Iranian*, March 7 (2000).

50   Esmaeil Zeiny, Peivand Zandi & Khalil Mahmoodi, "Reconstructing the Society: Iranian Women's Movements." *The NIEW Journal*, 4, December (2012).

51   Badr Al-Moluk Bamdad, *Zan-e Irani az Enqelaab-e Mashrootiyat taa Enqelaab-e Sefid (Iranian Women from the Constitutional Revolution to the White Revolution)*. Tehran: Ibn Sinaa Publications, 1968.

52   Hamideh Sedghi, *Women and Politics in Iran: Veiling, Unveiling and Reveiling*. (Cambridge University Press, 2007), 61.

53   Ibid., 70.

54   Sedghi, *Women and Politics*.

this law of unveiling despite the violence of this action.[55] They were per-
suaded that it was a "progressive" measure necessary for confronting clerical
misogynistic approaches to women's concerns. This forceful act of unveiling
was applauded by the *Kanoon-e Banovan* as an epitome of social progress. The
Kanoon was, indeed, the key organization in bolstering the underpinnings of
the state's preferred image for the "modern" Iranian woman. This Unveiling Act
'ostensibly liberated women while denying them the freedom to choose how
to present themselves in public.'[56] The Unveiling Act was later abolished and
the ban was lifted with the 1941 Reza Shah's coerced abdication and enthroning
of his son Mohammad Reza Shah. This became a period when women formed
many women's organizations and associations for their political and cultural
demands, of which the followings were the most influential: *Jamiat-e Nesvan-e
Vatankhaah-e Iran* (The Patriotic Women's League of Iran), *Tashkilat-e Zanan-e
Iran* (The Organization of Iranian Women), *Hezb-e Zanan* (Women's Party),
and *Jamiat-e Zanan* (Women's League).[57] They developed close ties with different political parties as well.

Sazmane Demokratike Zanan (Women's Democratic Organization) of Tudeh
Party, *Nehzate Zanane Pishro* (Women's Progressive Movement) of Society of
Iranian Socialists, and *Komiteh-ye Zanaan* (Women's Committee) of Nation's
Party of Iran were the three important political parties that women joined in
great numbers. Besides requesting equal rights, education, abolition of polygamy, and the discriminatory policies towards veiled/unveiled women, these
women were actively engaged in the national struggle against foreign forces.[58]
Supported by the Shah and founded in 1954, *Anjoman-e Rah-e No* (The New
Path Society) became the most important women organization focusing on
the political rights of women, family law and universal suffrage. Five years
later, the organization was renamed to *Shora-ye Ali-ye Jamiat-e Zanan-e Ira*n
(the High Council of Iranian Women's Association) including seventeen other
women's associations.[59] Although all women's socio-political activities and
demonstrations were channeled through this government-controlled organization, they succeeded to finally secure the women's enfranchisement in 1963
granted by the government in the face of direct opposition by the *ulama* of

---

55   Nima Naghibi, *Rethinking Global Sisterhood: Western Feminism and Iran*. (London: Univer-
      sity of Minnesota Press, 2007), 44.
56   Ibid., 45.
57   Ruth F. Woodsmall, *Women and the New East*. Washington, D.C.: Middle East Institute,
      1960.
58   Mahdi, "The Iranian Women's Movement."
59   Zeiny, Zandi & Mahmoodi, "Reconstructing the Society."

the time. In 1966, the organization was renamed to *Saazeman-e Zanan-e Iran* (Women's Organization of Iran) and lasted until the end of the Pahlavi regime in 1978. As the only legal women's organization campaigning for legal reforms and offering "literacy, abortion, job counseling and youth programs," the organization served as the umbrella organization for 55 women's organizations with 70,000 members, 350 branches and 113 centers.[60]

It has been argued that this was not a feminist organization and it took preventive measures to curb feminist activities. Whether it had a feminist trajectory or not pales in comparison with the fact that women were now basically and literally involved in politics and directed institutes and organizations. Their involvement became more conspicuous in 1963 when 6 women were elected as deputies in the Parliament and in 1965 when a woman was appointed as a minister. The presence of these women in the legislative body of the government paved the way for the 1967 Family Protection Law which transmuted several aspects of law in favor of women. Fast-forward to the 1978–79 Revolution period, Iranian women became a major force for change. As socio-political and economic discontent escalated in the country in the late 70s, many women participated in strikes and demonstrations against the Shah. To mobilize a strong force against the Pahlavi regime, the *ulama* resorted into the reservoir of religious women and asked them to participate in the demonstrations.[61] Seeing the massive outpouring of women against the Shah, many young and secular Iranian women voluntarily wore the *chador* in a symbolic defiance of the Shah's Westernization policies and participated in the demonstrations.[62] For these women, *chador* became the mark of resistance, agency and cultural membership.[63] Soon women from all walks of life, veiled and unveiled, with different ideological inclinations participated in these anti-Shah demonstrations.

These strikes and anti-Shah demonstrations led to the overthrowing of the Shah in 1979. The 'participation of women in the Iranian revolution of 1979 was historically unparalleled, both in terms of the depth and breadth of their commitment.'[64] Yet, their achievements in the immediate post-revolution period were far away from their expectations. Immediately after the establishment

---

60   Ibid.
61   Mehrangiz Kar, *Hoqooqe Siyaasi-ye Zanaane Iran* (*Political Rights of Iranian Women*). Tehran: Roshangaran & Women Studies Publishing, (1376, 1997).
62   Farah Azari, "The Post-Revolutionary Women's Movement in Iran," in *Women of Iran. The Conflict with the Fundamentalist Islam*, ed. Farah Azari. London: Ithaca Press, 1983.
63   Naghibi, *Rethinking Global Sisterhood*.
64   Mahdi, "The Iranian Women's Movement," 435.

of Mehdi Bazargan's Interim Government, Ayatollah Khomeini demanded the abolition of Family Protection Act, ordered the implementation of *Sharia* and issued a decree demanding women not to wear miniskirts to work and wear the Islamic form of modest dress to which women responded massively and angrily. Hundreds of thousands of women poured into the streets and chanted slogans against the forced *hijab* and the abolition of the Family Protection Act. All these demonstrations and activities of women made the government retreat and caused a delay in enforcing the Veiling Act. However, in 1983, Ayatollah Khomeini ratified the Veiling Act which forbade women to appear unveiled in public. Women, who played a significant role in the 1979 Revolution were no longer free to choose either to veil or not to veil but their active role was once again recognized at the outset of the Iran-Iraq war when the authorities asked them to defend the country alongside Iranian men.[65] Hundreds of thousands of women contributed to the war effort serving in combat roles, battlefield nurses, doctors and surgeons, and they drove trucks to the war zones.

Another episode which is illustrative of women's significant role in refashioning the country is the 2009 Green Movement. As the first popular uprising after the 1979 Revolution, women, traditional and secular, religious and non-religious, young and old formed the forefront of these protests against the rigged presidential election. Women took to the streets in thousands defying the government in a non-violent manner through chanting, holding hands, and carrying banners. Iran witnessed no withdrawals from these women although they were aware of the consequences. Neda Agha-Soltan, a twenty-six-year-old student, was one of these women who took part in a peaceful demonstration and was shot to death. Her last moments were filmed with a cellphone and spread to the four corners of the world through social media. Since then, her image epitomizes both the victimization of Iranian women and their bravery, agency and self-determination in refashioning their country. The massive presence of women in the Green Movement was ultimately suppressed by the government but it demonstrated the tenacity of women to prove their existence in public sphere and it also spoke volume of the feminine power of the nation. For years many of these women have carried out subtle campaigns of civil disobedience as well. One such campaign is the social media campaign of "White Wednesday" through which Iranian women have been removing their headscarf in public or wearing a white headscarf as a symbol of protest against the compulsory dress code.

---

65   Esmaeil Zeiny, "Visual Discourses of (Un)veiling: Revisiting Women of Allah," in *Seen and Unseen: Visual Cultures of Imperialism*, eds. Sanaz Fotouhi & Esmaeil Zeiny. Brill: Leiden, 2018.

This social movement began to take center stage amidst the street demonstrations of January 2018 when a thirty-one-year-old woman, Vida Movahed, removed her headscarf and tied it to a stick waving it like a flag while standing on a platform in the Revolution Street in Tehran. This image of her silent protest went viral on social media and turned her into a symbol for women who oppose the compulsory dress code. The Iranian women in different parts of the country repeated her non-violent protest which soon has been named as "The Girls of Revolution Street." This has been the quietest protest Iran has probably ever seen but it may turn into the most effective strategy in pushing the boundaries set by the government. It ignited debates on Iran's mandatory hijab regulations. Despite being jailed, these women are continuing their battle against the discriminatory policies. They are not just fighting for the freedom to remove their headscarf or choose what to wear but also to change the political face and the paternalistic culture of the country which resists gender equality and favors males over females. For instance, blood money (*diyah*) is paid to women at half the rate paid to men; a court testimony by a woman is deemed half as valuable as that of a man. All the Iranian women's movements led to a breakthrough in societal attitudes towards women which has positive implications for the future of Iran. Their willpower to refashion the country is shaping the democratic aspirations of the nation in content, method and philosophy and challenges the Western rhetoric of "saving Muslim women." They counter the often misleading impression put forward by the West and challenge the homogenous representation of Iranian women as voiceless and submissive depicted by the diasporic life narratives. This thwarts the diasporic narratives' orientalist representations of Iranian women as passive and submissive.

4   Counter-discourses of the Rehistoricized Narratives

The surge of diasporic writing and cultural production by Iranian women in which women have become increasingly the subject of imperialist pity, fear and fascination continue to this day. Given the proliferation of these diasporic rehistoricized narratives, finding the effective counter-discourses – discourses that offer a positive alternative, deconstruct and delegitimize one-sided views in diasporic narratives – is crucial. Just as there are narratives that perpetuate the currency of Orientalist writing and representation, the response, direct or indirect, by Iranian women writers pushing back against these reductive mainstream stories that have been told about Iranian women has been equally overwhelming. For instance, Fatemeh Keshavarz's *Jasmine and Stars: Reading More than Lolita in Tehran* (2007) reframes the position of Iranian women and

corrects the Orientalist assumption about Iranian women.[66] She starts this re-
framing right from the cover where unlike the typical cover of passive women
gazing down or staring at the viewer, her cover illustrates two smiling Iranian
girls wearing sunglasses and holding up signs which read 'We, women want
equal rights, and 'violence against women is tantamount to violence against
humanity.' Keshavarz's book is an intimate exploration of Iranian literature
and society wherein she introduces Western readers to two modern Iranian
women writers, Forough Farrokhzad and Shahrnush Parsipour, whose strong
personalities and articulate voices belie the stereotypical perception of Iranian women as passive and victims in Iran. Keshavarz admits that her book
is a response to the 'writings addressed to the educated but nonexpert reader'
who 'is consuming these works in vast quantities.'[67] Calling these narratives as
'nonspecialized, eyewitness accounts' and 'New Orientalist narrative,' her goal
in writing *Jasmine and Stars* is to 'provide an alternative approach for learning
about an unfamiliar culture.'[68] *Jasmine and Starts* is a direct response to Azar
Nafisis's *Reading Lolita in Tehran* (2003) as the epitome of the Muslim women's
memoirs and seeks to challenge Nafisi's assertions about Iran, Iranian men and
women. In this light, Keshavarz employs counter-discursive strategies which
are in tandem with Helen Tiffin's observation that 'counter-discursive strategies involve a mapping of dominant discourse, a reading and exposing of its
underlying assumptions, and the dis/mantling of these assumptions from the
cross-cultural standpoint of the imperially subjectified 'local.'"[69] In this respect, *Jasmine and Stars* can be seen as an alternative memoir and a counter-
discourse of the rehistoricized narratives.

There are also many counter-discourses written by Iranian women inside
the country in an attempt to break the stereotypes that surround Iran and
Iranians. This sort of counter-discourse resonates well with Terdiman's definition of counter-discourse in relation to a dominant discourse by referring to it
as a passion to 'displace and annihilate a dominant depiction of the world.'[70]
A prominent example is Masoumeh Ebtekar's *Takeover in Tehran: The Inside Story of the 1979 U.S Embassy Capture* (2000) through which she tries to
break the stereotype of Iranians as violent hostage takers.[71] Currently the Vice

---

66   Keshavarz, *Jasmine and Stars*.
67   Ibid., 2.
68   Ibid.
69   Helen Tiffin, "Post-colonial Literatures and Counter-Discourse." *Kunapip*, 9 (13) (1987): 23.
70   Richard Terdiman, *Discourse/Counter-Discourse: The Theory and Practice of Symbolic
       Resistance in Nineteenth-Century France*. (New York: Cornell University Press, 1985), 12.
71   Masoumeh Ebtekar, *Takeover in Tehran: The Inside Story of 1979 U.S Embassy Capture*. Van-
       couver: Talonbooks, 2000.

President of Iran for Women and Family Affairs, Ebtekar was the spokeswoman for a group of young students who occupied the American Embassy on November 1979, took the diplomats and intelligence personnel hostage, and sparked an international incident. The accounts about this Hostage Crisis before the publication of Ebtekar's memoir have all been from the Western perspective, reflecting 'not a single Iranian viewpoint, not a single Iranian voice'[72] and later from the viewpoint of Iranians in diaspora who mostly reiterated the Western account. *Takeover in Tehran* is a writing-back to those accounts; it is an illustration of Ebtekar's perspective and the perspective of those who participated in the hostage-taking. This book is an attempt to shed light on the reasons for the takeover and planning for it. It portrays the students' motivation, frustration, fear and insecurity, youthful sincerity, doubt and idealism. Ebtekar writes that her book 'which breaks the silence for the first time in print – is intended as a long-needed corrective to the stereotypical account' of the hostage-taking and it is 'an antidote to the distorted images conveyed by the world media not only during and immediately after the capture of the embassy, but right up to this day.'[73] This memoir rectifies the biased media perception of the takeover and has been written in the hope of engaging the two nations in a "constructive dialogue." She writes,

> Can the misconceptions and misjudgments which have been created by years of conscious disinformation ever be put right, I wondered, as I began the task of sifting through my notes, diaries and memories? Can the American and Iranian peoples ever hope to overcome the barriers of propaganda and fiery rhetoric that now stands between them, and finally come to understand one another? The only way – and this is the ultimate aim of my account of the fateful events of 1979 and 1980 in Tehran – to alleviate tensions between the two nations, is to engage the two diverse and different cultures in a constructive dialogue.[74]

This alternative view of the Hostage Crisis written in the hope of opening "understanding and dialogue" between the United States and Iran did not get enough attention and went unnoticed especially with the events of 9/11 and President Bush's "Axis of Evil" speech. Although it has been written before the emergence of post-9/11 Muslim women memoirs, *Takeover in Tehran* can be considered a valuable addition to the counter-discourses of the rehistoricized

---

72   Ibid., 34.
73   Ibid.
74   Ibid.

narratives. Another prominent example but equally less noticed life narrative outside the borders of Iran is Masoumeh Ramhormozi's *Eternal Fragrance* (2003).[75] It is an account of Iran-Iraq war, the fall and the subsequent conquest of Khorramshahr, told by a fourteen-year-old girl who worked as a social worker in the front. This memoir breaks the exclusive grips that men had in the literary production of "Sacred Defense"[76] in which women were almost always portrayed as faithful housewives and mothers of the martyrs. It brings to the fore the fact that although the eight years of Sacred Defense is replete with stories of men who stood up and defended their geographical and religious boundaries, it is also the saga of endurance and sacrifice of the Iranian women, secular and religious, Muslim and non-Muslim, on the fronts. It highlights the roles of Iranian women who participated in the Iran-Iraq war and it is suggestive of the fact that Iranian women do not have a lower position than men in defending the country. This memoir, indeed, protests against views that women are weak and submissive. For instance, Masoumeh questions the existing patriarchal assumption that 'men are women's guardians on the front.'[77] In this vein, she challenges both the Iranian patrilineal cultural patterns and the Orientalist assumptions of Iranian women who are regarded as victims and stripped of agency.

As one of the early works by and about Iranian women who have participated in the Iran-Iraq war, *Eternal Fragrance* was ranked the second book in the 9th Sacred Defense Book of the year awards. It has been enthusiastically received by the Iranian readers and paved the way for the publication of similar works. However, its English version translated by Farahnaz Omidvar and launched at the 66th Frankfurt Book Fair in 2014 has never received any sort of attention from media and reviewers. Within the genre of "Sacred Defense" literature, *One Woman's War: Da (Mother)* (2008) is another memoir told by Seyyedeh Zahra Hosseini about her experiences during the Iran-Iraq war as recorded by Seyyedeh Azam Hosseini.[78] This memoir contains three parts: the first past details the narrator's childhood in Iraq and her migration to Iran; the second part which is the core part of this memoir is a depiction of the seventeen-year-old Hosseini's volunteered activities such as nursing the wound,

75   Masoumeh Ramhormozi, *Eternal Fragrance*. Tehran: Sureye Mehr Publication, 2003.

76   The Iran-Iraq war is often called the 'Sacred Defense' or the 'imposed War' in the rhetoric of the Islamic Republic.

77   Ramhormozi, *Eternal Fragrance*, 201.

78   Seyyedeh Azam Hosseini, *One Woman's War: Da (Mother): The Memoirs of Seyyedeh Zahra Hosseini*. Tehran: Sureye Mehr Publication, 2008. For the English version, please see *One Woman's War: Da (Mother): The Memoirs of Seyyedeh Zahra Hosseini*. Trans. Paul Sprachman. Costa Mesa: Mazda Publishers, 2014.

washing the corpses of the dead, and her role as a combatant in defending Khorramshahr; and the last part details the narrator's recovery from shrapnel injury she received from the battlefield and it is an account of her married life. *Da* is among the few Iranian women's memoirs that criticize the traditional belief about war and challenge the stereotypical role of Iranian women. Hosseini is constantly challenging the patrilineal culture of the society through reinstating her agency. For instance, in part two of the memoir where she is going to inform the authorities of what is going on and ask for more people to come and wash the copses, Zeinab says, 'who would listen to you? ... This is men's job. Men should go and bring more personnel.'[79] In response, Zahra says, 'How long should we wait for men? What is wrong with us? Are we dump?[80]

In another scene, Zahra defies one of the top military male officers asking her and her friend to leave the front because it is dangerous. She states 'we won't go back. Who are you to tell us that we should go back? We came here on our own and we know what we are going to do.'[81] These excerpts and many other examples in the memoir show that Zahra has not been dominated by any man. Her tough, tenacious, brave and ready-to-help-at-any-time personality exemplifies the role of Iranian women during the war. Although this war memoir is state-sponsored, it still challenges the patriarchy and the gendered discrimination in the country. *Da* has been received well in the country and has seen 156 reprints as of late 2017 according to the publisher. Having become the biggest best seller in the shortest period, *Da* has outsold and gone through more reprints than any other memoir in the genre of "Sacred Defense." Thus far, it has been the focus of 11 theses, 220 news pieces, 150 interviews, and 70 sessions of review. Iranian Scholars such a Javadi Yeganeh and Sohofi examined the reasons for the popularity of the memoir.[82] Similarly, Laetitia Nanquette, in her paper 'An Iranian Woman's Memoir on the Iran–Iraq War: The Production and Reception of Da,' studied the production, distribution and reception of this memoir of "Sacred Defense."[83] *Da* has received several awards including the 2009 Jalal Al-e Ahmad Award, the 2009 Book of the Year Award,

79   Ibid., 123.
80   Ibid.
81   Ibid., 500.
82   Mohammad Reza Javadi Yeganeh & Seyed Mohammad Ali Sohfi, "Revayate Zanan-e az Jang: Tahlile Enteghadi-e Ketabe Khaterate *Da*" (Women's Narrative of War: Critical Analaysis of Da). *Naghde Adabi*, 6 (21) (1392, 2013): 85–110.
83   Laetitia Nanquette, "An Iranian Woman's Memoir on the Iran–Iraq War: The Production and Reception of Da." *Iranian Studies*, 46(6) (2013): 943–957.

and the 2009 Shahid Qanipour Prize.[84] The memoir was translated to English by Paul Sprachman and published by Mazda Publishers in 2014. The popularity of the memoir speaks volume about the positive changing of societal and cultural attitude towards women. This memoir defies the Orientalist stereotypes of the "Muslim woman" as a passive victim in need of saving as depicted in diasporic rehistoricized narratives. The impact of all these counter-discourses is to delegitimize the one-sided depictions of events, and to empower and give agency to the women.

5   Conclusion

Jasmine and Stars, Takeover in Tehran, Eternal Fragrance, Da and many other memoirs of this ilk are counter-discourses to those of diasporic rehistoricized narratives and challenge many dominant perceptions about Iran and Iranian women that have served towards dehumanizing and rendering invisible the Iranian other. In this alternative space, these narratives take a different path in interrogating the conditions that have historically placed women under erasure which is why these narratives are not vulnerable to criticism of reiterating Orientalist stereotypes. Whereas the diasporic rehistoricized narratives constantly represent women as submissive, passive victims and voiceless and blame the Islamic Republic and its imposed restrictions on women, these narratives question the imposed cultural restrictions and bring up potent female characters in an effort to improve their status in the society and to counter the Orientalist stereotypes of female passivity. In this space, the author of these counter-discourses empower an alternative way of knowing, filtered through what Barbara Harlow describes as specific 'conditions of observation'[85] and others refer to as experience. These authors write from, what Nancy Hartsock calls, a 'standpoint epistemology' which is 'an account of the world as seen from the margins, an account which can expose the falseness of the view from the top and can transform the margins as well as the center... an account of the world which treats our perspectives not as subjugated or disruptive knowledge, but as primary and constitutive of different world.'[86] Thus, these counter-discourses have the power to threaten the stereotypical

---

84   Da, An Emotional narrative of a Mother on Iran-Iraq War. https://roozame.com/detail/4627113.

85   Barbara Harlow, (1986). "Introduction," in *The Colonial Harem*, Malek Alloula. Trans. Myrna Godzich & Wlad Godzich. (Minneapolis: University of Minnesota Press, 1986), xxii.

86   Nancy Hartsock, 'Foucault on Power: A Theory for Women?" in *Feminism/Postmodernism*, ed. Linda J. Nicholson. (New York: Routledge, 1990), 171.

representations perpetuated and controlled by the conditioned way of seeing and they have the potential to produce a new way of seeing. This positive shift in vision produces a positive social change and even creates a new identity. Reading or writing counter-discourses is part of a process of decolonization which delegitimizes the narratives that are widely accepted, regularly read, repeated and studied in mainstream education. Therefore, these counter-discourses are the decolonizing voices that disturb the dominant discourse and furnish an alternative lens through which Western readers are invited to reconsider the stereotypical representations of Iran and Iranian women.

Bibliography

Alfred, Gerald Taiaiake. Colonialism and State Dependency. *Journal de la Sante Autochtone*, November, (2009): 42–60.

Ashcroft, Bill. *Post-colonial Transformation*. London: Routledge, 2001.

Ashcroft, Bill. "Remembering the Future: Utopianism in African Literature." *Textual Practices*, 32 (5) (2009): 703–722.

Ashcroft, Bill., Griffiths, Gareth, and Tiffin, Helen. *The Post-Colonial Studies Reader*. London: Routledge, 1995.

Azari, Farah. "The Post-Revolutionary Women's Movement in Iran." In *Women of Iran. The Conflict with the Fundamentalist Islam,* edited by Farah Azari. (London: Ithaca Press, 1983), 190–225.

Bamdad, Bar Al-Moluk. *Zan-e Irani az Enqelaab-e Mashrootiyat taa Enqelaab-e Sefid* (*Iranian Women from the Constitutional Revolution to the White Revolution*). Tehran: Ibn Sinaa Publications, 1968.

Buss, Helen. M. *Repossessing the World: Reading Memoirs by Contemporary Women*. Wilfrid Laurier University Press, 2002.

Clarke, Cathryn. Fuller Image. *The Iranian*. September 12 (2003).

Connerton, Paul. *How Societies Remember*. Cambridge: Cambridge University Press, 1989.

Dabashi, Hamid. *Brown Skin, White Mask*. New York: Pluto Press, 2011.

Ebtekar, Masoumeh. *Takeover in Tehran: The Inside Story of 1979 U.S Embassy Capture*. Vancouver: Talonbooks, 2000.

Fanon, Frantz. *Black Skin, White Masks* (Richard Philcox, Trans.). New York: Grove Press, 1967.

Fotouhi, Sanaz. *The Literature of Iranian Diaspora: Meaning and Identity since the Islamic Revolution*. London, New York: I.B.Tauris, 2015.

Guppy, Shusha. *The Blindfold Horse: Memories of a Persian Childhood*. London: Heinemann, 1988.

Gusdorf, George. "Conditions and Limits of Autobiography." In *Autobiography: Essays Theoretical and Critical,* edited by James Olney. (Princeton, NJ: Princeton University Press, 1980), 28–49.

Harlow, Barbara. "Introduction." In *The Colonial Harem,* Malek Alloula. (Myrna Godzich & Wlad Godzich, Trans.). (Minneapolis: University of Minnesota Press, 1986), ix–xxii.

Hartsock, Nancy. "Foucault on Power: A Theory for Women?" In *Feminism/ Postmodernism,* edited by Linda J. Nicholson. (New York: Routledge, 1990), 157–175.

Ho, Christian. "Responding To Orientalist Feminism." *Australian Feminist Studies*, 25 (66) (2010): 433–439.

Hosseini, S.Z. *One Woman's War: Da (Mother): The Memoirs of Seyyedeh Zahra Hosseini.* (Paul Sprachman, Trans.). Costa Mesa: Mazda Publishers, 2014.

Javadi, Yeganeh, Mohammad Reza & Sohfi, Seyed Mohammad Ali. "Revayate Zanan-e az Jang: Tahlile Enteghadi-e Ketabe Khaterate Da" (Women's Narrative of War: Critical Analaysis of Da). *Naghde Adabi*, 6 (21) (1392, 2013): 85–110.

Kar, Mehrangiz. *Hoqooqe Siyaasi-ye Zanaane Iran (Political Rights of Iranian Women).* Tehran: Roshangaran & Women Studies Publishing, (1367, 1997).

Keshavarz, Fatemeh. *Jasmine and Stars: Reading More than "Lolita" in Tehran.* Chapel Hill: The University of North Carolina Press, 2007.

Mahdi, Ali Akbar. "The Iranian Women's Movement: A Century Long Struggle." *The Muslim World*, 94,(2004): 427–448.

Marandi, Seyed Mohammad. & Pirnajmuddin, Hossein. 'Constructing an Axis of Evil: Iranian Memoirs in the "Land of the Free."' *Ajiss,* 26 (2) (2009).

Mottahedeh, Negar. "Off the Grid: Reading Iranian Memoirs in Our Time of Total War." http://www.merip.org/mero/interventions/mottahedehinterv.html, (2004).

Nafisi, Azar. *Reading Lolita in Tehran.* New York. Random House, 2003.

Naghibi, Nima. *Rethinking Global Sisterhood: Western Feminism and Iran.* London: University of Minnesota Press, 2007.

Nanquette, Laetitia. "An Iranian Woman's Memoir on the Iran–Iraq War: The Production and Reception of Da." *Iranian Studies*, 46(6) (2013): 943–957.

Nemat, Marina. *Prisoner of Tehran.* Simon & Schuster: New York, 2007.

Price, Massoume. "Women's movement; A brief history 1850–2000." *The Iranian,* March 7 (2000).

Rahimieh, Nasrin. "Marking Gender and Difference in the Myth of the Nation: a Post-revolutionary Iranian Film." In *The New Iranian Cinema: Politics, Representation and Identity,* edited by Richard Tapper. (London, New York: I.B. Tauris, 2002), 238–252.

Ramhormozi, Masoumeh. *Eternal Fragrance.* Tehran: Sureye Mehr Publication, 2003.

Random House. Teacher's Guide for Reading Lolita in Tehran. (2006). http://www.randomhouse.com/catalog/display.pperl?isbn=9780812971064&view=tg.

Reid, Mehry & Reid, Thomas. *Snake's Marble: A Persian Memoir*. Veradale: Vantage Press, 1995.

Rowe, Carlos J. "Reading 'Reading Lolita in Tehran' in Idaho." *American Quarterly*, 59 (2) (2007): 253–275.

Satrapi, Marjaneh. *Persepolis: The Story of a Childhood*. New York: Pantheon Books, 2003.

Sedghi, Hamideh. *Women and Politics in Iran: Veiling, Unveiling and Reveiling*. Cambridge University Press, 2007.

Sium, Aman, Desai, Chandni & Ritskes, Eric. "Towards the 'tangible unknown': Decolonization and the Indigenous future." *Decolonization: Indigeneity, Education & Society*, 1 (1) (2012): i–xiii.

Terdiman, Richard. *Discourse/Counter-Discourse: The Theory and Practice of Symbolic Resistance in Nineteenth-Century France*. New York: Cornell University Press, 1985.

Tiffin, Helen. "Post-colonial Literatures and Counter-Discourse." *Kunapip*, 9 (13) (1987): 17–34.

Whitlock, Gillin. *Soft Weapons: Autobiography in Transit*. Chicago, University of Chicago press, 2007.

Woodsmall, Ruth F. *Women and the New East*. Washington, D.C.: Middle East Institute, 1960.

Zeiny, Esmaeil. "Neo-colonialism as an Imperialistic Project: A Critique of Three Iranian Diasporic Memoirs." National University of Malaysia, Dissertation, 2013.

Zeiny, Esmaeil. "Diasporic Muslim Discourses: Re-visiting & Challenging the Stereotypes." *Islamic Perspective, London Academy of Iranian Studies*, 17 (2017): 1–14.

Zeiny, Esmaeil. "Visual Discourses of (Un)veiling: Revisiting Women of Allah." In *Seen and Unseen: Visual Cultures of Imperialism,* edited by Sanaz Fotouhi & Esmaeil Zeiny. (Leiden: Brill, 2018), (143–171).

Zeiny, Esmail, Zandi, Peivand & Mahmoodi, Khalil. "Reconstructing the Society: Iranian Women's Movements." *The NIEW Journal*, December (4) (2012): 125–137.

CHAPTER 5

African Literature: Leadership, Plight of the Majority and Hope

Masumi Hashimoto Odari and Ciarunji Chesaina

1 Introduction

This chapter is a discourse of fundamental issues on African literature as a tool of protest against the marginalization and oppression of the majority of the masses due to inhumane leadership. One of the important arguments in the chapter is that, if African literature is a mirror of social reality, then it must truthfully depict this reality from the standpoint of the majority of the people.

The question of leadership is at the heart of African literature. Chinua Achebe (1983), one of the fathers of the African novel, argues that the trouble with Nigeria is not the Nigerian character or its land and climate; it is 'simply and squarely failure of leadership.'[1] The African writer sees literature as a dialogue. The writer is not writing in a vacuum, but he/she is writing to an audience or for an audience. The issue of writing for an audience was well articulated by Wole Soyinka, one of Africa's fathers of drama and 1986 Nobel Prize winner for Literature. With reference to his plays, he says,

> I write in the firm belief that there must be at least a hall full of people who are sort of on the same wave-length as mine from every stratum of society and there must be at least a thousand people who are able to feel the same way as I do about something.[2]

The African writer also sees himself/herself as a liberator. The role of African writers as liberators was behind the poetry of Mozambique and Angola poets during their struggle for liberation from Portuguese colonialism. Aghostino Neto, who later became the first President of Angola, was not satisfied with only spearheading the Popular Liberation Movement of Angola (MPLA), but he wrote poetry to inspire his people to protest against the fetters of colonialism.

---

1 Achebe, Chinua. *The Trouble with Nigeria*. (London: Heinemann Educational Books, 1983), 1.
2 Quoted in Dennis Duerden & Cosmo Pieterse (eds). *African Writers Talking*. (London: Heinemann, 1972), 177.

In the contemporary era, Micere Mugo of Kenya centers her poetry on the oppression of the masses by neo-colonial African leaders. She states that she has no apologies to make to her American readers who claim that her poetry is too focused on the oppression of the masses.[3] It is noted that some African writers have deliberately deviated from European forms of writing to articulate their positions with regard to inhumane leadership in both the colonial and postcolonial periods.

This chapter views good leadership as that which is geared towards uplifting the welfare of the masses or the majority of the people. The writers examined in this chapter write from the standpoint of criticizing oppressive leadership and articulating the masses' aspirations and hope for leadership that regards them as human beings. The masses are therefore viewed as, "the rest." Although the masses and marginalized groups are shown to be weighed down by burdens of exploitation, discrimination and dehumanization emanating from oppressive leadership, African writers recognize that the oppressed are not passive beings with no hope about tomorrow. This chapter, therefore, ends with comments on the rest voicing out their aspirations and hope for better leadership.

2   The Colonial Context

The colonial powers termed Africa "The Dark Continent." This was a justification of encroaching on the continent with a false mission of cultural illumination through Christianity, education and the so-called "civilization." Africa was also portrayed as a land riddled with poverty, ignorance and disease. Hence the civilizing mission included raising the living conditions of African people through eradication of poverty and disease, while at the same time putting in place preventive measures. The rest write back to demolish these myths that were used for colonization purposes.

In "Western Civilization," Neto writes back to the colonizers, on behalf of the masses, in relation to the colonial powers' lies about the so-called civilizing mission.[4] Neto's poem satirizes the whole notion of civilization and better living conditions for Africans. Through the poem, Neto asks a number of questions on behalf of the masses. Is this the light, to illuminate the "Dark Continent"? Is this the success of raising the living standards of the sons and

---

3   Micere Mugo, *My Mother's Poem and Other Songs*. (Nairobi: East African Educational Publishers, 1994), xii.

4   Aghostino Neto, "Western Civilization," in *When Bullets Begin to Flower*, ed. Margaret Dickinson. (Nairobi: East African Educational Publishers, 1992), 63.

daughters of Africa? Is this the eradication of poverty? Is this the medicine to cure African people's diseases and to raise their lifespan? The poem is quoted in full below in order to facilitate thorough scrutiny of the above questions,

> 'Western Civilization'
> Sheets of tin nailed to posts
> driven in the ground
> make up the house.
>
> Some rags complete
> the intimate landscape
>
> The sun slanting through cracks
> welcomes the owner
>
> After twelve hours of slave
> labour.
>
> breaking rock
> shifting rock
> breaking rock
> shifting rock
> fair weather
> wet weather
> breaking rock
> shifting rock
>
> Old age comes early
>
> a mat on dark nights
> is enough when he dies
> gratefully
> of hunger.[5]

The colonialist pretended that civilization was marked by what he termed "permanent houses." But do sheets nailed to posts which are merely driven in the ground make up a permanent house? This house can hardly protect the owner from the elements. Instead of the mud we used traditionally to fill in

---

5   Ibid.

the cracks, now we are forced to use rags. Similarly, the house cannot protect the owner from extreme heat. Like an uninvited guest, the sun welcomes the owner through slanting cracks. And the house is too small, as reflected by the irony in the words, 'intimate landscape.'

The poet unveils the real motive of the colonialist. It was not "civilization of the native" but exploitation of the native. The man is subjected to twelve hours of slave labor; this means that the whole day he has no time to attend to his human needs or the needs of his family. And as we know about slavery, it is unpaid labor. Notice how hard the labor is; Neto uses alliteration and ono-matopoeic language through the repetition of 'breaking rock /shifting rock' to underscore not only the strenuousness of the labor but also its monotony and hazardous nature. It is the kind of labor which dehumanized African people, demanding them to work as robots or machines. The worker's human needs are not taken into consideration; hence the work has to be done regardless of the weather conditions – 'fair weather/wet weather.'

What of poverty eradication pretence? The worker's house is a poor hovel and the furniture in it harmonizes with the rags on the wall. Instead of a bed, the man sleeps on 'a mat on dark nights.' This also means that there is no lamp. Talk of bringing light to the uncivilized dark continent! Neto's satire cannot be missed. What of eradication of disease and increasing life expectancy of the native? The whole scenario is a contradiction. The worker is exposed to pre-mature aging and the subsequent premature death. Notice that this is actually a premature aging and premature death that could be avoided. The prema-ture aging and death result from diseases that can be avoided. The diseases are caused by deprivation of basic human needs – rest, food, human relationships. The poet ends the poem with a punch line full of pathos –

> a mat on dark nights
> is enough when he dies
> gratefully
> of hunger.[6]

What irony! A man who has to toil from dawn to dusk has nothing to show for it, except for miserable death from starvation. The irony is poignant; that the man dies 'gratefully / of hunger.' He is grateful because death is the only thing that rescues him from the harsh and hazardous existence which has been his lot hitherto. Note further irony; that the mat which has been his bed is equally

---

6   Ibid.

"enough" as his coffin. His body will probably be rolled in this mat and thrown into the bush like a dog's. Western civilization indeed! Neto's final message is that if colonial leadership is allowed to continue, death is the only thing that Angola will harvest.

Just as in "Western Civilization," Neto evokes death in his other poem, "Contract Workers."[7] Again here, the death of Angolan people is seen as the only payment from Portuguese colonial leadership. The poem is written through a fusion of modern (written) and traditional (oral) poetry. It reads (or sings) like a dirge, a traditional funeral song. The contract workers form 'a long line of bearers' which evokes the picture of pallbearers. But who has died? Whose death? We deduce the contract workers are mourning their own looming death. They are being killed slowly as they work on Portuguese projects, and carry heavy burdens on their bare backs. We are told, 'they sprinkle the roadside dust/with their sweat.'[8] If their sweat is enough to sprinkle the roadside dust, then the dehydration they are exposed to must be extreme, and life is slowly but surely being squeezed out of them. No wonder, their mouths are described as, 'gaping mouths,' like mouths of dead people.

A similar criticism of Portuguese leadership is elucidated in Antonio Jacinto's "Letter from a Contract Worker."[9] This poem is a vivid illustration of how the rest has used poetry to write back and lay bare the emotional wounds inflicted on indigenous African people through lies about illuminating "The Dark Continent." The poem captures the trauma contract workers experienced due to displacement and family disintegration. These workers were forcefully uprooted from their homes and families to go and work in territories that were completely foreign to them. The pain of having to live separated from their loved ones is captured right from the onset,

> I wanted to write you a letter
> my love
> a letter to tell
> of this longing
> to see you
> and this fear
> of losing you
> of this thing which deeper than I want, I feel

---

7   Aghostino Neto, "Contract Workers," in *When Bullets Begin to Flower*, ed. Margaret Dickinson. (Nairobi: East African Educational Publishers, 1992), 39–40.

8   Ibid., 39.

9   Antonio Jacinto, "Letter from a Contract Worker" in When Bullets Begin to Flower, ed. Margaret Dickinson. (Nairobi: East African Educational Publishers, 1992), 51–53.

a nameless pain which pursues me
a sorrow wrapped about my life.[10]

The longing, even for a mere look at the loved one, is so deep that it has translated itself into fear, pain and sorrow. It cuts deep like the emotional torment that haunts an individual after the death of a close member of the family. And indeed the longing makes the persona experience deep fear of losing his lover, both physically and emotionally. The persona's nostalgia for his homeland is captured through his longing for the beauty of the environment he has been forced to leave behind. The poet parallels the beauty of the loved one with that of the environment, hence underscoring the nostalgia forced on the persona. His memories evoke,

your lips as red as the tacula fruit
your hair black as the dark diloa fish
your eyes gentle as the macongue
your breasts hard as young maboque fruit.[11]

The persona's nostalgia and longing for his loved one make his emotions run wild. He recalls his intimacy with her and wishes that he could recapture the madness of their passion in the letter he wanted to write.

The letter would have been like no other that has ever been read in Kilombo, the home area of the two lovers. It would have been so captivating and so passionate that the loved one would have had to hide it from her parents because of the language the contract worker would have used and the emotions it would have aroused on the recipient. Even nature – the plants and the animals – would have "heard" it and would have empathized with the two lovers 'pitying [their] sorrow.'[12] The poet leaves the clincher to the very end and it hits the reader's mind, heart and all, arousing not only empathy but also anger. The poem ends with the message that the poet all along was preparing to convey on behalf of the rest,

I wanted to write you a letter
But my love, I don't know why it is,
Why, why, why it is, my love,
But you can't read
And I – oh the hopelessness – I can't write.[13]

---

10   Ibid., 51.
11   Ibid.
12   Ibid., 52.
13   Ibid., 53.

The contract worker cannot write, and even if he could, his loved one cannot read. What a situation in a dark continent that was supposed to be illuminated through education! The irony in the above ending of the poem is a punch from the rest on the face of colonialists. The rest are telling the colonialists that they unearthed the colonial motives and pretences long ago.

The colonialists denied Africans education deliberately. The Portuguese kept the indigenous people illiterate to facilitate the real motive – exploitation. It is significant that the "letter" is from a contract worker, because it brings in another irony. If the contract worker was illiterate, how did he enter into a contract? A contract is naturally between two parties; both parties must understand the contract and must agree to its terms. It is a mutual agreement between the parties involved. Contract workers were mere slaves working on forced labor terms. The letter, as it stands is not to the loved one since, as mentioned above, she cannot read anyway. The letter is to the colonialists from the rest telling the oppressors their pretence has been uncovered. Their leadership is sham and this leadership is doomed to die.

Before Alex La Guma wrote his famous novella, *A Walk in the Night* (1967);[14] very little, if at all, was known about the Coloureds of South Africa. In fact, when La Guma wrote this novella, his major intention was to let the world know about the plight of the Coloureds during apartheid South Africa. In his interview with Robert Serumaga in 1972, the writer states,

> Writers have tried to describe the situation in South Africa in general but very little has been said about the different 'national' groups and the people who live in South Africa. For instance I don't think a great deal has been said about the Coloured community or about the Indian community and *I think that even within a framework of racial separateness there is a task which writers have to perform. That is at least letting the world know what is happening – even within their compartments.*[15] (italics ours)

Even today very little is known about the Coloureds of South Africa. Some people dismiss them as *individuals* born from a union between a white man and a black woman and *vice versa*. Coloureds are a race, and by writing about them La Guma is writing back to the colonizer telling him to look at the product of

---

14   Alex La Guma, *A Walk in the Night & Other Stories*. London, Heinemann Educational Books, 1967.
15   Quoted in Duerden & Pieterse, *African Writers Talking*, 93.

his hypocrisy as well as his savagery. Why hypocrisy? Why savagery? Yes, indeed the Coloureds are the products of the union between whites and blacks. When the Boers arrived in South Africa from Holland and started stealing large tracks of land from Africans and forcing them to work on this very land as slaves, they regarded themselves as a superior race; a chosen race – chosen by God. They, for instance, insisted that as a chosen race they had to keep their race pure – pure by not mixing with other races. The black race was far from being regarded as a race; it consisted of savages, according to the Boers. This was one of the reasons behind the Immorality Sex Act which forbade sex relations between members of different races. How did it then happen that a whole race was born out of forbidden sex relations?

The resulting race of Coloureds in the first instance shows the hypocrisy of the Boers as a chosen race. They wanted to keep their race pure but this Puritanism was merely theoretical. Secondly, the Boers had considered themselves as a superior cultured race while regarding Africans as uncultured savages. Their rape of African women to the extent of producing a race of Coloureds would indicate that the Boers' cultural superiority was a myth. Men who rape women *en masse* can only be described as savages. La Guma sees it as his task to show the world the plight of the Coloured race. In *A Walk in the Night,* the writer gives a voice to Coloureds to write back to their "fathers" and remind them they fathered them and then abandoned them. La Guma writes from the point of view of the Coloureds and quite often in the novella he uses dialogue spoken in the lingua of the ordinary Coloureds.

The Coloureds are very conscious of their rejection and lack of identity. The young derelicts keep referring to themselves as "us bastards." And the police cannot let them forget their lack of distinct status as they call them Hottentots. This lack of distinct identity has led the Coloureds into developing an inferiority complex. Willieboy is an epitome of this inferiority complex. He tries to make himself feel like somebody of worth by dressing and walking flamboyantly. He puts on an air of nonchalance, yet deep down he is extremely unhappy. Michael Adonis as well has developed an inferiority complex from being mistreated by his white foremen at work. His ideal woman is one who has smooth hair like the white woman; he assumes getting himself a woman close to white would uplift him to be somebody of worth.

La Guma exposes the Coloureds as a race that is extremely poor and lives in extremely poor neighborhoods. Their areas are infested with cockroaches and other creatures which are neighbors of poverty-stricken people. As a result, the Coloureds are exposed to diseases as La Guma's use of disease imagery vividly describes. But in apartheid South Africa, it is deemed perfect for Coloureds to live in such areas. When the white policeman discovers that the dead Mister Doughty is white, he is shocked and wonders why a white man would be living in a place like that. The implication is that white people should never live in such places, but poverty and squalor are perfect for Coloureds.

Worse still the Coloureds have neither freedom nor human rights. Michael Adonis is dismissed from his job for going to the toilet while on duty which means that he is denied even the right to attend to natural processes. They have no right to move from one place to another and the police make sure such freedom is curtailed. The police brutalize the Coloureds and regard all of them as drug addicts and thieves. They are searched on a whim and shoed off the streets as in Michael's case when he is strolling home.[16] The Coloureds are cowed and they have to learn not to provoke the police, even by looking at them,

> You learned from experience to gaze at some spot on their uniforms, the button of a pocket, or the bright smoothness of their Sam Browne belts, but never into their eyes, for that would be taken to be an affront by them.[17]

The Coloureds are denied not only freedom to move around, but also the right to live in a place they can call their own. Whenever an area is declared "For Whites Only" the Coloureds are evacuated without any regard as to where or how they go. They end up as nomads in their own country, like the character named Joe. This leads to the disintegration of families. Joe has no idea where the rest of his family live. In frustration, his father leaves the family because of nomadic existence and poverty-stricken life. The next time the family was evacuated Joe also decided to go separately and fend for himself. However, his existence is nothing to be proud of. He ends up as a scavenger and a beggar, a creature La Guma describes as something that has been left in a junkyard.

Denial of rights to the Coloureds leads not only to physical disintegration of families but also to psycho-social disintegration. Franky Lorenzo and his wife Grace love each other dearly as a couple. However, Franky's frustrations and denial of rights at his workplace affect the couple's relationship. Having been denied rights at work and in the world outside the home, he comes to view sex as a right rather than intimacy with his wife. Like the derelicts who find comfort in cheap sex, Franky finds solace in sex with his wife. Subsequently, the

---

16   La Guma, *A Walk in the Night*, 11–12.

17   Ibid., 11.

Lorenzos end up with too many children whom they cannot give reasonable care and upbringing.

Other male characters like Willieboy's father end up battering their wives. Since Willieboy's father cannot stand up to his white bosses he oppresses his wife, while the latter who cannot stand up to her husband oppresses her son Willieboy. Others such as Abrahams end up acting as informers, selling their own people to the police but reaping rebuff from the latter. Hence a community of scapegoats develops. The Boers who crafted the apartheid type of leadership justified dividing South African society into racial groups by arguing that such a color discrimination policy would assist the various races to develop at their own pace. In *A Walk in the Night*, La Guma is asking on behalf of the Coloureds as the rest: is oppression through police brutality and denial of rights at work and in the streets development? Is being forced to live in poverty and squalor development? What about the inevitable family and community disintegration? What of being forced into a nomadic life in one's own country? What of living as a vagrant and a beggar in one's own country? The rest as the Coloured race is asking through the writer – is this really humane leadership or respect for human dignity?

Ferdinand Oyono in *The Old Man and the Medal* (1972)[18] writes back to the French colonizers questioning their sincerity as "leaders." Oyono uses Meka, an old man from a village and his wife Kelara to bring his views of how the French colonizers were hypocrites who cared less for the African people. The story begins where Meka is busy preparing to receive a medal from the Great Chief of the White Man in recognition of his sacrifice for the country. Kelara is also excited that, by virtue of her husband receiving the medal from a "white man," she is also being elevated to the status of a "white woman."[19] From this, and the reaction of the villagers, the Africans seemed to have believed that being closer to the "white men" meant prestige and prosperity. Did Meka forget that he and his wife's two sons fought for the white men and lost their lives? Did he forget that he gave his land to the "white men"? Was giving a medal to Meka all that the Great Chief of the White Man could offer for the loyalty and sacrifice Meka made for them? Interestingly, it is Kelara who wakes up to the realization that a medal from a white man was not worth their sacrifice and leaves without witnessing the event.

Meanwhile, Meka is excited that by receiving a "medal," he has become the "white man's" friend. During the reception at the African Cultural Centre, he even offers to host the High Commissioner in his village as he uses the proverb

18   Ferdinand Oyono, *The Old Man and the Medal*. London: Heinemann, 1972.
19   Ibid., 34.

'If you want to know what your friend thinks of you, drink a few glasses with him.'[20] The use of a proverb shows Meka's pride in the African custom. However, by using proverbs, Oyono writes back to the colonialist that they do have wisdom that talks to humanity. It is evident that the Whites have no intention of being friends with the Africans; the white men all sit on the dais by themselves and do not share the same food with the Africans; the white men do not have one to one conversation with the Africans; the medal that Meka receives is different from that of the Greek man, Pipiniakis; the manner in which each receives his medal is also different. There is a certain distance between the white men and the Africans.

Meka gets too drunk during the reception and is left alone sleeping when a raging storm strikes the town. He loses his medal in the rain and gets lost in the darkness. He finds himself in a prohibited area where he is arrested by the police and brutally beaten. It is ironical that a man who was honored with a medal a few hours ago by the "white man" was now treated like a criminal simply because he was drunk and was found in a white man's area. After all, he was simply an old man. What harm would he have been to anybody? Meka is finally released but he feels humiliated. As Mulenda Kapanga claims, Meka's 'civic privileges, his religious affiliation, and his adopted French manners cannot shield him from the degrading restrictions of the Code de l'indigenat (Indigenousness Code).'[21] No matter what he does to please the "white men" and sacrifice for them, he will always remain an African who can never be like the "white man" and can never be accepted by them. Meka returns to his village half dead. But through this hurtful experience, Meka realizes that the white men are just hypocrites who do not have the least regard for the African people.

Hypocrisy of Christianity is also touched on in this novel. When Meka tries to ask Father Vandermayer for directions to the African Culture Centre, Father Vandermayer gives Meka 'an angry glance and waves him to go away.'[22] Little did Meka know that Father Vandermayer was hiding behind the mask of hypocrisy. As a religious leader, Father Vandermayer tries to show how caring and compassionate he is towards the Africans, but his sense of superiority towards Meka in front of his fellow white men cannot be hidden.

The story ends with Meka's last words, 'I'm just an old man now'[23] and there seems to be no hope at the end for Africans to achieve their own dreams

20   Ibid., 106.
21   Kasongo Mulenda Kapanga, "Ferdinand Oyono," in *Contemporary African Writers*, ed. Tanure Ojaide, (New York: Gale, 2011), 232–235.
22   Oyono, *The Old Man*, 97.
23   Ibid., 167.

and aspirations. However, Meka and his fellow village people realize that the "white men" after all, were nothing more than hypocrites who simply used the Africans for their own gains. Oyono writes back to the white colonizers that the masses were not ignorant; they have come to the realization that the whites were only exploiting the Africans for their own gains. The medal was merely a prize to make Meka believe that the whites appreciated the sacrifices Africans made to the colonial powers. But he realizes that the medal can neither better their lives nor bring back his dead sons. The realization by the Africans may suggest the beginning of a new era which in turn becomes hope for a new nation.

3   The Neo-colonial Context

From the mid-20th century, African countries were gaining independence, one after another. The Africans were excited to see their countries freed from colonialism and hopeful that finally, they would enjoy their freedom for which they worked so hard. The first African leaders made great inaugural speeches during the independence celebrations. One such person was the President of Nigeria, Nnamdi Azikiwe. In his inaugural speech on 16th November 1960, he stated,

> Without respect for the rule of law permeating our political life Nigeria would degenerate into a dictatorship with its twin relatives of tyranny and despotism ... Any justification of such untrammelled exercise of political power is, to me, an outrage on human conscience and a gross violation of human rights. I submit that respect for human dignity is the challenge which Africa offers to the world.[24]

Statements such as the above represented the aspirations of the African masses for what independence would bring. But were these aspirations fulfilled? The purpose of this section is to discuss the response of the masses or the marginalized (as the rest) to this question. The writers selected here write back, on behalf of the masses, to the African leaders who led and continue to lead independent African states. The leaders are portrayed as masqueraders and betrayers of the people's hopes.

---

24   Excerpts from Inaugural Speech of Nnamdi Azikiwe on November 16 1960. Paragraph 4. Retrieved from http:// www.educationalresourceproviders.com/excerpts-from-inaugural -speech-of-nnamdi-azikiwe-nov-16-1960/.

Micere Mugo says that her poem "We will Rise and Build a Nation" was written,

> In defiance of neo-colonial dictators,
> reminding them that even the darkest
> of nights breaks into daylight and
> that their days are truly numbered![25]

Mugo writes the poem in the first person plural, "we." The persona, "we" are the masses whom Mugo gives a voice to write back to their neo-colonial leaders. The first part of the poem analyzes how the masses feted the leaders at the attainment of independence. The middle part looks at the betrayal of the masses by their leaders during the neo-colonial period, while the last part states categorically the action the masses will take to build the betrayed nation.

The masses 'garlanded' their leaders 'with embracing hearts.'[26] These embracing hearts denote how strongly the masses believed in the leaders. They believed in them so strongly because they felt that the leaders' memories could not have been so short as to forget the pain the masses had had to endure living under colonialism. It was not only the hearts of the masses that believed in these new leaders but also the minds. By stating that the masses celebrated the leaders with 'earnest minds,'[27] the poet indicates how the masses believed in these leaders, body and soul. The masses recalled how they had had to endure years of psychological trauma under colonialism.

The masses felt betrayed because, instead of settling down to build a better environment for the masses, the leaders embarked on amassing wealth through transnational businesses with their former oppressive powers. The poet uses the symbol of a serpent to describe the neo-colonial leaders in this position of pretending to be working for the masses, while bartering meaningful independence and throwing the masses' hopes into the gutter,

> colonial collaborators, snatched
> our national liberation flag
> highjacking our independence
> with cunning serpentine imposture
> twisting into a rope

---

25   Micere Mugo, *My Mother's Poem and Other Songs*. (Nairobi: East African Educational Publishers, 1994), 68.
26   Ibid., 68.
27   Ibid.

with which they strangulated our hopes
leaving us under neo-colonial barrenness.[28]

The masses expected that once independence was attained they would have provisions and opportunities to cater for their families, unlike during the colonial era when their labor was exploited and they suffered deprivation. But, as the poet says above, their hopes were 'strangulated' and they were thrown into 'neo-colonial barrenness.' All the promises they were given were null and void.

It was hoped that after attainment of independence, the African leaders would unite the masses into one nation which would work together for social, political and economic progress. Hence, together they would build a national identity, thus demolishing the ethnic divisions that had been created by the colonialist's policy of divide and rule. But, the poet observes, the neo-colonial leaders are using the same divide and rule policy, killing the aspired national identity, with 'ethnic subtraction and division.'[29] Worse still, these neo-colonial leaders visit the masses with the same terror, injustice and inhumanity that characterized the colonial era.

The last part of "We Will Rise and Build a Nation" reveals Micere Mugo's conviction that the masses will work towards building a real meaningful independence. They are not bound to lie low and watch their independence die and be buried. The poet writes back to the neo-colonial leaders on behalf of the masses that the changes the latter mean to bring will not be attained through peaceful means; the masses are prepared for a revolution. Notice the implication of violence in the repetition of "fury" as illustrated below,

We swirl
with the sweeping fury
of a dust storm...
To-morrow
We will rise
with the sweeping fury
of a dust storm.[30]

Henry Barlow's poem "Building the Nation" is a satire on neo-colonial leaders' pretences about their role in (re) building African nations after the ravages

---

28   Ibid., 69.
29   Ibid.
30   Ibid., 70–71.

of colonialism.[31] Permanent Secretaries (PS) were the drivers of building the nations. There was a PS who acted as the Chief Executive Officer in every government ministry. The implementation of policies lay on his shoulders. It was expected and hoped that these men would assist the country stand on its legs in progress and development. In "Building the Nation," Barlow shows that this was not to be. Barlow makes the persona a driver of one of these PS to tell us exactly how the latter took their responsibilities. It is significant that it is a driver observing the PS because drivers were the ones who knew every detail about where the PS went and what he did. Hence the rest writes back through this driver.

The PS takes the prestige that the position offers, but does not give even a thought to the work or responsibilities demanded. It is an opportunity to show off at the international hotels. The colonial administrators dined and wined at the Vic and our PS simply wants to feel how they felt. No wonder while there he engages in aspects of colonial officers' culture – 'small talk,' 'hollow laughs,' and 'stereotype jokes.'[32]

The poet is, bitterly satirical about these leaders' superficial attitude towards their responsibilities. The luncheon is the important meeting the PS has come to attend. The first priority is "to eat," which symbolizes egocentrism, self- interests and self-aggrandizement. It is no wonder the PS talks condescendingly to his driver, 'Did you eat any lunch friend?' Of course, he knows very well the driver did not have any lunch, as on so many occasions before this one. He and his lot have no regard for the masses and the question is part of the "small talk."[33] This poem illustrates neo-colonial leaders' lack of concern for the masses. They know about the food insecurity in their respective African countries. They also know the masses suffer hunger-related illnesses, but they camouflage this knowledge by talking about their non-existent deprivation and exhaustion from non-existent labor of building the nation – 'the pains we suffer building the nation.'[34] The poet gives a voice to the rest to speak out that they are the ones who actually build the nation, and on empty stomachs, while listening to the leaders' empty talk,

> So the PS had ulcers too!
> My ulcers I think are equally painful

---

31   Henry Barlow, "Building the Nation," in *Poems from East Africa*, eds. Cook David & David Rubadiri. (2010). (Nairobi: East African Educational Publishers, 2010), 14–15.
32   Ibid., 14.
33   Ibid.
34   Ibid.

> Only they are caused by hunger,
> Not sumptuous lunches![35]

Chinua Achebe's *A Man of the People* (1984) articulates the voice of "the rest."[36] Leaders such as the Minister of Culture, Nanga, have proven to be uncouth and immoral leaders who feel nothing but self-importance. In this case, the title of the novel, *A Man of the People* is a satirical statement. Achebe ridicules a "Minister of Culture" who is not only illiterate but who has no shame of seducing girls and other men's wives. When leaders like Nanga impose themselves on the masses with money and power, it is such a tragedy that all these leaders have forgotten the sacrifices made by the people to realize independence and freedom.

Achebe (1984) uses the proverb 'The man who carried the carcass of an elephant on his head and searching with his toes for a grasshopper.'[37] Proverbs are commonly used by African writers as a medium to press home the truth of matters. Achebe demonstrates how leaders such as Nanga are spending time on trivial matters that have nothing to do with the country's prosperity or the welfare of the people. They are only engrossed in self-preservation. Though Nanga explains that a Minister is expected to be a servant and that his motto is 'do the right and shame the Devil,'[38] the irony is that he does the opposite. These leaders have no intention of winning the people's hearts by doing what is right. Instead, they use their might.

While incompetent leaders like Nanga are given high positions in the government, Achebe focuses his hope on "the enlightened youth" to respond to the corrupt and malevolent leaders. Max, a young intellectual who launches the Common People's Convention desires to change the nation from one that has been led by 'corrupt and mediocre politicians'[39] to a nation that is led by visionary leaders. Sadly, Max is killed at the end for fighting back the corrupt government. He condemns the leaders for establishing 'themselves as the privileged class sitting on the back of the rest of the people.'[40] Nevertheless, Max represents the voices of the "rest" responding to the neo-colonial leaders who betray their people.

In *Smouldering Charcoal* by Tiyambe Zeleza (1992), two men from different social classes; Mchere, a bakery worker and Chola, a reporter for a newspaper,

---

35   Ibid., 15.
36   Chinua Achebe, *A Man of the People*. London: Heinemann, 1984.
37   Ibid., 71.
38   Ibid., 11.
39   Ibid., 77.
40   Ibid., 124.

share a similar destiny of exposing the tyrannical government under which they live.[41] The African leaders are described as brutal, corrupt and hypocritical and individuals who have no apology to make for using the masses for their own selfish gains. During the colonial era, the colonized African people were treated harshly, but one day, they said enough was enough. There were men like Mchere's father who fought for freedom and independence. They fought so hard to make their dreams a reality for all,

> my sons, never shy away, never run from injustice. Injustice cannot destroy, it merely seeks to reproduce itself, until those who have been wronged by it, starved because of it, gone mad because of it. Been crippled in body and maimed in spirit because of it, stand up and fight.[42]

These were men who genuinely believed in freedom for all and genuinely desired to build a nation of their own that they could be proud of. However, nothing has changed much in terms of poverty, exploitation and degradation. It was their own African men who sold their own people as slaves, or 'collaborated with the invaders to subjugate their people.'[43] Chola fearlessly makes his point when he says, 'Independence did not alter the conditioning, In fact, it grew under the new rulers whose only path to material wealth was through national plunder and the use of terror and repression.'[44] For Chola, the African leaders are worse than the White expatriates. Because of fighting for the right cause, men like Mchere's father were imprisoned and killed.

The author uses the oral tradition of performance to show how power can become too sweet for those in power that before long one becomes 'corrupt so that what had earlier been perceived by others as cleverness became cunning.'[45] The author does this effectively by introducing the play, "The Great Famine," in the novel. It conveys the writer's message of how power can be addictive to the extent that a fertile land becomes barren due to power. Corrupt leaders cling to power at any cost.

Too many leaders seem to make promises they never have the intentions to fulfill. To please women, the party leader in the novel will enthusiastically claim that 'women were the backbone of society and they must be respected.'[46] Ironically, When Mchere's wife, Nambe, goes to the party leader for help to save

41   Tiyambe Zeleza, *Smouldering Charcoal.* Essex: Heineman, 1992.
42   Ibid., 89.
43   Ibid., 23.
44   Ibid., 51.
45   Ibid., 86.
46   Ibid., 45.

her son who fell from a tree, he despises her and wonders how she could come asking him, 'a party leader,' to take her sick son to the hospital. He was not an ambulance. He was 'a leader, and a leader could not afford to be soft and sentimental.'[47] What he pronounces and what he does are two different issues. The religious leaders are not spared of the attack either. When Nambe goes to her church leader for help to take her son to the hospital, the man of God could only say, 'we will pray for you. The Lord is with you.'[48]

Chola represents the youth who are against any forms of oppression; he represents the "rest." Like Max, in *A Man of the People*, Chola does not hide his honest opinions about his leaders. When Chola's closest friend, Dambo who was an activist and a competent lawyer is killed by the government, Chola tries to go to exile abroad but he is arrested and imprisoned. Just as in the case of Max, there is a tendency to silence those who speak out or actively take the initiative to advocate for change.

Kongi in Soyinka's *Kongi's Harvest* (1967), is a dictator in whose leadership, the interests of the masses are alien.[49] His organizing Secretary who knows his character well helps Kongi prop up his image as that of a 'benevolent father of the nation.'[50] But Kongi is nothing close to this. A benevolent father leads as a servant of the people and is deeply conscious of their needs. Kongi does not even care about people's basic human needs such as food. His Aweri's (council of advisers) are starved. The only 'fee' the Fifth Aweri begs for is food because he cannot last any longer without food.[51] If the people who handle Kongi's dirty jobs are starved, what hope have the masses?

Kongi cannot stand suggestions, criticism or divergent points of view. That is why he issues directives over the radio, which does not offer opportunities for the people to respond. Rather than a benevolent father, he is a malevolent leader who imprisons and assassinates anyone he considers a threat to his dictatorship. Segi's father is a case in point and he is a representative of the rest. Segi's father is presumably the leader of the men awaiting execution. We are not told what they did to deserve detention, but it is clear that detention without trial must emanate from opposition to Kongi's schemes. Segi's father is on the traditional ruler's side and traditional rule caters for the welfare of the masses. The masses are given opportunities to voice their needs.

---

47   Ibid.
48   Ibid., 43.
49   Wole Soyinka, *Kongi's Harvest*. London: Oxford University Press, 1967.
50   Ibid., 18.
51   Ibid., 30.

The traditional ruler, Oba Danlola is a complete contrast to Kongi. Where Kongi does not tolerate even a single response from the people, we are told that 'in Oba Danlola's palace his sons/speak their minds.'[52] Whereas Kongi is murderous and does not respect life, Danlola's regime protected life,

> They complained because
> The first of the new yams
> Melted in an Oba's mouth
> But the dead will witness
> We drew the poison from the root.[53]

But the person who is the real antithesis of Kongi is Daodu, the heir apparent of Oba Danlola. It is Prince Daodu whom the masses want *in lieu* of dictators. Hence when Soyinka introduces Daodu in his play, he is writing back to the neo-colonial dictators to pave way for the Daodus of Africa. Daodu, combines the best from the traditional culture's leadership and the best from the modern. Daodu has embraced Western education, but not education *per se*. His education is applied education. It is this education Daodu has utilized in his farming projects whereby he has involved the masses. Notice that unlike Kongi who has personal interests in leadership, Daodu has the interests of the majority at heart. His leadership is a leadership of service to the community not a leadership of self-aggrandizement like Kongi's. His involvement in agricultural projects ensures that there is food security for the majority of the people.

Like the traditional leaders who were concerned with and respected life, Daodu has the life of the people at heart. In this way, he contrasts sharply with Kongi. Daodu's giant yam that wins at the harvest festival is symbolic. The yam as a crop is a symbol of life. The fact that Daodu has spent years perfecting his agricultural expertise to produce a giant yam would, therefore, symbolize leadership that is truly dedicated to enhancing and protecting the life of the nation; the life of the majority. And the masses are no fools; they know that this is the leadership that should be supported.

A further illustration of the neo-colonial dictators the masses write back to is Boss in Francis Imbuga's *Man of Kafira* (1984).[54] Boss is cut from the same cloth as Kongi, but something has been added on top. Like Kongi, Boss suffers from megalomania and he will stop at nothing to maintain his absolute power in Kafira. He has even extended his power to include the Church as one

---

52   Ibid., 58.
53   Ibid., 7.
54   Francis Imbuga, *Man of Kafira*. Nairobi: Heinemann, 1984.

of his territories. He murders Archbishop Lum Lum for following the church's doctrines: the doctrine of "one man one wife." Hence he eliminates Lum Lum when the latter refuses to solemnize his marriage to his second wife in church.

In *Man of Kafira,* Imbuga uses elements from traditional oral narratives to emphasize neo-colonial dictators' devaluation of human life. The playwright portrays Boss as an ogre, a cannibalistic half-man half-animal creature. These were mythic creatures which thrived on terrorizing and killing human beings. Boss is sadistic and thrives on the destruction of life. He has refused to eat vegetables, deeming them to be lifeless. His use of body internal organs for his special diet is the playwright's satire against neo-colonial African leaders' inhumanity. They maintain their political power through throttling lives of the citizens the way ogres did in traditional oral narratives.

Imbuga uses Boss as a caricature of neo-colonial African leaders. This arrogance about his grandeur simply serves as self-criticism of which he is unaware. He boasts of being the African Hitler saying, 'I am Hitler, you know, a black Hitler I am Shaka too, and when men tremble at the mention of my name, don't doubt them. They are not merely acting.'[55] On behalf of the masses, Imbuga exposes neo-colonial African dictators as leaders who lead through instilling fear, instead of working with the citizens to build their nations. They alienate themselves further from the masses through misuse of the law of the land. Instead of using the law to lay down parameters of the right things to do in creating a just society, they take the law in their own hands and assume that they are above the law. It should be noted that Boss is used as an epitome of all post-independence African leaders. The play is about the "man of Africa" as in the title whereby "Kafira" is a creative rewriting of "Afrika."

As expressed above, "the rest" is represented by the oppressed people under the neo-colonialist African rulers. The African leaders, at independence, promised to build nations of equality, liberation and peace for all, which the colonizers were unable to provide. However, as the creative works suggest, the African leaders superseded their foreign masters in their art of greed, lies and oppression. "The rest" are not the African leaders who spoke out to the "white men" that they can run their countries more efficiently than the "Whites" with the true spirit of democracy and equality. Rather, "the rest" are the new generation of Africans voicing their concerns towards their malevolent African leaders who have no intentions of listening to them. The voices of the rest are the true voices of revolt against their selfish leaders.

---

55   Ibid., 32.

4   Voices of Hope

The question to consider when we read the foregoing is that of the way forward after the writers have written back about oppression of the masses during the colonial era and betrayal of their hopes in the neo-colonial era. To end with the above gloomy picture would be to ignore the realism of our writers in portraying the plight of the masses and the marginalized. It would also be to ignore the attitude of our writers towards the masses. The masses are seen, not as passive stupid beings but intelligent people who are actively involved in weaving their own destiny. Their voices of hope are reflected in various writings.

Writers writing back with regard to the colonial period reveal that, although the masses do not own guns like the colonialists, they are prepared to resist oppression. The latter part of Neto's "Contract Workers" portrays workers who are weighed down by exploitation, but they are building resistance to the status quo.

> They go full of homesickness
> and dread
> – but they sing...[56]

During the struggles for independence, African people used the song as a strategy for protesting. Freedom fighters would communicate messages to one another using songs whose words and intentions the oppressors could not understand. The repetition of the phrases, 'but they sing' and 'and they sing' shows how seriously the workers take the singing.[57] The song is also a strong thread of unity. The poet says, that they may be 'full of injustice/silent in their inmost souls,'[58] but they still sing. Notice that this silence is another strategy to camouflage their resistance. It should also be noted that the poem ends with the sad songs being lost in the distance. The reader presumes that as the sad songs get lost, happy songs replace them. Hence the emphatic ending, 'Ah!/They sing!'[59]

In his novels, Alex La Guma conveys hope for the masses through symbolism. In the novella *A Walk in the Night* (1967) the author narrates about the horrors of living as a Coloured in apartheid South Africa.[60] Extreme poverty, victimization by the police and dehumanization may be their plight, but their

---

56   Neto, "Contract Workers," 39.
57   Ibid.
58   Ibid., 40.
59   Ibid.
60   La Guma, *A Walk in the Night*.

eyes are opened to the hope that lies in unity against oppressive forces. Hence towards the end of the novella, they show that they are reaching a point when they are ready to show resistance. One of their own, Willieboy a mere boy has been victimized and treated in a most inhuman manner. The crowd cannot take it any longer and they even scare the police. Resistance is shown when 'firsts thumped on the metal bodywork and a shower of brick bars rained suddenly down on it...'[61]

In addition, the rest realizes that they have to unite if they have to bring down an oppressive leadership. Abrahams, who has been telling on his own people to the police, undergoes a transformation. He realizes he has to stop being the police's collaborator and instead be on the side of his people. La Guma's view is that the rest are capable of building a better future for themselves. Hence he ends the novella with the baby Franky Lorenzo and his wife Grace are expecting. The baby is to be born at dawn, which signifies a new dawn for the Coloureds.

In *Kongi's Harvest,* (1967) Soyinka deliberately leaves the audience to make their own conclusion.[62] It is true that Prince Daodu does not take over leadership from Kongi. This would have been too easy and too unrealistic an ending for Soyinka. It is also true that the assassination of the dictator Kongi is thwarted and instead Segi's father has been assassinated. This is where the hope lies, albeit symbolically. The presentation of Kongi with a dead man's head portends his own death. Symbolically it portends the death of dictatorial and oppressive regimes. Rather than be depressed about the death of Segi's father and the failure of their plans, Daodu and Segi will stop at nothing in working towards instituting measures to put in place a more meaningful post-independence regime that has the masses' lives at the core. In any case, Kongi's assassination of Segi's father has ignited greater inspiration to work for a regime that respects life.

In "We Shall Rise and Build a Nation," Micere Mugo protests on behalf of the masses against betrayal of their hopes for what independence was expected to bring – humane leadership.[63] Although most of the poem raises issues of gross oppression of the masses, at the end the poet lets these marginalized majority of the people voice out how they will overturn the situation and build the kind of nation they want – one that takes cognizance of their humanity. The poem is used by the poet to project the masses' warning to neo-colonial leaders that they will confiscate the steering wheel and drive the nation towards

---

61   Ibid., 89.
62   Soynika, *Kongi's Harvest.*
63   Mugo, *My Mother's Poem.*

their desired destiny. They will take up this responsibility with fury and demolish oppressive instruments that the neo-colonialists have inherited as legacies
from the colonialists. They will transform prisons into people's parks and children's playgrounds while they bring back exiled citizens to play part in nation
building. They will also work towards putting back the economy on its feet.[64]

The poem ends on a note of hope,

> We will rise
> and build a nation
> moulding from the pieces
> of an oppressive history
> an unassailable monument
> grafted with justice for all
> enshrined with limitless hope.[65]

Henry Barlow, in "Building the Nation" portrays the rest (the masses) as the
ones capable of building the nation.[66] The rest are shown to be eagle-eyed
through the representation of the Permanent Secretary's driver. The rest can
see through the callousness, carelessness and superficiality of the leaders and
that the latter's engagement in building the nation is empty talk. At the end of
the poem, the writer tells us that there are two nation builders who play their
role differently. The poet leaves us to choose who the better nation builder is
and his choice is obvious,

> So two nation builders
> Arrived home this evening
> With terrible stomach pains
> The result of building the nation –
> – Different ways.[67]

At the end of *A Man of the People,* Odili states that suffering must be for a positive purpose.[68] 'Suffering should be creative, should give birth to something
good and lovely.'[69] Though Max is killed at the end for following his heart to
do right for the country, his death is believed to achieve greater things in life.

---

64   Ibid., 71.
65   Ibid., 72.
66   Barlow, "Building the Nation."
67   Ibid., 15.
68   Achebe, *A Man of the People.*
69   Ibid., 104.

Max's girlfriend Eunice avenges his death by shooting Chief Koko and ends up in prison. The story ends with the words 'you died a good death if your life had inspired someone to come forward and shoot your murderer in the chest – without asking to be paid.'[70] Achebe seems to give hope by suggesting that Max's death is not in vain. It will inspire other young people to fight the evil that robbed the masses of their freedom.

In *Smouldering Charcoal*, Chola decides to write a book about the raping of a dream, the subversion of the aspirations of independence and about how the dreams and aspirations were vested in the wrong people's hands.[71] The death of his friend Dumbo gave him strength and a sense of mission to write about Dambo, Mchere and their families as well as himself and many other people, "their inadequacies and frustrations, their lives and struggles to break out of the monstrous concentration camp that is independent Africa.'[72] Although he ends up being killed in prison, his girlfriend Catherine will send the information she receives from the prisoners outside the country and to the Movement's headquarters in one of the neighboring countries for publication. The voices of the suppressed people are finally heard. The newspapers outside the country publish scathing articles on the country's repressive institutions. Catherine also receives a manuscript with a letter from Chola asking her to publish his life in detention, his hopes and fears.[73] With the help of Mchere who was in prison with Chola, she will publish his story. She says that Chola did not die in vain and that the charcoal continues to smoulder. In other words, the 'future has begun.'[74]

Another interesting point to raise is the role of women in this change. In *Smouldering Charcoal*, it is Catherine who becomes the agent of the voice of the rest to create a change. It is through her that the ills of the country are disseminated. The wives of the prisoners also walk a great number of miles to join the procession at the prison. The writer makes an incredible comment about these women. Though the guards did not allow them in and simply ignored their plight, "their lives were undergoing a profound transformation. They were discovering resilience and fortitude and other qualities they had never thought they possessed.'[75] Adversity can give birth to strength and the will that one may have never believed she had. In *A Man of the People*, it is Eunice who takes the

---

70   Ibid., 149.
71   Zeleza, *Smouldering Charcoal*.
72   Ibid., 106.
73   Ibid., 180.
74   Ibid., 182.
75   Ibid. 138.

bold action to rid the ills of the society represented by Chief Koko.[76] Under the leadership of Segi, the women's corps in Soyinka's *Kongi's Harvest* defect from Kongi's Carpenters Brigade to align themselves with Daodu's farmers.[77] As intimated above, Prince Daodu is concerned with food security for the masses. He works with the masses to produce the award-winning yam that symbolizes life for the masses. Hence women are seen taking sides with the leadership that is benevolent to the masses. Women are the ones who give birth and feed the family. Subsequently, they are writing back to neo-colonial murderous leaders like Kongi to tell them that they divorce them and welcome life-giving and life-protecting leaders such as Prince Daodu.

In Imbuga's *Man of Kafira* (1984), it is a woman (Regina) who assassinates Boss.[78] As he is dying, Boss is humiliated and cannot believe that he has been killed by a woman, 'she has ... she has stabbed me. She has ... oh, no, not a woman.'[79] Imbuga's message is similar to that of Soyinka – even the most oppressed gender will rewrite history by cleansing Africa of its indigenous murderous leaders in order for more humane leaders to be born.

5   Conclusion

This chapter has examined the question of the rest writing back to their political leaders in the African Continent, during the colonial and neo-colonial eras. In the chapter, the rest refers to the masses or the marginalized people of Africa. The chapter is based on the significance of political leadership in African literature and the pertinent issue of the relationship between the leaders and the masses in political leadership. The chapter critically observed that the colonial powers were not interested in benefitting the masses by "illuminating" the so-called dark continent of Africa and eradicating ignorance, poverty and disease as they claimed when they encroached on Africa. Writing on behalf of the masses as the rest, selected African creative writers reveal that the colonizers' real motive was to enrich themselves through exploiting the indigenous African people. The so-called illumination of the continent through education was a myth. The colonial leaders ensured that the rest did not know how to read and write in case they learned about their rights, hence becoming difficult to subjugate.

---

76   Achebe, *A Man of the People.*
77   Soynika, *Kongi's Harvest.*
78   Imbuga, *Man of Kafira.*
79   Ibid., 70.

The chapter also examined neo-colonial leaders' betrayal of the masses' hopes about the kind of leadership that they would enjoy in post-independence Africa. It was observed how these hopes were declared at the inauguration of first African presidents. The masses were promised humane leadership that would heal the wounds inflicted on them during the colonial era. Selected creative literature was examined in which the masses as the rest write back to express the disillusionment with their African leaders and to expose the latter's real motive in leadership. Lastly, the chapter ends with a section on hope for the masses. The rest write back from a united front, conveying the message that they are ready to work and fight for leadership that can restore their hopes and human dignity.

Bibliography

Achebe, Chinua. *A Man of the People*. London: Heinemann, 1984.

Achebe, Chinua. *Hopes and Impediments: Selected Essays 1965–1987*. London: Heinemann International, 1988.

Achebe, Chinua. *The Trouble with Nigeria*. London: Heinemann Educational Books, 1983.

Chesaina, Ciarunji. *Notes on Francis Imbuga's Man of Kafira*. Nairobi: Heinemann Kenya, 1984.

Cook, David & David Rubadiri (Eds.). *Poems from East Africa*. Nairobi: East African Educational Publishers, 2010.

Dickinson, Margaret (Ed). *When Bullets Begin to Flower*. Nairobi: East African Educational Publishers, 1992.

Duerden, Dennis & Cosmo Pieterse (Eds.). *African Writers Talking*. London: Heinemann, 1972.

Excerpts from Inaugural Speech of Nnamdi Azikiwe Nov 16 1960. Retrieved from http://www.educationalresourceproviders.com/excerpts-from-inaugural-speech-of-nnamdi-azikiwe-nov-16-1960/.

Imbuga, Francis. *Man of Kafira*. Nairobi: Heinemann, 1984.

Kapanga, Kasongo Mulenda. "Ferdinand Oyono." In *Contemporary African Writers*, edited by Tanure Ojaide. Dictionary of Literary Biography. (New York: Gale, 2011), 232–235.

King'ei Kibwa & Henry Indangasi (Eds.). *Writers Speak: Essays on Literature and Democracy*. Nairobi: Writers Association of Kenya, 1997.

La Guma, Alex. *A Walk in the Night & Other Stories*. London, Heinemann Educational Books, 1967.

Mugo, Micere. *My Mother's Poem and Other Songs*. Nairobi: East African Educational Publishers, 1994.

Ngugi wa Thiong'o. *Writers in Politics*. London: Heinemann, 1981.

Ngugi wa Thiong'o. *Decolonizing the Mind*. Nairobi: Heinemann Kenya, 1986.

Ojukwu, Chinyelu F.(Ed.). *Critical Issues in African Literature: Twenty-First Century and Beyond*. Port Harcourt, University of Port Harecourt Press, 2013.

Oyono, Ferdinand. *The Old Man and the Medal*. London: Heinemann, 1972.

Soyinka, Wole. *Kongi's Harvest.* London: Oxford University Press, 1967.

Soyinka, Wole. *Myth, Literature and the African World*. Cambridge: Cambridge UP, 1990.

Zeleza, Tiyambe. *Smouldering Charcoal*. Essex: Heinemann, 1992.

CHAPTER 6

Aesthetic Hospitality: Mustafa Saʾeed as Guest in Tayeb Salih's *Season of Migration to the North*

Hiba Ghanem

Let us say yes *to who or what turns up,* before any determination, before any anticipation, before any *identification,* whether or not it has to do with a foreigner, an immigrant, an invited guest, or an unexpected visitor, whether or not the new arrival is the citizen of another country, a human, animal, or divine creature, a living or dead thing, male or female.[1]

1   Introduction

Ever since its publication in 1966, Tayeb Salih's *Season of Migration to the North* has been read as a postcolonial text that "writes back" to the empire.[2] In all these readings, however, little attention has been paid to the fact that the novel takes the figure of the "immigrant," who is educated in Britain and returns to Sudan, as its focal point. The migrant aspect is central to the two main characters: the narrator and Mustapha Saʾeed. The narrator is an anonymous character who finishes his Ph.D. in English Literature in Britain and returns to the Sudanese village of Wad Hamid. Mustapha Saʾeed is the stranger whom the narrator meets in Wad Hamid, Sudan, and who has had a similar past to that of the narrator; he has studied and taught Economics in Britain. United in their experience of displacement after their return from Britain, the two

---

1   Jacques Derrida, *Of Hospitality: Anne Dufourmantelle invites Jacques Derrida to respond.* Trans. Rachel Bowlby. (Stanford, California: Stanford University Press, 2000), 77.

2   Tayeb Salih, *Season of Migration to the North.* Trans. Denys Johnson-Davies. (New York, New York Review of Books, [1969] 2009; In "The Empire Renarrated: 'Season of Migration to the North' and the Reinvention of the Present," Saree S. Makdisi claims that Salih's novel writes back to the empire by reinventing the present. It forsakes the limitations of 'traditionalism of the Arab past' as well as the 'future that imperial Europe, through the ideology of modernity, once held out to its victims' (p. 817). In such a present, "Mustafa's problem-and the narrator's-is that they are neither black nor white, but grey; neither wholly Eastern nor wholly Western, neither completely European nor completely Arab" (p. 814). This chapter thus invests in the ambiguousness of these "grey characters," the narrator and Saʾeed, to investigate how such a state could indicate a state of promise and potentiality.

characters rewrite the postcolonial experience through that of the migrant in both settings.

As displaced migrants, these two characters become guests in search of a host to welcome them, a host who would 'say yes' to them. By 'say yes,' Derrida refers to a state of hospitable welcoming that is 'an art and a poetics.'[3] Adopting the framework of Derridean hospitality as a form of art, this chapter asks: how does the category of the "guest" rewrite the postcolonial categorization of social alienation in terms of the master and the slave? Who plays the role of the host in the novel and what is the significance of this role? How do Britain and Wad Hamid differ in their manner of extending hospitality to the foreign guest? And do they really differ? And, finally, what role does aesthetics or art play in the novel and how does it redefine the experience of hospitality?

This chapter argues that by re-reading this novel in terms of hospitality, the novel highlights the role that Sa'eed and the narrator play in redefining the cultural encounter between East and West. The chapter is specifically interested in how the hospitality rituals of eating, drinking and entertainment provide these two characters with the means to rewrite the colonial narrative and develop an 'active sense of self' that has been 'eroded by dislocation, resulting from migration.'[4] In Britain, Sa'eed is tried for the killing of his wife, Jean Morris, and for his role in the suicide of his other three lovers, Ann Hammond, Sheila Greenwood and Isabella Seymour. His love relationships are narrated in terms of eating and drinking. As a 'desert of thirst,' Sa'eed seeks the 'North and the ice' of his lovers who also reciprocate in alimentary terms.[5] While Jean Morris is said to 'bite' into his arm,[6] Ann Hammond 'feeds' him with lies.[7] These alimentary relationships are read as Derridean attempts by Sa'eed, the guest, to take his British lover as 'hostage,' thus, challenging their sovereignty as both colonizers and owners of the land.[8] In his love relationships, the host and guest switch places in a political act of appropriation.

This political act of appropriation extends to the Old Baileys or the British court of justice where Sa'eed is tried for his role in the death of his lovers. Instead of exercising its political sovereignty over Sa'eed, the British court's decision lays bare a Derridean process of decision-making that Sa'eed rewrites in terms of hospitality. Politically speaking, the court executes justice by

---

3   Jacques Derrida, "The principle of hospitality." *Parallax*, 11 (2005): 7.
4   Bill Ashcroft, Gareth Griffiths, & Helen Tiffin, *The Empire Writes Back: Theory and Practice in Post-Colonial Literatures.* (London; New York: Routledge, 2002), 9.
5   Salih, *Season of Migration*, 155.
6   Ibid.
7   Ibid., 144.
8   Derrida, *Of Hospitality*, 107.

sentencing Sa'eed to seven years in prison, a decision that Sa'eed abhors as he desires to join Jean Morris. Despite his desire to kill himself in order to join his lover, Sa'eed has previously failed to execute this decision. This failure lays bare a Derridean 'undecidability' that is a feature of every 'act of decision-making.'[9] By undecidability, Derrida refers to the state where 'a subject can never decide anything' because every decision is subject to rules and laws that cannot guarantee justice as an ethical standard beyond the rule of law.[10] In this sense, the court's sentence serves to reinforce the undecidability within Sa'eed's decision-making. This is why Sa'eed describes the court's decision as 'justice, the rules of the game, like the laws of combat and neutrality in war. This is cruelty that wears the mask of mercy.'[11] Although the court seems to execute a legal decision, it is actually 'refusing to take the decision which he should have taken of his own free will.'[12] The court's decision, in this sense, becomes a vehicle within Sa'eed's negotiation of his own process of decision-making.

By releasing Sa'eed after imprisonment, the court prolongs Sa'eed's torturous indecision, a state that he describes as an 'apology, not for killing her, but for the lie that was [his] life.'[13] By narrating these incidents to the narrator, Sa'eed presents his narrative as an attempt at making an apology or seeking forgiveness, thus introducing unconditionality into hospitality. In unconditional hospitality, Derrida describes how 'whoever asks for hospitality, asks, in a way, for forgiveness and whoever offers hospitality, grants forgiveness' for both are always 'lacking hospitality.'[14] As a site of political justice, the court of justice falls prey to the guest's political act of decision making that acquires an ethical significance of seeking forgiveness. Sa'eed thus introduces this court of justice to unconditional hospitality through redefining decision-making and law in terms of an ethical attempt at seeking and granting forgiveness in which guest and host engage.

While Britain extends to Sa'eed a conditional form of hospitality that Sa'eed redefines, Wad Hamid seems more open in receiving Sa'eed as a stranger who is allowed to settle down and marry a local woman, Husna Bint Mahmoud. In Wad Hamid, the ceremonial aspect of hospitality plays a role that is similar to that which it has in Britain. However, the hospitality practices of drinking

---

9   Jacques Derrida, "Force of Law," in Acts of Religion, ed. Gil Anidjar. (New York: Routledge, 2002), 253.
10   Ibid.
11   Salih, *Season of Migration*, 68.
12   Ibid., 68–69.
13   Ibid., 29.
14   Jacques Derrida, "Hostipitality," in *Acts of Religion*, ed. Gil Anidjar. (New York: Routledge, [1997] 2002), 308.

and entertainment, specifically the recitation of poetry, assume a more active political role in defining the identities and the decision-making of the host and the guest. Poetry displays the confusion of the categories of "host" and "guest" through the two returned migrants, Sa'eed and the narrator. In an event of hospitality initiated by Mahjoub, the narrator's childhood friend, the narrator is surprised by Sa'eed's sudden recitation of poetry in English.[15] He describes how it seems as if 'the ground suddenly split open and revealed an *afreet* standing before [him], his eyes shooting out flames.'[16] Through this poetic surprise, Sa'eed evokes the image of the *afreet*, a supernatural entity, thus reducing the narrator to a state of shock in the presence of the unknown. Sa'eed thus introduces the narrator to the state of openness in the presence of the 'absolute other,' which characterizes unconditional hospitality.[17] This is why the narrator feels that 'the men grouped together in that room – were not a reality.'[18] In that event of hospitality, all the characters experience an erasure of identity as "absolute other[s]," a process that is initiated by the guest's poetic recitation. In that sense, poetry becomes the medium elected by Sa'eed and the narrator for narrating and overcoming their 'crisis of identity' that characterizes postcolonial societies.[19]

Through introducing the narrator to unconditional hospitality, Sa'eed lays bare the conflict between hospitality as an ethics of openness to the other and hospitality as a politics concerned with the rules that a sovereign imposes upon a guest.[20] In terms of sovereignty, Sa'eed becomes the guest who takes his host as a hostage, thus practicing sovereignty over his host. In their confusion of identities, however, poetry unites the guest and host where the narrator feels compelled to complete the poetry verse that Sa'eed starts before his death. In Sa'eed's 'wax museum,' the narrator finds that Sa'eed has left behind him a few verses of poetry, so he embarks on completing the poem by adding a verse.[21] While Sa'eed has been 'awed when face to face with art,' the narrator embraces art and embarks on the poetic mission.[22] This incident shows how poetry provides the guest and host with complementary identities. In the hospitality of poetry, both host and guest are unified as non-entities that poetry can define through complementation.

---

15   Salih, *Season of Migration*, 12.
16   Ibid., 14.
17   Derrida, *Of Hospitality*, 26.
18   Salih, *Season of Migration*, 14.
19   Ashcroft, Griffiths & Tiffin, *The Empire Writes Back*, 8.
20   Derrida, *Of Hospitality*, 25.
21   Salih, *Season of Migration*, 154.
22   Ibid., 152.

As poetry assumes an active role, it redefines the political act of decision-making in aesthetic terms. In the final scene, while swimming in the river, the narrator considers the choice of either following the example of Sa'eed and allowing the river to drown him, or of living. However, he finally decides to 'choose life,' and his decision to live is described in terms of 'hunger, a thirst.'[23] In this sense, the narrator chooses to live in a perpetual state of hospitality. However, the critical point here is that the narrator enacts the decision in an artistic form by becoming 'a comic actor shouting on a stage' as he seeks help to enact his decision.[24]

In aesthetic hospitality, the narrator describes how place, specifically the desert, comes to indicate the 'land of poetry and possibility;' poetry becomes a characteristic pertaining to the landscape where the displaced migrants seek refuge. In that land, the narrator feels that all characters are 'brothers; he who drinks and he who prays and he who steals and he who commits adultery and he who fights and he who kills.'[25] In this event of hospitality, the Divine seems not to 'care' or 'not [to be] angry.'[26] The narrator's view runs counter to the local custom of asking forgiveness of the Divine as 'when they laugh they say 'I ask forgiveness of God' and when they weep they say 'I ask forgiveness of God."[27] In this sense, the land of genies and poetry seems to conflate ethical standards and dispense with the discursive act of asking for forgiveness. In this 'land of despair and poetry but there is nobody to sing,' possibility lies in the act of reciprocation through singing.[28] In this sense, poetry illustrates the 'dialectic of place and displacement' that distinguishes post-colonial societies.[29] In the land of the possible, poetry represents the attempt of migrants to demand a language that would allow them to express the 'sense of Otherness in a positive and creative way.'[30] Through the act of poetic recitation, the narrator and Sa'eed illustrate a post-colonial sense of 'liberation' that is initiated by the 'artist in exile' and 'political figure between domains' where 'all things are indeed counter, original, spare, strange.'[31] Poetry, this chapter argues, rewrites the categories of master/slave that define post-colonial social alienation by

23 Ibid., 168.
24 Ibid., 169.
25 Ibid., 112.
26 Ibid.
27 Ibid., 130.
28 Ibid., 112.
29 Ashcroft, Griffiths & Tiffin, *The Empire Writes Back*, 11.
30 Ibid.
31 Edward Said, *Culture and Imperialism*. (New York: Vintage Books, 1994), 332.

introducing the guest/host relationship as a vehicle for liberating the potential of the self to define its Otherness through poetic creativity.

2   The Politics of Hospitality

As a theoretical paradigm, hospitality has a religious, moral and ethical significance that have made it increasingly relevant to recent political debates on immigration. In its earlier formulations, hospitality has assumed the moral and religious significance of 'mutual hospitality between guest and stranger.'[32] The Abrahamic religious scriptures present hospitality as a moral concept through the figure of Abraham, the 'prototype of hospitality' in Christianity, Judaism and Islam.[33] In its religiously moral version, hospitality conflates the guest, traveler and stranger and identifies them only in terms of their reception of the host's welcome.

Among the many philosophers, however, who would later theorize hospitality and highlight its political relevance is Kant. Kant distinguishes between the public dimension of hospitality to a stranger and the private dimension of hospitality to the guest. In *Perpetual Peace: A Philosophical Sketch*, Kant defines the natural right of hospitality as 'the right of a stranger not to be treated with hostility when he arrives on someone else's territory.'[34] This natural right is contrasted with the right of the guest to be entertained and that would 'require a special friendly agreement whereby he might become a member of the native household for a certain time.'[35] By referring to "hostility," "territory" and the necessity of "agreement," Kant draws attention to the political significance of hospitality.

Building on Kant's works, Derrida more recently investigates the political significance of hospitality in relation to immigration. Derrida claims that 'debates on immigration' deal with an 'unstable site' that is defined by a 'double law of hospitality.'[36] Hospitality, for Derrida, involves an 'antinomy,' for it indicates absolute ethical or unconditional welcoming that should also involve calculating

---

32   Mona Siddiqui, *Hospitality and Islam: Welcoming in God's Name.* (New Haven; London: Yale University Press, 2015), 23.

33   Ibid., 22.

34   Immanuel Kant, "Perpetual Peace: A Philosophical Sketch," in *Kant: Political Writings*, ed. Hans Reiss. Trans. H.B. Nisbet. (Cambrindge, UK: Cambridge University Press, [1795] 1970), 105.

35   Ibid., 106.

36   Derrida, "The Principle of Hospitality," 6.

risks and politically restricting that welcome.[37] Hospitality 'calculate[s] the risks, yes, but without closing the door on the incalculable, that is, on the future and the foreigner.'[38] For Derrida, the calculation of risks indicates 'a politics of hospitality, a politics of *capacity*, of *power* [*pouvoir*]' that is concerned with the 'power of the *hôte over* the *hôte*, of the host over the guest or vice versa.'[39] Derrida builds this argument on Levinas's differentiation between an ethics of hospitality, or the 'face,' which indicates the private space of the household and a politics of hospitality concerned with the public realm.[40] For Levinas, hospitality is 'attention to speech or welcome of the face'[41] which starts with language where 'language is hospitality.'[42] By language, Derrida refers to the appeal to the other that should be without conditions, whether linguistic or political. The central concern of Derrida and Levinas, then, is how to build a politics of hospitality that maintains its ethical dimensions.

While these philosophers engage with the political significance of hospitality, they give little attention to the role that the rituals of hospitality play in this respect. This chapter thus investigates how the hospitality rituals of eating, drinking and entertainment or reciting poetry redefine the politics of hospitality. Instead of being a concern with power, the politics of hospitality comes to indicate the potential of these rituals to negotiate the dynamics of power between the guest, Sa'eed, and the host, regardless of the setting or the cultural context. Rituals of hospitality assume the power to redefine the roles that the guest and host play, whether within the multicultural context of London or the Muslim culture of Wad Hamid. It is in this sense that we can read Edward Said's claim that Tayeb Salih's *Season of Migration to the North* is a 'masterpiece [that] is necessarily to be viewed' as 'enlarging, widening, refining the scope of a narrative form at the center of which had heretofore always been an exclusively European observer or center of consciousness' by engaging with issues of '[e]xile, immigration, and the crossing of boundaries.'[43] By narrating the experience of the migrant as a guest through the figure of Mustapha Sa'eed, the novel refines the scope of this narrative form through making hospitality fundamental to the postcolonial narration of the migrant experience.

---

37   Ibid., 7.
38   Ibid., 6.
39   Jacques Derrida, *Adieu to Emmanuel Levinas*. Trans. Pascale-Anne Brault & Michael Naas. (Stanford, Calif.: Stanford University Press, 1999), 18.
40   Ibid., 22.
41   Ibid.
42   Derrida, *Of Hospitality*, 135.
43   Edward Said, *Reflections on Exile and Other Literary and Cultural Essays*. (London: Granta, [2001] 2012), 638.

3   Between Conditional and Unconditional Hospitality: Sa'eed as
         'Guest' in Britain

In his recollection of his life in Britain, Sa'eed takes the court of justice as the
focal point for his narration. By trying Sa'eed for the killing of his wife, the
British court highlights the crucial role that the law plays in framing Sa'eed's
identity as an immigrant-guest who is hosted by a sovereign country. Britain,
in this sense, extends to Sa'eed a conditional form of hospitality whereby a
'sovereign' host imposes a set of rules upon this guest.[44] Instead of following
these rules, however, Sa'eed invests in the dynamics of hospitality, specifically
the ritualized practices of eating, drinking and entertainment, to challenge the
conditionality of British hospitality within that trial.

     In the British court of justice, Sa'eed carries out his first attempt at intro-
ducing the category of the "guest" into the colonial discourse on the master/
slave relationship. From the colonial discourse, he borrows the category of the
'invader' as he recollects the 'rattle of swords in Carthage and the clatter of
the hooves of Allenby's horses desecrating the ground of Jerusalem.'[45] Besides
'invader,' Sa'eed chooses to call himself the 'intruder' or the unwelcome guest
'whose fate must be decided.'[46] As an 'intruder' and an 'invader,' Sa'eed introduces the category of the "guest" in his recollection of the colonial past that
builds on the master/slave relation. He fuses the two discourses in describing
his trial for the killing of his lover-wife, Jean Morris, and his possible role in
causing the suicide of his other lovers. This fusion features in the person of the
Public Prosecutor and the defense lawyer. The Public Prosecutor, Sir Anthony
Higgins, Sa'eed's former Criminal Law teacher, appeals to the authority of the
law to indict him. On the other hand, Professor Maxwell Foster-Keene, 'one of
the founders of the Moral Rearmament movement in Oxford, a Mason, and a
member of the Supreme Committee for the Protestant Missionary Societies
in Africa,' defends Sa'eed by reinforcing the colonial discourse.[47] Foster-Keene
argues that Sa'eed has been the victim of displacement brought on by cultural
confrontation between the West and the East in order to 'save [him] from the
gallows.'[48] The argument of Foster-Keene builds on the construction of binary oppositions between 'two worlds,' between the East or Africa and Western
civilization.[49] Whether on the side of the prosecution or the defense, Professor

---

44   Derrida, *Of Hospitality*, 25.
45   Salih, *Season of Migration*, 94–95.
46   Ibid., 94.
47   Ibid., 93.
48   Ibid., 32.
49   Ibid., 33.

Maxwell Foster-Keen and Sir Arthur Higgins both enact their roles as masters who have the right to enforce the law and decide the fate of this foreigner, letting him live or die. In the prosecution, he is only allowed to say 'Yes' and 'I don't know.'[50] Although he desires the court to sentence him to death, Sa'eed ends up being imprisoned for a 'mere seven years' and pardoned for all his possible roles in the suicide of his other lovers.[51] He describes the court's decision as 'justice, the rules of the game, like the laws of combat and neutrality in war. This is cruelty that wears the mask of mercy.'[52] Forgiveness by the court is a torture for Sa'eed as it denies him the end that he desires: death to join his lover.

Despite the conditionality of the trial where the master sentences Sa'eed to prison, the court becomes a setting for an event of ritualized hospitality of eating and drinking. The trial becomes a 'ritual' that is 'being held primarily because of' him.[53] In this ritual, Sa'eed feels that he is the 'colonizer' as an 'intruder whose fate must be decided.'[54] Instead of master, Sa'eed becomes an unwelcome guest or "intruder" whose host subjects him to the rule of law. In this ritualized hospitality, Sa'eed describes himself as the 'desert of thirst' and the 'werewolf' who is 'the reason for two girls committing suicide' and who has 'wrecked the life of a married woman and killed his own wife.'[55] Referring to death, Sa'eed turns the trial into a description of an event of hospitality, eating and drinking. Sa'eed refers to himself as the 'southern thirst'[56] or the desert traveler who is thirsty and needs the 'North and the ice'[57] from which he can drink. His love relationships thus become attempts on his side to drink and eat his lovers.

By eating and drinking his lovers, Sa'eed represents a Derridean attempt at internalizing his lovers to experience 'the foreigner in me.'[58] In his love relationships, Sa'eed represents how host and guest are inserted in a relationship of 'learning and giving to eat, learning-to-give-to-the-other-to-eat.'[59] With Isabella Seymour, Sa'eed finds that he has to reassure her that he is harmless and not a 'cannibal' by describing himself as an 'aged crocodile who's lost its teeth'

---

50   Ibid., 32.
51   Ibid., 68.
52   Ibid.
53   Ibid., 94.
54   Ibid.
55   Ibid., 32–33.
56   Ibid., 42.
57   Ibid., 30.
58   Derrida, "Hostipitality," 407.
59   Jacques Derrida, "Eating well: or the calculation of the subject," in Points…: interviews, eds. Werner Hamacher and David E. Wellbery. Trans. Peter Conor and Avitar Ronell. (Stanford: Stanford UP, 1995), 282.

and that 'wouldn't have the strength to eat' her.[60] Her wrinkles prove to him 'not that she had grown old, but that she had ripened.'[61] Sa'eed also uses the same imagery of eating and drinking in describing his love relationship with Sheila Greenwood, the country girl from the outskirts of Hull, who 'would lick [his] face.'[62] Greenwood displays how the other lovers take part in the event of eating and drinking. By turning these relationships into practices of hospitality, Sa'eed draws attention to the changing postcolonial dynamics where master and slave are actually learning to eat and drink together. Commenting on this relationship between Sa'eed and Isabella Seymour, the narrator wonders at the irony of the fact that '[j]ust because a man has been created on the Equator some mad people regard him as a slave, others as a god.'[63] Seymour expresses her adoration of Sa'eed by addressing him as a 'pagan god.'[64] In his narration of their love relationships, Sa'eed describes how Seymour looks at him as a 'symbol rather than reality' of the 'Arab soldiers' first meeting with Spain.'[65] By referring to the Arab soldiers' meeting with Spain, Sa'eed echoes the colonial category of the master as a god. He appears to take the seduction of women as a 'reclamation of masculinity [...] and a metonymic equivalent of conquering territory.'[66] However, his descriptions of these lovers also include events whereby he allows his British lovers to metaphorically share in the experience of eating and drinking.

In Sa'eed's narration of his love relationship with Ann Hammond, the young 'Oriental languages' student at Oxford, Sa'eed gives ritualized hospitality practices an aesthetic dimension: theatre.[67] Theatre is taken to indicate the hospitality ritual of entertaining the guest that rewrites the colonial experience. Hammond employs colonial categories when she addresses Sa'eed as 'Mustafa, my master and my lord' while calling herself 'Sausan, [his] slave girl.'[68] However, Sa'eed describes how their encounter takes the form of a performance where both are on 'a stage surrounded by actors who were performing minor roles' while he is 'the hero and she the heroine.'[69] Sa'eed redefines the colonial

---

60   Salih, *Season of Migration*, 40.
61   Ibid.
62   Ibid., 139.
63   Ibid., 108.
64   Ibid.
65   Ibid., 42–43.
66   Wail S. Hassan, "Gender and Imperialism: Structures of Masculinity in Tayeb Salih's Season of Migration to the North." *Men and Masculinities* 5 (3) (2003): 311.
67   Salih, *Season of Migration*, 30.
68   Ibid., 142.
69   Ibid., 144.

master/slave encounter into that of a theatrical performance. Theatre or play-acting becomes a leitmotif that reveals the 'struggle to draw the line between truth and illusion, identity and role, authentic face and mask.'[70] In this theater, the master and the slave are roles and masks that the colonial powers and the colonized accept to play. Echoing Sa'eed, the narrator carries out a similar redefinition of these roles by describing the colonial encounter in dramatic terms of a melodrama and a tragedy. Colonial history becomes 'a melodramatic act which with the passage of time will change into a mighty myth.'[71] In all these descriptions, Sa'eed and the narrator perceive the colonial encounter in terms of the hospitality practice of entertaining a guest through playacting.

As melodrama and myth, however, the colonial encounter as an event of hospitality relies upon the conflating of reality and illusion to achieve this redefinition. In his theatrical performance, Sa'eed describes how 'moved by poetry and drink,' Hammond willfully assumes the role of the slave girl.[72] Sa'eed and Hammond start their relationship by discussing the wine poetry of Abu Nuwas. Quoting verses from the latter, Sa'eed refers to wine as a weapon of war as 'with wine we kill and our dead with wine we bring to life.'[73] Although this verse refers to war, it relegates the mission of killing and reviving the enemy to wine. In his version of hospitality, Sa'eed chooses wine to affect the experience of blurring reality and illusion to lure his lovers into believing the 'fantasy'[74] that he offers them as an 'Arab-African' from the South.[75] This confusion is also carried out in theatrical terms. Hammond, the slave girl, is said to 'feed' him with 'sweet lies' as lies 'are turned into truth.'[76] He feels 'that somehow [he] meant what [he] was saying and that she too, despite her lying, was telling the truth.'[77] The theatre of imperial encounters presents the friend and enemy in an event of hospitality defined by the sharing of wine and the poetry of Abu Nuwas. In this event, 'true war' is defined by Abu Nuwas's poetic verse where 'death [is] in pleasure' instead of 'strife.'[78]

---

70 As'ad Khairallah, "The travelling theatre or the art of entertaining a doomed caravan with amusing stories," in *Tayeb Salih's Season of Migration to the North: A Casebook*, ed. Mona Takieddine Amyuni. (Beirut, Lebanon: American University of Beirut, 1985), 107.

71 Salih, *Season of Migration*, 60.

72 Ibid., 145.

73 Ibid.

74 Ibid.

75 Ibid., 38.

76 Ibid., 144–145.

77 Ibid., 144.

78 Ibid., 145.

The main feature of this aesthetic hospitality lies in the death of all these lovers, and especially Jean Morris, the wife whom he kills and because of whom he is brought to trial. In colonial terms, Sa'eed seems to translate his 'anti-colonial anger' through the suicide and murder of these 'unsuspecting British women.'[79] However, this anger is rewritten as a dynamic fundamental to hospitality. Similar to all his other love relationships, Sa'eed and Jean Morris practice hospitality in alimentary terms. In this relationship, Morris shares in the activity of eating. Although she is the 'mountain of ice' that could quench his thirst, she is described as biting into 'Sa'eed's arms.'[80] He feels that she chews at his liver when she has 'chewed and spat out' a rare Arabic manuscript that he owns.[81] Sa'eed finds that he has to 'swallow' the agonies of her humiliation of him, just like 'the man fasting swallows the agonies of the month of Ramadan when it falls in the scorching heat of summer.'[82] In her rage, she 'would break any crockery that came to hand.'[83] Their alimentary relationship, however, reaches the epitome of hospitality when Sa'eed finally quenches his thirst by killing her. By surviving Morris and refusing her invitation to join him in death, Sa'eed tinges his life after her death with regret; his life becomes an 'apology, not for killing her, but for the lie that was [his] life.'[84] Sa'eed thus experiences the 'failing, fault, offense, even sin, to be forgiven on the very threshold [...] of hospitality.'[85] His anti-colonial anger lends itself into a sense of regret at his failing, a failing that he expresses through the poetry that he leaves behind after his death: 'Deep silence has embraced the vestiges of prayer/ Of moans and supplications and cries of woeful care.'[86] He seems to issue a Derridean prayer for forgiveness that is integral to asking for and granting hospitality. In its Derridean form, forgiveness 'must be infinite or it is nothing,' for it is 'excuse or exchange' where 'the welcoming one must ask for forgiveness from the welcomed one even prior to the former's own having to forgive for one is always failing, lacking hospitality.'[87] In hospitality, both host and guest, Sa'eed and his

---

79   Catherine Rashid, "Academia, Empathy, Faith: Leila Aboulela's The Translator," in *Postcolonialism and Islam: Theory, Literature, Culture, Society and Film,* eds. G. Nash, K. Kerr-Koch & S.E. Hackett. (London and New York: Routledge, 2014), 132.

80   Salih, *Season of Migration,* 155–156.

81   Ibid., 157.

82   Ibid., 160.

83   Ibid.

84   Ibid., 29.

85   Derrida, "Hostipitality," 380.

86   Salih, *Season of Migration,* 153.

87   Derrida, "Hostipitality," 380.

lovers, are inserted in a relationship of prayer for forgiveness that exceeds the state of the law or the conditionality of hospitality.

In this prayer of forgiveness, Sa'eed revisits the conditionality of hospitality that Britain extends to him. Although he describes how his 'life achieved completion that night' in killing Jean Morris, Sa'eed delays taking the decision of realizing his desire to join his loved one even when 'there was no justification for staying on.'[88] By imprisoning him, the British host refuses to take the 'decision which he should have taken of his own free will.'[89] The court's decision, in this sense, becomes one more delay mechanism that Sa'eed, the guest, has activated upon killing Morris. His delay of the decision starts at the moment he faces 'undecidability'[90] and could not take the decision to join Jean Morris who implores him to 'come with' her.[91] Even upon his release from prison, Sa'eed wanders 'from place to place, from Paris to Copenhagen to Delhi to Bangkok, as he tries to put off the decision.'[92] In this act, Sa'eed shows how the conditionality of the hospitality that Britain has extended to him through the trial acquires an unconditional form. While the court makes a decision as law, it indirectly discloses the delay mechanism within decision making, or the "undecidability," which the guest has initiated.

4   From Unconditional to Aesthetic Hospitality: The "Guest" in Wad Hamid

While Britain extends to Sa'eed a conditional form of hospitality, Wad Hamid seems to be more open to receiving Sa'eed as a perfect stranger. Despite being a stranger, Sa'eed chooses and marries one of its local inhabitants, Husna Bint Mahmoud. As in Britain, the ceremonial aspect of hospitality plays a significant role in Wad Hamid. As returned migrants, Sa'eed and the narrator, however, display the aesthetic features of unconditional hospitality where the hospitality practices of eating, drinking and entertainment through poetry and singing assume a more active role in redefining the roles of the guest and the host, as well as of the locals of Wad Hamid.

The hospitality practices of singing, poetry and wine-drinking play a critical role in disclosing Sa'eed as a guest with a political agenda of challenging

---

88   Salih, *Season of Migration*, 92.
89   Ibid., 68–69.
90   Derrida, "Force of Law," 253.
91   Salih, *Season of Migration*, 165.
92   Ibid., 69.

the sovereignty of the host. Upon his return to Wad Hamid, the narrator is intrigued by Sa'eed who is 'not a local man but a stranger' and whose past no one seems to know about.[93] The narrator is acquainted with Sa'eed more intimately through a traditional hospitality event of wine-drinking which is organized by Mahjoub, the 'Chairman of the Agricultural Project Committee.'[94] Drunk, Sa'eed reduces the narrator to a state of shock when he recites poetry in English. Instead of being a source of entertainment, the traditional hospitality practice of reciting poetry becomes an element of undesirable surprise. By reciting poetry in a different language, Sa'eed lays bare his status as a stranger who seems to be hiding a secret. In this sense, poetry defies the conditionality of this event of hospitality whereby the host would know the 'name and family name' of the guest.[95] When he 'suddenly heard him reciting English poetry in a clear voice and with an impeccable accent,' the narrator demonstrates the surprise of the Derridean host.[96] As a host, the narrator is 'overtaken' and surprised 'in a fashion almost violent' by this unknown guest.[97] In this sense, hospitality becomes a political concern whereby Sa'eed, the guest, threatens the narrator, the host, as a master in his own land of Wad Hamid. This is why the narrator 'shouted at him: 'What's this you're saying? What's this you're saying?''[98]

Overtaken by this unknown guest, the narrator perceives Sa'eed as a threat to all the participants in this hospitality event. This incident highlights the Derridean conflict between hospitality as an ethics, an openness to the absolute other, and hospitality as a politics, as a set of rules that a sovereign imposes upon a guest.[99] In political terms, Sa'eed places his host, the narrator, at 'risk [of] becoming [his] hostage.'[100] For Derrida, the host or the 'inviting one' becomes the 'hostage of the guest' who threatens the sovereignty of the host as the ruler of his own home.[101] As a guest in Wad Hamid, Sa'eed plays a significant political, specifically colonial, role in the Sudanese community. He is the stranger who submits the inhabitants of Wad Hamid to the authority of the law. He mimics the colonial role of the master as a 'man whose approach to life includes a healthy respect for, and protection of, the law allied with a superior,

93   Ibid., 2.
94   Ibid., 12.
95   Derrida, *Of Hospitality*, 25.
96   Salih, *Season of Migration*, 14.
97   Derrida, "Hostipitality," 361.
98   Salih, *Season of Migration*, 15.
99   Derrida, *Of Hospitality*, 25.
100   Ibid., 55.
101   Ibid., 53–55.

specialized intellect inclining to science.'[102] He advises the Agricultural Project Committee to 'submit to the rules of the project.'[103] He further reinforces the power of the law by warning the Sudanese community against the chaos that will ensue from not heeding to that law, for 'if they were to contravene the law they would be punished like anyone else.'[104] For Mahjoub, Sa'eed is worthy of being a minister in the government because he has 'great mental capacity.'[105] Even ministers in Khartoum remember him as the 'President of the Society for the Struggle for African Freedom' who will 'liberate Africa.'[106] His association with the Sudanese politicians and their desire to liberate Africa illustrates the political role that Sa'eed plays by mimicking the colonizers. In his political role, Sa'eed threatens the sovereignty of the Sudanese inhabitants of Wad Hamid over their own lands. By submitting them to the rule of law, he manages to take his hosts as hostages who willingly welcome him amongst them.

Sa'eed's political role displays the dynamics of the conditional form of hospitality whereby the narrator himself is also taken as a hostage. Besides colonial mimicry, appeal to social customs and the *Shari'a* law are among these dynamics of conditional hospitality that Sa'eed carries out. Before his disappearance, Sa'eed divulges to the narrator the secret of his previous life in Britain and makes him 'promise on oath' that he will not let anyone know.[107] By committing the narrator 'irrevocably' by this secret,[108] the Derridean "guest" lays down upon the narrator as host a law that the latter 'has to choose to obey.'[109] As a hostage, the narrator later finds out that he has also been assigned the guardianship of Sa'eed's children after the latter's sudden disappearance. The narrator receives this posthumous assignment in an 'envelope sealed in red wax.'[110] In this assignment, Sa'eed appeals to a social and religious custom to maintain his bind over the narrator, for the role of the guardian is a social and religious role which is mandated by the 'Shari'a law in the Sudan' which assigns a *wasi* or legal guardian to insure that 'minors with property are not left unprotected.'[111] However, Sa'eed redefines this legal form of guardianship in

---

102   Said, *Culture and Imperialism,* 152.
103   Salih, *Season of Migration,* 12.
104   Ibid.
105   Ibid., 102.
106   Ibid., 120.
107   Ibid., 18.
108   Ibid., 154.
109   Derrida, *Of Hospitality,* 60.
110   Salih, *Season of Migration,* 154.
111   Carolyn Fluehr-Lobban, *Islamic Law and Society in the Sudan.* (New York and London: Routledge, 2008), 219.

terms of hospitality. He requests that the narrator give 'his kind attention, and to be a help, a counselor and an adviser' to his two sons in order to 'spare them the pangs of wanderlust.'[112] As an adviser and counselor, the narrator's assigned guardianship is defined in terms of hospitality.[113] Through the narrator, Sa'eed tries to protect his children from the social alienation that wanderlust causes; his children should not relive the experience of their father, the guest, who is always in search of hospitality.

By taking the narrator as his hostage, Sa'eed employs the hospitality practice of poetry recitation to further alienate the narrator. In a conversation between Sa'eed and the narrator, Sa'eed dismisses the value of the narrator's degree in poetry because other disciplines, such as 'agriculture, engineering or medicine,' are more practical for the people of his village.[114] Sa'eed employs the first person plural pronoun "we" to refer to the inhabitants of Wad Hamid. This argument infuriates the narrator who feels that he has become a "stranger" through his association with poetry.[115] Through poetry, Sa'eed immerses the narrator in his own experience of foreignness as a "guest" despite 'being with a background, with roots, with a purpose.'[116] The narrator later describes this alienation, evoked by Sa'eed, in his sense of living 'superficially' in his own village where he has 'no room' and where he feels the need to 'pack up and go.'[117] The narrator thus becomes the guest, the alienated one in his own hometown, the 'image' of which he sees through 'the eye of [his] imagination.'[118] His hometown becomes a mirage that promises him nourishment but provides none.

Although poetry has been politically employed by Sa'eed to reinforce alienation, it evokes in the narrator a recollection of a native cultural belief in supernatural entities, the *afreet* or genie. Poetry, in this sense, assumes a seemingly imaginative role that redefines the state of political alienation as an

---

112   Salih, *Season of Migration*, 65.
113   Ahmad A. Nasr claims that Salih juxtaposes "popular Islam" with 'Western civilization in general' (p. 94). By popular Islam, he refers to the grandfather's mysticism and the principles accepted by society, such as guardianship, specifically that of a man over a woman (p. 99). For Nasr, the narrator 'harmoniously united' the two in order to highlight the 'value of popular Islam' (p. 103). For further details on this, please see Ahmad Nasr, "Popular Islam in Al-Tayyib Salih," *Journal of Arabic Literature* 1, (1980): 88–104. This chapter thus builds on Nasr's conclusion to show how the narrator's attempt at establishing unity is actually an attempt at redefining popular Islamic practices, such as guardianship, through local hospitality practices.
114   Salih, *Season of Migration*, 9.
115   Ibid.
116   Ibid., 1.
117   Ibid., 219.
118   Ibid., 49.

attempt to reconnect with indigenous beliefs. When Sa'eed recites the poetic verse, the narrator feels as if 'the ground suddenly split open and revealed an *afreet* standing before [him], his eyes shooting out flames.'[119] Confronted with Sa'eed's appearance as a supernatural entity, the narrator finds himself in a state of openness to the 'absolute, unknown, anonymous other' or the Derridean unconditional form of hospitality.[120] Upon this revelation, the narrator confuses and momentarily forgets Sa'eed's name and addresses him as the 'man.'[121] Sa'eed thus becomes an anonymous being who is later described as a 'lie' and 'the Prophet El-Kidr, suddenly making his appearance and as suddenly vanishing.'[122] However, this state of absoluteness does not affect Sa'eed alone. The narrator describes how he, himself, feels that even 'the men grouped together in that room – were not a reality.'[123] As a host, the narrator doubts the identity of all the fellow guests at that moment of unconditional hospitality initiated by poetry. In a sense, poetry seems to have exposed the absoluteness of all characters, even those who take on the role of the host. Absoluteness, here, refers to a state of non-identity or potentiality for identity that has not been defined as yet. The suddenness of the poetic surprise recalls the suddenness of the Derridean 'gift of the poem' that 'comes along without [his] expecting it, cutting short the breath.'[124] Poetry, here assumes a revelatory force, for it is only through poetry and drinking that the absoluteness of all characters is disclosed. In the novel, poetry becomes a creative medium that revives the pre-colonial, indigenous cultural belief in the supernatural, the *afreet*, in the post-colonial society.[125] However, this pre-colonial belief assumes an ethical power insofar as it introduces absoluteness of the unknown to that event of hospitality.

Poetry's ethical role of disclosing absoluteness affects the narrator as well. Just as Sa'eed comes to indicate a state of absoluteness in his being an *afreet*, the narrator experiences a state of confusion about his own identity. This takes place when the narrator enters the locked room, or 'a graveyard. A mausoleum. An insane idea. A prison. A huge joke. A treasure chamber,' which Sa'eed leaves behind after his disappearance.[126] Upon entering this 'wax museum' or

---

119   Ibid., 14.
120   Derrida, *Of Hospitality*, 25–26.
121   Salih, *Season of Migration*, 15.
122   Ibid., 107.
123   Ibid., 14.
124   Jacques Derrida, "Che cos'è la poesia!" in *A Derrida Reader: Between the Blinds*, ed. Peggy Kamuf. (New York: Columbia University Press, 1988), 235.
125   Salih, *Season of Migration*, 115.
126   Ibid., 137–138.

the locked room that Sa'eed has left behind, the narrator describes how he is met with a 'frowning face with pursed lips' which he confuses with that of Sa'eed. The narrator, however, discovers that it 'is not Mustafa Sa'eed – it's a picture of [him] frowning at [his] face from a mirror.'[127] In this sense, the narrator confuses his identity with that of Sa'eed.[128] This is why he wonders, at an earlier point, if 'it [is] likely that what had happened to Mustafa Sa'eed could have happened to [him]?'[129] By switching roles, the guest and host cease to have separate identities but define themselves in terms of hospitality. When he finds the few verses of poetry that Sa'eed has left behind in his "wax museum," the narrator decides to finish the poem by adding a verse. While Sa'eed had been 'awed when face to face with art,' the narrator embraces art and embarks on the poetic mission. Although the narrator criticizes Sa'eed's poem as a 'poor poem that relies on antithesis and comparison' and lacks 'genuine emotion,' he feels compelled to complete it with a verse of his own.[130] This incident shows how poetry plays a crucial role in relegating both identities to a state of absoluteness where only art matters. Both guest and host play a complementary role of writing a verse of poetry and in doing so become unified as non-entities that art defines through complementarity. In this way, poetry seems to provide the narrator and Sa'eed with the refuge, roots and identity which they lack.

---

127   Ibid., 135.

128   For Ahmad Elnimeiri (2017), Mustapha Sa'eed is 'a character that exists only in the narrator's mind, invented by him to enable him to face in an effective manner the implications of the actual and closer contact with the colonial experience that he had evaded during his stay in London.' Elnimeiri argues that 'the combination of allegory and irony in [Sa'eed's] name makes it more reasonable to doubt his existence' (p. 5). Please see Ahmed Elnimeiri, "At an Impasse: The Discourse of Recession in Tayeb Saleh," *The Victorian* 5(2) (2017): 1–9. While this chapter does not adopt Elnimeiri's argument, it holds that the non-existence of any of the characters is a matter of relegating to absoluteness that the hospitality practice of poetry recitation allows.

129   Salih, *Season of Migration*, 49.

130   Ibid., 75–79; Barbara Harlow (1985) argues that the novel is an illustration of "*mu'arada*" or Arabic "literary opposition" as a 'formula whereby one person will write a poem, and another will retaliate by writing along the same lines, but reversing the meaning' (p. 75). Please see Barbara Harlow, "Sentimental Orientalism: Season of Migration to the North and Othello," in *Tayb Salih's Season of Migration to the North: A Casebook*, ed. Mona Takieddine Amyuni. (Beirut, Lebanon: American University of Beirut, 1985), 75–79. While Harlow uses this analogy to show how the novel adopts the same poetic technique of *mu'arada* to rewrite and reverse the conventions of tragedy within Shakespeare's Othello, this chapter perceives this instance of the narrator's completion of the poetic verse as a direct application of *mu'arada*. However, instead of focusing on the reversal, the chapter is interested in the first instance of completion to which the narrator feels he has to succumb to despite his apparent dislike of the poem.

If poetry plays a double role as an ethical agent that relegates to absolute-ness, all politically alienated characters, including Sa'eed and the narrator, it also plays an aesthetic role whereby art unifies those absolute characters. In this confusion of identities, the narrator displays the aestheticizing of the po-litical role that decision-making plays in hospitality. In the final scene, while swimming in the river, the narrator considers the choice of following the ex-ample of Sa'eed and allowing the river to drown him. He reflects 'that if I died at that moment, I would have died as I was born – without any volition of mine.'[131] The narrator thus equates death and an inability for decision-making. However, this wakes him up to his own ability to 'choose life' as 'there are a few people I want to stay with for the longest possible time and because I have duties to discharge.'[132] His decision to live is described in terms of 'hunger, a thirst,'[133] thereby transforming decision-making into a desire for hospitality. By deciding to live, the narrator chooses to become a traveler in search of hos-pitality. However, in screaming for help, the narrator becomes 'a comic actor shouting on a stage'[134] and thereby enacts his decision in artistic form. His artistic enactment becomes his final statement on decision-making as he de-clares that if he is 'unable to forgive,' then he 'shall try to forget.'[135] In aesthetic hospitality, travelers dispense with the need to ask for forgiveness. In the state of absoluteness, both Sa'eed and the narrator find their refuge and hospitality in art, and even political acts such as decision-making or ethical forgiveness-seeking become purely aesthetic.

5   Conclusion

To return to the question of how the category of the "guest" rewrites the post-colonial categorization of master/slave, I would argue that the guest stands for the infinite, the Derridean absolute, which challenges categorization as a colonial discursive act. The hospitality practices of eating, drinking and poetry recitation constitute a locale for creating possibilities in redefining social alienation that characterizes postcolonial cultures. In the hospital-ity of poetry, Sa'eed and the narrator become absolute entities that can only be defined aesthetically. They come to indicate Edward Said's 'migrant, [...]

---

131   Ibid., 168.
132   Ibid.
133   Ibid.
134   Ibid., 169.
135   Ibid.

whose consciousness is that of the intellectual and artist in exile' and the 'political figure between domains, between forms, between homes, and between
languages.'[136] As migrant-artists, the two characters rewrite the post-colonial
as an experience of the in-between. This experience of in-between-ness is best
exemplified in the novel in the desert that the narrator calls the 'land of poetry
and the possible' where he feels that 'we are all brothers; he who drinks and he
who prays and he who steals and he who commits adultery and he who fights
and he who kills.'[137] Previously described as the 'land of despair and poetry but
there is nobody to sing,' the desert can only acquire its potentiality as the 'land
of the possible' when it becomes a locale for poetic hospitality and reciprocity
through singing.[138] In this artistic state of the in-between, the artist 'lies not
in the middle, paralyzed between north and south, but in presenting all the
contradictions.'[139] The narrator, through Sa'eed, becomes such an artist who
transposes the contradictions of north and south, through the native people of
that south, into the land of poetry. The Sudanese desert, in this sense, constitutes the mirror image of the British land/ courtroom as locales for hospitality
practices. In these locales, the master/slave colonial relationship is re-written
through the lens of the "guest." As guests in the hospitality of poetry, master
and slave, the colonizer and colonized, forsake the Derridean need for apolo-
gizing or seeking forgiveness for their lack of hospitality. In this sense, it could
be said that Salih has intentionally chosen to keep the matter of the narrator's
survival and Sa'eed's death unknown in order to carry on poetic hospitality.
In poetic hospitality, even the novel itself becomes a dramatic poem.[140] The
narrator and Sa'eed take the role of the absolute guest, the *afreet*, whose actual

---

136   Said, *Culture and Imperialism*, 332.

137   Salih, *Season of Migration*, 112.

138   R.S. Krishnan (1996) argues that Salih, in this novel, 'reinscribes the 'truth' of colonial
      encounter from the perspective of the colonized.' (p. 15). For Krishnan, Salih's 'rejection
      of colonial ideology' is communicated in his 'reiteration of the national and cultural iden-
      tity' of the native culture (p. 14). By doing as such, Salih 'draw[s] new maps of reality, to
      throw some much needed light on the dark center of colonial discourse' (p. 15). In this
      sense, the 'land of poetry and possibility' that render Bedouins into a tribe of genies is
      the new map of reality that challenges colonial discourse and rewrites it creatively. For
      further details, please refer to Krishnan, R.S., "Reinscribing Conrad: Tayeb Salih's Season
      of Migration to the North," *The International Fiction Review*, 23 (1–2) (1996): 7–15.

139   Peter Nazareth, "The Narrator as Artist and the Reader as Critic in Season of Migration
      to the North," in *Tayb Salih's Season of Migration to the North: A Casebook*, ed. Mona
      Takieddine Amyuni. (Beirut, Lebanon: American University of Beirut, 1985), 132.

140   Ali Abdalla Abbas, "Notes on Tayeb Salih: Season of Migration to the North and The
      Wedding of Zein," *Sudan Notes and Records*, 55 (1974): 46.

presence invites the reader to poetic hospitality before migrating in search of the hospitality of another reader.

Acknowledgements

The author wishes to thank Dr. Francesca Cauchi and Dr. Esmaeil Zeiny for their remarks on the initial drafts of this chapter.

Bibliography

Abbas, Ali Abdalla. "Notes on Tayeb Salih: Season of Migration to the North and The Wedding of Zein." *Sudan Notes and Records*, 55 (1974): 46–60.

Ashcroft, B., Griffiths, G., & Tiffin, H. (2002). *The Empire Writes Back: Theory and Practice in Post-Colonial Literatures*. London; New York: Routledge, [1989] 2002.

Derrida, Jacques. "Che cos'è la poesia!" In *A Derrida reader: between the blinds,* edited by Peggy Kamuf. (New York: Columbia University Press, 1988), 221–237.

Derrida, Jacques. "Eating well: or the Calculation of the Subject." In *Points…: interviews, 1974–1994.* Edited by Werner Hamacher and David E. Wellbery. (Peter Conor and Avitar Ronell Trans.). (Stanford: Stanford University Press, 1995), 255–287.

Derrida, Jacques. *Adieu to Emmanuel Levinas.* (Pascale-Anne Brault and Michael Naas. Trans.) Standford, California: Stanford University Press, 1999.

Derrida, Jacques. *Of Hospitality: Anne Dufourmantelle invites Jacques Derrida to respond.* (Rachel Bowlby, Trans.). Stanford, California: Stanford University Press, 2000.

Derrida, Jacques. "Force of Law." In *Acts of Religion,* edited by Gil Anidjar. (New York: Routledge, 2002), 230–298.

Derrida, Jacques. "Hostipitality." In Acts of Religion, edited by Gil Anidjar. (New York: Routledge, [1997] 2002), 356–420.

Derrida, Jacques. "The Principle of Hospitality." *Parallax*, 11, (2005): 6–9. DOI: 10.1080/1353464052000321056.

Elnimeiri, Ahmed. "At an Impasse: The Discourse of Recession in Tayeb Saleh." *The Victorian,* 5 (2) (2017): 1–9. Retrieved from http://journals.sfu.ca/vict/index.php/vict/article/view/250/127.

Fluehr-Lobban, Carolyn. *Islamic Law and Society in the Sudan*. New York and London: Routledge, 2008.

Harlow, Barbara. "Sentimental Orientalism: *Season of Migration to the North* and *Othello*." In *Tayb Salih's Season of Migration to the North: A Casebook,* edited by Mona Takieddine Amyuni. (Beirut, Lebanon: American University of Beirut, 1985), 75–79.

Hassan, Wail S. "Gender and Imperialism: Structures of Masculinity in Tayeb Salih's Season of Migration to the North." *Men and Masculinities* 5 (3) (2003): 309–324.

Kant, Immanuel. "Perpetual Peace: A Philosophical Sketch." In *Kant: Political Writings*, edited by Hans Reiss. (H.B. Nisbet, Trans.). (Cambrindge, UK: Cambridge University Press, [1795] 1970), 93–130.

Khairallah, As'ad. "The Travelling Theatre or the Art of Entertaining a Doomed Caravan with Amusing Sories." In *Tayeb Salih's Season of Migration to the North: A Casebook*, edited by Mona Takieddine Amyuni. (Beirut, Lebanon: American University of Beirut, 1985), 95–112.

Krishnan, R.S. "Reinscribing Conrad: Tayeb Salih's *Season of Migration to the North*." *The International Fiction Review*, 23 (1–2) (1996): 7–15.

Makdisi, Saree S. "The Empire Renarrated: *Season of Migration to the North* and the Reinvention of the Present." *Critical Inquiry*, 18 (4) (1992): 804–820. DOI: 10.1086/448657.

Nasr, Ahmad A. "Popular Islam in Al-Tayyib Salih." *Journal of Arabic Literature* 1, (1980): 88–104. DOI: 10.1163/157006480X00108.

Nazareth, Peter. "The Narrator as Artist and the Reader as Critic in *Season of Migration to the North*." In *Tayeb Salih's Season of Migration to the North: A Casebook*, edited by Mona Takieddine Amyuni. (Beirut, Lebanon: American University of Beirut, 1985), 95–112.

Rashid, Catherine. "Academia, Empathy, Faith: Leila Aboulela's *The Translator*." In *Postcolonialism and Islam: Theory, Literature, Culture, Society and Film*, edited by G. Nash, K. Kerr-Koch & S.E. Hackett. (London and New York: Routledge, 2014), 131–141.

Said, Edward. *Culture and Imperialism*. New York: Vintage Books, 1994.

Said, Edward. *Reflections on Exile and Other Literary and Cultural Essays*. London: Granta, [2001] 2012.

Salih, Tayeb. *Season of Migration to the North*. (Denys Johnson-Davies, Trans.). New York, New York Review of Books, [1969] 2009.

Siddiqui, Mona. *Hospitality and Islam: Welcoming in God's Name*. New Haven; London: Yale University Press, 2015.

CHAPTER 7

The Rest in the White West: After the Empire is Buried, *Shadows of Your Black Memory* Are Born

JM. Persánch

You discovered us, now you got us.[1]

∴

1   Introduction

Equatorial Guinea, under Spanish rule since 1778, proclaimed its independence from Spain in 1968, which situates us in a period when the push for decolonization was at its peak, and twenty-three years after the UN was founded.[2] After the independence in 1968, firstly Francisco Macías Nguema between 1968 and 1979, and later his cousin Teodoro Obiang Nguema, 1979 to present, established Afro-fascist dictatorial regimes.[3] Between 1969 and 1979 Macías Nguema transformed Equatorial Guinea 'in a gigantic concentration camp, a 'Great Cage' and the immediate result was an alienated, fragmented and traumatized country.'[4] Nguemismo, as an equatorial Guinean variation

---

1   James Baldwin, "Interview Néelandaise de James Baldwin – 1981" (sous-tirée en français), *Vpro Zomer Gasen.* [Video file] (1981).

2   Equatorial Guinea mainly integrates six ethnic groups of which two of them are majoritarian. Overall national make-up the Fangs are a group who belong to the Bantu tribe, settled in the Equatorial coast, and most of the continental zone of Rio Muni. The other majoritarian ethnic group, whose had intent of achieving independence from the repressive Fang system, are the Bubis, established in the Island of Fernando Poo, currently called Bioko, they are different than the Fang because they are a Sudanese race. Both Macías Nguema and his cousin Obiang Nguema belong to the Fang ethnic's Mongomo clan. Present day, among the 100 MP seats only one is a Bubi: Plácido Micó. For details, please see Rodríguez Núñez, Á., "La antigua Guinea Española: Análisis y perspectivas," Semanario del centro superior de Estudios de la defensa nacional (CESEDEN). Compostela, Universidad de Santiago de Compostela. (n.d.): 4.

3   Please see Max Liniger-Goumaz, *De la Guinée Equatoriale Nguémiste. Eléments pour le dossier de l'Afrofascisme. Les Editions du Temps,* (1983) which analyzes the situation of Equatorial Guinea's Afro-fascist society.

4   Mbaré Ngom, "Afro-fascismo y creación cultural en Guinea ecuatorial: 1969–1979," *Revista Canadiense de Estudios Hispánicos,* 21(2) (1997): 386. "[S]e transformó en un gigantesco

of Afro-fascism, imposed a tribal hegemony of the Fang ethnic group. This 'fanguinization of Guinea reached such extremes that Macías and the 'fang-esangui' came to be identified as the State itself.'[5] The overall outcome was a fanguinization of Guinean everyday life, politics, and culture. This process of fanguinization mimicked the *modus operandi* of persecution and repression of the dictatorship of Francisco Franco in Spain, toward the defeated republicans even after the Spanish Civil War (1936–1939). In the Guinean process of nation-al homogenization, 'control over the 'Other' meant to terminate it or, where that was not possible, forcing its invisibility.'[6] To reach this goal, nguemismo articulated its power around two axes: one, an open discrimination exercised against the Bubi ethnic group which wrecked their traditions and ended any aspirations of independence of the Island of Bioko from Equatorial Guinea; and, two, Macias refuted anything that came from Spain which was seen as an imperial signifier. Interestingly enough, during the first ten years of nguemis-mo, Equatorial Guinea became a concomitant part of the communist bloc, thus establishing an alliance with one of the enemies of Franco's contubemio judeomasónico (an international Masonic Jewish collusion with the commu-nist) in Spain.

This rupture with the Afro-Hispanic cultural tradition and the estrange-ment regarding the Spain Government of the time persisted until the *coup d'état* of 1979 held by the dictator's cousin. Once in power Obiang Nguema 'tried to disassociate himself, from the anti-colonialist ideology of his uncle Macías, approaching Spain again and asking for help to foster the Hispanic cul-tural field.' Obiang made this turn in Equatorial Guinean's international rela-tions as a strategy to avoid the assimilation of the nation into the francophone bloc.[7] Also, by evoking the Spanish imperial past in Equatorial Guinea, Obiang made Spain invest in international cooperation. According to Álvaro Rogrí-guez Núñez, an estimated worth of '15,000 million of pesetas in concept of the countries' reconstruction aid between 1979 and 1983.'[8] This financial strategy

---

campo de concentración, una 'Gran Jaula' y el resultado fue un país enajenado y trauma-tizado." (All the translations from Spanish have been done by JM. Persánch unless another source is indicated.)

5   Ibid. "fanguinización' de Guinea alcanzó tales extremos que Macías y los 'fang-esangui' llega-ron a ser identificados con el Estado.'

6   Ibid., 387. 'el control del 'otro' pasaba por su eliminación o, en su defecto, su invisibilidad.'

7   Núñez, "La antigua Guinea Española," 24. 'desmarcarse de la ideología anticolonialista de su tío, el dictador Macías, acercándose más a España y solicitando su ayuda [con objeto de] fomentar los factores culturales hispánicos para evitar las ansias territoriales de los países vecinos, todos ellos del área francesa.'

8   Ibid., 25. '[...] 15.000 millones de pesetas en concepto de ayudas a la reconstrucción del país' (25) entre 1979 y 1983.'

would be the one the regime pursued practically until its economic integration in the francophone Africa, and later findings of oil reserves in 1995.[9] However, for Equatorial Guineans this change in politics and the economy meant nothing. In fact, one of the direct consequences of the repressive, discriminatory and racializing politics of nguemismo, was that thousands of Equatorial Guineans, and virtually all the intellectuals went in exile.

Donato Ndongo-Bidyogo was one of these diasporic intellectuals who decided to remain in Spain after Equatorial Guinean independence. He would not set foot back in Guinean territory until 1979, that is, eleven years after proclaiming independence, and right after the coup d'etat which overthrew Macías. In one of his multiple interviews, Ndongo-Bidyogo (interviewed by Tènon, 2013) explained the feeling of anguish that he felt upon his return, 'I faced a tremendous, terrible situation. It inflicted me a serious trauma. I stayed over two months in my country, before I returned to Spain (...) in the Guinean colonial times that I remembered, everyone was well-dressed and were well-stocked;' 'now I met specters, naked people, skeletal, toothless, shabby, very dirty people; they lacked everything.'[10] This traumatizing experience was the germ which made him write *Las tinieblas de tu memoria negra* (1987), translated in English in 2007 by Michael Ugarte as *Shadows of Your Black Memory*,[11] and usually compared to Chinua Achebe's *Things Fall Apart* (1958).[12]

2   Shadows of Your Black Memory

Set towards the end of Spanish law in Equatorial Guinea, *Shadows of Your Black Memory* recalls the voice of an African boy as well as his adult memories to revisit his childhood and colonial past. This way Ndongo-Bidyogo reveals the racial, cultural, religious, conflicts between Africa and Spain, as well as European internal contradictions dismantling their discourse of superiority. The author

---

9   The Discovery of petrol reserves in 1995 made the Equatorial Guinean economy enter in a period of exponential GDP growth, going from a negative 5% in 1979 to a 34% growth in 1996 and a 95% growth in 1997 according to international economic studies. Please see Data in *Expansión* GDP growth rate chart, "PIB de Guinea Ecuatorial" available in its subsidiary web *Datos Macros*.

10   K. Tènon, "Site du Geal," March 9 (2013): 4–5. 'la situación que encontré fue tremenda, terrible. *Me produjo un serio trauma*. Estuve unos dos meses en mi país, y regresé a España (...) en la época colonial que yo recordaba, todos iban vestidos y estaban nutridos; 'y yo encontre espectros, gente desnuda, esqueletica, desdentada, harapienta, sucisima; faltaba de todo.'

11   Donato Ndongo-Bidyogo, *Shadows of Your Black Memory*. Trans. M. Ugarte. Chicago, Swan Isle Press, [1987] 2007.

12   Chinua Achebe, *Things Fall Apart*. Heinemann, 1958.

values his ancestral worship equating it with Catholicism, and contraposing African traditions to European modernity. Overall, the novel reflects upon the divided African self. In Ndongo's words, 'the novel captures the interiority of the Guinean soul, besieged and haunted by the ghosts of colonization,' a fascist colonization.[13] In the same interview he would describe the reasons why he wrote it in the following terms:

> The exhumed superstitions by a fake traditionalist obscurantism, and the stifling Catholic orthodoxy established since the Council of Trento… the upheaval in postcolonial Africa, the Cold War… the pulsing tension between the African traditions reviled by the invaders and a modernity not assumed by the colonized… perhaps all this hodgepodge could explain the inexplicable… I do not know. I was confused, almost terrified. This is how the idea of writing *Las tinieblas de tu memoria negra* came across, my first novel, in which I reflect upon our identity.[14]

In words of Joseph-Désiré Otabela and Sosthène Onomo-Abena (2009), Ndongo-Bidyogo 'decided then to deal with the collective history of the Guinean people to delve in his soul and find the answers that had led to such extreme horror.'[15] Thus, *Las tinieblas de tu memoria negra* responds to the need to externalize an emotional anguish, a literary working through to overcome both his own trauma, and that of his generation. Ndongo-Bidyogo's experience projected the autobiography of a generation, reflecting upon the state of devastation and abandonment of Equatorial Guinea. His work is invaluable because, as Michael Ugarte (2010) put it, on the one hand,

---

13   Tènon, "Site du Geal," 5. "[U]na interiorización en la profundidad del alma guineano, acosado por fantasmas como la colonización" – una colonización fascista."

14   Ibid. 'las supersticiones exhumadas por el oscurantismo falsamente tradicionalista, y un catolicismo de una ortodoxia asfixiante, impuesta desde el Concilio de Trento … Las convulsiones del África poscolonial, la 'Guerra Fría' … La pulsante tensión entre las tradiciones africanas denostadas por los invasores y una modernidad no asumida por los colonizados … Quizá toda esa mezcolanza pudiera 'explicar' lo inexplicable …, no sé. Estaba confuso, casi aterrado. Así surgió la idea de escribir *Las tinieblas de tu memoria negra*, mi primera novela, en la que se reflejan todos estos componentes de nuestras señas de identidad.'

15   Joseph-Désiré Otabela and Sosthène Onomo-Abena, *Entre estética y compromiso: La obra de Donato Ndongo-Bidyogo*. (Madrid, Universidad Nacional de Educación a Distancia, 2009), 109. 'decidió entonces abordar *la experiencia colectiva del pueblo guineano* para bucear en su alma y extraer las claves que lo habían llevado a estos extremos de horror.'

> Donato Ndongo is 'Western' in two specific senses: he is from the region of central west Africa, an area that includes the nations of Senegal, Cameroon, Gabon, and Nigeria. But he is also 'European' (...) Ndongo might be considered European in the postmodern or postcolonial sense in much the same way as are African writers steeped in the so-called 'Western tradition.'[16]

On the other hand, as Aponte and Rizo (2014) rightfully claimed, 'the literature of Equatorial Guinea is positioned at the crossroads of the black Atlantic and Hispanism, and it emerges as a connecting space that not only covers Latin America but also other areas where the black and Hispanic experiences converge.'[17] They continue that 'this literature has thus a transnational and postcolonial conscientiousness ... it is African, as pointed earlier, but it is also Western.'[18] In other words – as I shall put it – what Ugarte, and Aponte and Rizo seemed to indicate is how Ndongo-Bidyogos's novel announced the presence of the Rest *in* the white West.

Ndongo-Bidyogo claims that this literature 'is much-needed as a tool for reflection, as a collective memory, as a depositary of society's consciousness. And, therefore, as an indispensable vehicle for change, for transformation. For I believe in the power of subversion, of anticipation.'[19] Through inventiveness, fantasy, and the imagination, this literature aims to reach out to the consciousness of great numbers of people, as an instrument for social transformation.

It is precisely because of his understanding of literature as a collective work and a reflection tool, that the protagonist in *Las tinieblas...* has no name: his anonymity easies the reader in the process of identification. This narrative technique favors a collective identification that is also reinforced by a narrator in second person singular. The use of the subject pronoun *tú* [you] appeals directly to the reader as part of the narrative *yo* [I]. Ndongo-Bidyogo seems very aware of the need to get the reader involved in the process of construction and interpretation of the story as an accomplice. This way both the author and reader come to identify with the anonymous boy-narrator, who embodies the Equatorial Guinean people. In the same vein, the adult character-narrator symbolizes the new Equatorial Guinean's divided soul between the traditions of a Black Africa and European modernity's cultural ethnocentrism. Deploying

---

16   Michael Ugarte, "An Introduction to Spanish Post-Colonial Exile: The Narrative of Donato Ndongo," *Arizona Journal of Hispanic Cultural Studies*, 8(1) (2010): 177.

17   Dolores Aponte Ramos & Elisa Rizo, *Guinea Ecuatorial como pregunta abierta: Hacia el dialogo entre nuestras otredades.* (Pittsburgh, University of Pittsburgh, 2014): 747–748.

18   Ibid.

19   Tènon, "Site du Geal," 6.

this dialectical tension, Ndongo-Bidyogo questions Spanish colonialism, de-nounces its atrocities, and illustrates the postcolonial trauma embedded in Equatorial Guinean-ness caused by its cultural dislocation. Regarding this la-tent cultural dislocation, Otabela and Onomo Abena (2009) assume that 'the sentimental education of the Equatorial Guinean is motivated by the evoca-tion of a Spanish Empire which only existed now in the minds of the colonizers.' They further argue that 'to this regard, the ideology of a Trident Catholicism and the vestiges of African beliefs overlapped whilst being replaced by a suf-focating modernity.'[20] For these reasons, Ndongo-Bidyogo chose to narrate the story of a fang boy who grew up in colonial Equatorial Guinea to tackle this transculturalized reality.

According to Ugarte (2010), 'this novel takes the form of an Afro-Spanish bildungsroman narrated by a first/second person in search of racial, cultural, linguistic, existential identity, all very much within a socio-historic colonial structure.'[21] This narrative voice exposes the relations within the tribe as well as his initial devotion to catholic rites. From this intermediate position be-tween two distinct cultural traditions, years later, the adult character-narrator recalls his colonial experiences. From a structural standpoint, Alice Driver (2009) remarked how,

> the chapters are structured so that memories of the two cultures are jux-taposed. For example, after a chapter describing the rite of initiation into the Fang tribe, the protagonist describes his first communion. Chapter zero marks the beginning of the new hybrid nation, and is the moment in which the protagonist reaches adulthood and fully understands the two cultures which have influenced his personal and intellectual growth.[22]

The book presents in this fashion situations of internal contradictions to expose the fallacy of dichotomies between a black atavist Africa and the al-mighty white modernity of Europe. This ideological clash is expressed through

---

20   Otabela and Onomo-Abena, *Entre estética y compromiso*, 110. 'la educación sentimen-tal del guineano estaba motivada por la evocación de un Imperio español que ya solo existía en las mentes de los colonizadores, todo ello amplificado por la parafernalia del movimiento nacional sindicalista que era el Partido Único que gobernaba en la España de Franco; a esto se superponía por un lado la ideología de un catolicismo tridentino y los restos caducos de unas creencias africanas que estaban siendo reemplazadas por esa modernidad asfixiante.'

21   Ugarte, "An Introduction to Spanish Post-Colonial Exile," 178.

22   Alice Driver, "The Construction of National Identity in Donato Ndongo's Las tinieblas de tu memoria negra," *Divergencias: Revista de estudios lingüísticos y literarios*, 7(2) (2009): 4.

his father, his uncle Abeso and Father Ortíz. The narratological structure essentially relies on these four characters.

Formally, the book has nine chapters. Each one is a conglomerate of stories that both the anonymous protagonist and the narrator evoke by contrasting past to present. Overall, the chapters' development reevaluates the colonial experience of Equatorial Guinea through the anonymous' reconstruction of memory, as the book title explicitly indicates by the use of words *tinieblas* de tu *memoria* negra [*Shadows* of Your Black *Memory*]. For Baltasar Fra-Molinero (2000),

> the protagonist-narrator explains his fight to stay loyal to both worlds, to create a synthesis which contradicts the dividing model found at the heart of all European cultural constructions since the 18th century. For the Europe of the Enlightenment, the concepts of race and culture are intertwined. The European culture is not only superior, but it justifies the conquest and exploitation of the defeated, inferior races, whose cultures are equally of a second class.[23]

Conceptually, the novel establishes a *bildungsroman*, a term that arose in eighteenth-century German literary criticism and coined by Karl Morgenstern, to refer to texts which focus on the coming of age, maturation and/or the main character's psychological and moral development, conducted or articulated by means of social or sexual encounter.[24] Based on this conceptualization, the main character's evolution in *Las tinieblas...* coincides with the progressive acquisition of the reader's awareness of simultaneous realities that are imbricated in Africanity.

Note that the boy is traditionally a literary figure associated with innocence and inexperience. It becomes the perfect vehicle to express the internal struggle resulting from cultural and religious syncretism, as well as the identitarian transculturalization of the Equatoguinean. To contravene this feeling of alienation derived from a coercive transculturalization of the boy's innocence and

---

23   Baltasar Fra-Molinero, "La educación sentimental de un exiliado africano: Las tinieblas de tu memoria negra de Donato Ndongo-Bidyogo," *Afro-Hispanic Review*, 19(1) (2000): 50. 'El protagonista-narrador relata su lucha por permanecer fiel a dos mundos, crear una síntesis que contradiga el modelo separador que está en la base de todas las construcciones culturales europeas desde el siglo XVIII. Para la Europa de la Ilustración, los conceptos de raza y cultura van unidos. La cultura europea no solo es superior, sino que justifica la conquista y explotación de las razas vencidas e inferiores, cuyas culturas son igualmente de segundo orden.'

24   Please consult Karl Morgenstern, Wilhelm Dilthey and Goethe.

inexperience, Ndongo-Bidyogo incorporates the boy's adult experience as the voice of the narrator. This contrast between the child's voice of the past and the adult's memories in the present establishes a continuum in time to denounce how, for Africans and blackness 'the time has stopped.' Any European -in general, except honorable exceptions- continue to treat Africans as 'not-so-equal-beings' to them. (Ndongo-Bidyogo interviewed by Gautier Carmona, 2011).[25] The atemporality of blackness situates the African body as the quintessential subaltern subject of the West. This atemporal problematization of both blackness and the non-white west as racially, culturally, politically, and socially inferior has been revisited recently by Decolonial Theory to describe the state of Latin Americans, Africans and Asians' permanent coloniality.[26] Also as part of this south-to-south dialogue, Achille Mbembe has alerted us of the global presence of a "post-colonized" – instead of a post-colonial – African subject.[27] In addition, it is precisely because of these structures which replicate atemporality, permanent coloniality, and post-colonized subjects, that the blackness/whiteness paradigm reveals the process how both identities gain meaning when they encounter each other, and how whiteness becomes naturally superior by constructing the images of black people as inferior. To neutralize this trend, Ndongo-Bidyogo will make the boy appropriate Spanish cultural whiteness to make it implode.

In the latter sense, Ndongo-Bidyogo reminds us that in colonial Equatorial Guinean 'the priesthood was presented as the only way to equate with whites.'[28] From this prism, the boy's initial devotion to become a priest entails

---

25   Gautier Carmona, "Un viaje a las tinieblas de tu memoria," *Siglo* XXI, July 17, (2011). 'el
       tiempo se ha detenido. Cualquier europeo – por lo general, salvo honrosas excepciones-
       sigue tratando a los africanos como seres 'no tan iguales' a ellos.'
26   Decolonial theorists like Walter Mignolo, Enrique Dussel, Anibal Quijano, defend the
       need to rethink the relations of minoritized groups with modernity to offer an alternative
       discourse regarding power relations. They aim to push forward a plural notion of knowl-
       edge and validates the idea of parallel modernities.
27   Achille Mbembe explains that the determination of the conditions upon which the Afri-
       can subject could acquire conscience of itself found two ways of historicism that would
       annihilate them: an economicism which would use Marxists and nationalist categories
       to define the African discourse of authenticity's legitimacy; and the "metaphysics of dif-
       ference" that promotes the idea of a unique African identity which is identified with the
       black race. The central tenet is the conception of the human agency out of an alienated,
       split off, objectified, degraded subject by three historical events: slavery, colonialism and
       the apartheid. A subject that is not only recognized by an-Other but also recognized by
       itself." Please see Achille Mbembe, "The Banality of Power and the Aesthetics of Vulgarity
       in the Postcolony," *Public Culture*, 4(2) (1992): 2.
28   Ndongo-Bidyogo interviewed by Gautier Carmona, Carmona, "Un viaje a las tinieblas
       de tu memoria." 'el sacerdocio se presentaba como la única manera de igualarse a los
       blancos.'

a desire for social mobility and individual freedom. Nonetheless, the novel paradoxically begins when the boy decides to quit the seminary 'now or never, I'm ready to face everything, let the chalice of my early salvation come to me, let it recover who I am, individually and collectively.'[29] He continues, 'I must not go through this life without leaving something behind, but he won't believe it, he'll believe it's about something else.'[30] In this fashion, Ndongo-Bidyogo questions this path also as an effective integration. He conceives it as a transcultural coercion of the Spanish imperial whiteness because this tradition does not respond to the real needs of the nation,

> Africa doesn't only need priests, father. – Ndongo-Bidyogo writes – In my country, I continued timidly and humbly, there are barely any doctors, engineers, lawyers, and so forth... among the natives. These are crucial too, father, to achieve stability, progress, to construct a nation. Have come to realize this and... hi cut me off with just a hint of anger.[31]

The colonizer interrupts irascibly this realization of African needs and Africans. The interruption turns into a metaphor that conveys the violent domination exercised by the Spanish imperial whiteness, and it alludes to the power of silencing the point of view of the "Other." Silencing the "Other" is the first step toward a White transculturalization of the black soul, that one of the greatest consequences of it is the identitarian disorientation this coercion causes on the continent's negritude and Africanity,

> sometimes we are dis-personified, we live in a 'land of nobody,' because we have not assimilated into the exogenous values, firstly imposed by colonialism and now by a Neo-Imperialism, and at the same time we have become unfamiliar with the profound reason of our rites and traditions. [...] I believe that this disorientation explains many of the attitudes and phenomena which are taking place in Equatorial Guinea as well as everywhere in black Africa.[32]

---

29   Ndongo-Bidyogo, *Shadows of Your Black Memory*, 8.
30   Ibid.
31   Ibid., 10. Note that in the Spanish version Ndongo places the emphasis on '...*nuestra estabilidad, para nuestro progreso*... Our stability, for our progress.'
32   (Ndongo-Bidyogo interviewed by Gautier Carmona), Carmona, "Un viaje a las tinieblas de tu memoria." 'a veces que estamos despersonificados, vivimos en una 'tierra de nadie,' puesto que no hemos asimilado los valores exógenos, impuestos por el colonialismo y ahora por el neoimperialismo, y al tiempo desconocemos la razón profunda de nuestros ritos y de ciertas costumbres. [...] Creo que eso explica muchas actitudes y fenómenos que suceden no solo en Guinea Ecuatorial, sino en el resto del África negra.'

Paradoxically, the boy discovers his true roots in a seminary by practicing an array of white traditions. His change of attitude expresses the possibility of resistance as he refuses to become the driving force for African coercion for the interests of Spain. The hope underlying this refutation makes it possible to think that Africans can change the whites' biased conceptions of negritude, to restore Equatorial Guineans stability and to allow their progress, as well as African self-governance. There are many passages in which Ndongo-Bidyogo reflects this boy's symbolical resistance to being subsumed into Spanish whiteness. For example, at the beginning of chapter three, the boy pronounces how,

> It was shortly before I was nine when I got into the habit of saying Mass from a little alter I made for myself in my room in front of the crucifix Father Ortiz had given me and under the religious things I had on the wall: the Eye-of-God triangle and some prints that were brought to me by my father's white friends; the *Little Prayer Book* served as missal. Alone in my room, when no one was looking, when my little brothers succumbed to the midday sun, I got all dressed up and in a bed sheet and pretended it was a priest's chasuble and started to say Mass, *in nominee Paris et Filii et Spiritus Sancti*, I made the sign of the cross: I, a sinner, confess.[33]

The protagonist absorbs the religious discourse of the colonizers, only to then subvert it by celebrating a *fake mass*. This simulacrum induces us to think of the possibility of reverting the sway of Spanish imperial whiteness from within. In other words, Ndongo proposes to acquire the cultural practices of the West to defeat the West by the implosion of their own traditions. By appropriating the whites' cultural traditions, the boy can elaborate an ambivalent response thus creating a space from which to resist the West's hegemonic discourse, and even to subvert it, combating the subjugation of his black experience into whiteness. Another example of this ambivalence is when the boy is about to make his First Holy Communion,

> look at you, the sacrilege you have committed against the Body of Christ the very first day (…) the floodgate opened and came out the stream. The same way as in my dreams, I sensed the warmth in my underpants, then in my pants down into my thighs, knees, legs, socks, all the way to my white shoes, and the water made a trail to my place (…) and I felt deep

---

33   Ndongo-Bidyogo, *Shadows of Your Black Memory*, 57.

shame accompanied by a conviction that the Christ I had on my tongue
had decided not to enter me.[34]

It is noteworthy that the reception of the Body of Christ provokes vomiting in
him. This fact emulates the resistance to a possessed body being exorcized by
Christ. Beyond this obvious rejection of the religion of whites, Ndongo-Bidyogo
makes explicit the fact that the boy cannot help but pee on a *white shoe*. Whilst
the historical association of white with purity is well-known – a white meaning that Ndongo-Bidyogo tarnishes literally peeing on it–, the meaning of the
shoe could be a bit less known. Since ancient times, according to Las Heras
(2005), 'the footwear has been a symbol of freedom, whilst it also became a
prove of authority, control, and the warranty of property. This is why slaves
were forced to walk barefoot.'[35] Therefore, imploding the inherent values of
both the sacred host and the white shoe, Ndongo-Bidyogo enounces his refusal to accept the superiority of European beliefs and traditions, as well as the
rejection of the naturalization of a white transculturalism in Africa. What is
more, he contends that,

> Many European fashions and customs are pernicious. We Africans have
> exportable values. My literature is a constant proposal to reflect, and for
> us to know how to choose what is good for us, be it from our traditions
> or foreign [...] assuming everything uncritically will take us, in only a few
> years, to the disappearance of Africa as a concept. We black people will
> exist but reduced to caricatures of the Europeans, or the Chinese.[36]

In reaction to the latter statement, the protagonist is the one chosen to recu-
perate his tribe's collective memory and to restore their dignity, 'He had invoked the blessings of the forefathers on you as on all the males of your tribe,
and the ancestors had responded that you were no ordinary descendant, you

---

34   Ibid., 79–80.
35   Las Heras, *Sueños: El lenguaje onírico desvelado.* (Buenos Aires: Alhue, 2005), 117. 'el cal-
     zado era símbolo de libertad, a la vez que constituía una demostración de autoridad, de
     dominio y de garantía de propiedad. Por eso se obliga a los esclavos a caminar descalzos.'
36   (Ndongo-Bidyogo interviewed by Tènon), Tènon, "Site du Geal," 4. 'Muchas modas o cos-
     tumbres europeas son perniciosas. Los africanos tenemos valores exportables. Mi obra
     literaria es una constante propuesta de reflexión para que sepamos escoger lo que nos
     conviene, sea de nuestras tradiciones o del exterior (...) Asumirlo todo indiscriminada-
     mente llevará, en muy pocos años, a la desaparición de África como concepto. Seguire-
     mos existiendo los negros, pero reducidos a caricaturas de europeos, o de chinos.'

were the one chosen to bring back the glory of the tribe.'[37] With the wisdom of time, the adult-narrator will return to this moment in order to explain the actual impossibility of a white transculturalization of blackness,

> I identified with the martyr's early sufferings, a little like mine but infinitely more sublime, and I so yearned to have their faith, integrity, constancy, because more than anything, I wanted to be like them; yet I couldn't, I would never be. In the soul of a Little black boy like me, an animal in the wild, the vices of my primitive race were locked in.[38]

Given this impracticality of making the black soul white, Ndongo-Bidyogo reclaims the African right to make a black from a black. He argues that the Holy Bible teaches us that 'David defeated Goliath, not because he was stronger, but thanks to his astuteness. And this very same allegory does exist in our cultures: in the Fang fable, the turtle always ends up defeating or ridiculing the tiger.'[39] The author revalorizes African tradition equating it to that of Europeans and conceiving an independent negritude which has value *in* and *for* itself.

It is not surprising that Ndongo-Bidyogo places the boy between two fathers: one, his *biological* African father, the other Father Ortiz, a white *cultural* father. This contraposition of biology and culture illustrates how in Equatorial Guinea the values of Africanity and Hispanism were combined to craft a new man. Nevertheless, this tension between biology and culture is palpable in the "new" man throughout the novel despite the seemingly idyllic – unproblematized – combination. Father Ortíz represents the white Spanish missionary as well as the Western's tendency to impose its culture and values. In contraposition, the boy's biological father is characterized in appearance as a compliant black man who is fully assimilated into the cultural practices of whiteness, 'The image of my father: a tall, thin black man, a firm disposition; at a particular point in his life he decided to collaborate with the white colonizer.'[40] However, the boy learns that his biological father's pact with the white colonizer responds to a strategy of liberation: by not manifesting his resistance to whites, he gains their trust achieving social mobility in turn. This attitude toward the white

---

37   Ndongo-Bidyogo, *Shadows of Your Black Memory*, 38.

38   Ibid., 106–107.

39   (Ndongo-Bidyogo interviewed by Gautier Carmona), Carmona, "Un viaje a las tinieblas de tu memoria." 'la Biblia nos enseña que David venció a Goliat, no por ser más fuerte, sino por ser más astuto. Y esas mismas alegorías están en nuestras culturas: En las fábulas de mi etnia fang, la tortuga siempre termina venciendo o ridiculizando al tigre.'

40   Ndongo-Bidyogo, *Shadows of Your Black Memory*, 13.

colonizer grants him access to full emancipation, as insinuated in the following excerpt,

> It was clear to all, although no one said so, that my father had abandoned
> the traditions of his people for the sake of civilization. This is why my fa-
> ther is a black man who does everything on a grand scale, like the whites,
> and this is why he commands respect, perhaps even fear, and it's why the
> missionaries and the police in charge of our district stay at our house
> when they visit the village.[41]

This access to the enjoyment of the white colonizer's privileges pre-establishes
the optimal conditions from which to force the liberation of both his tribe and
nation. In this sense, Ndongo-Bidyogo argues the need for an instrumentalization of the colonizer's knowledge, practices and resources. Ndongo-Bidyogo
seems to agree on this point with the thesis of Niall Ferguson, who explains
the decline of the West or its contested hegemony, arguing that the things that
once set the West apart from the Rest are no longer monopolized by the West.[42]
Ndongo-Bidyogo suggests using western knowledge as a cultural weapon of
the invisible man's silent resistance,

> I understood his role. He had never been on their side, he was the link
> between the tribe and the occupiers, someone has to negotiate: someone
> has to talk to them to figure out how they should be treated, what foods

---

41   Ibid., 13–14.
42   In his book *Civilization: The West and the Rest* (2011), Niall Ferguson inquired of the rela-
      tionship between European knowledge and power. Specifically, his analysis scrutinized
      why the West came to dominate the Rest and not *vice versa*. To explain such matter, Fer-
      guson laments how the West is the loss of faith in the civilization the westerners inherited
      from their ancestor and develops a theory of what he termed "the six killer applications"
      to prove it. These killer apps are six fields that Western civilization had mastered, thus dif-
      ferentiating it from the Rest and marking it as unique and rather successful: competition,
      the scientific revolution (the freedom of thought as well as the scientific method), proper-
      ty (the rule of law and property rights as well as representative government, democracy),
      modern medicine, the consumer society, the work ethic (Protestantism). Please see Niall
      Ferguson, *Civilization: The West and the Rest*. New York: The Penguin Press, 2011. If the Rest
      has not overtaken the West yet – Ferguson contends – is because the West still have more
      of these institutional advantages than the Rest. 'The Chinese do not take political compe-
      tition. The Iranians do not have freedom of conscience. They get to vote in Russia, but the
      rule of law is a sham. However, what Ferguson failed to acknowledge – in his more than
      1000 pages – is that, since the beginning of the postcolonial era and particularly in the
      aftermath of globalization, the persistent dialectics of differentiation between the West
      and the Rest, or the West *vs.* the Rest, should now reference the most recent phenomena:
      The Rest is *in* the West.

they like and what bothers them, how they fornicate and how many cigarettes they smoke a day; *Someone should be with them to spy on them from the inside;* The tribe must store information on their movements and their ideas.[43] (Emphasis added)

In order for his father's silent resistance to be successful, others must sacrifice showing themselves openly against the white colonizers, so that they trust those supposedly assimilated. Uncle Abeso comes to symbolize this confrontational, as much as sacrificial, role. Ndongo-Bidyogo describes Abeso's role in the following terms, 'Your uncle was the resister; the one who refused to capitulate, the one who wanted to keep the torch burning; He was the light that your generation was dimming, little by little.'[44] Recalling the following argument with Father Ortiz, the narrator explains how 'the priest started praising the example of my baptized father, who had married through the Church without concubines or illegitimate children.'[45] These 'were virtues that God would compensate, since he had gained full emancipation, a condition allowing him to enjoy advantages out of the reach of stubborn heathens.'[46] Ndongo-Bidyogo takes advantage of a discussion between Father Ortíz and Uncle Abeso to evidence the internal contradictions of Western beliefs and religious cults, thus demystifying the presumably cultural superiority of European traditions. In opposition to stigmatization of polygamy, Uncle Abeso responds that 'he had heard the white man's god had told his people to be fruitful and multiply so that they would not disappear from the face of the earth because he had made them in his own image.'[47] And 'Tío asked the priest if he had too abided by God's mandate to be fruitful. The priest was exasperated and grew quite angry.'[48] By exalting chastity as a supreme value of purity, and having exposed the white man's contradiction, Uncle Abeso poses another question, 'Tell me, would you be telling me all this now if your mother and father were like you?'[49] In view of Uncle Abeso's frontal resistance, Father Ortíz, far from desisting, concludes he himself will baptize Uncle Abeso sooner or later. Once the white colonizer's religious superiority has been de-legitimized, Ndongo-Bidyogo (2007) continues to dismantle other cultural stereotypes like anthropophagy,

43   Ndongo-Bidyogo, *Shadows of Your Black Memory*, 126.
44   Ibid., 24.
45   Ibid., 93.
46   Ibid.
47   Ibid., 88.
48   Ibid.
49   Ibid.

> Surely you won't deny that eating your fellow beings, your brothers, is an ugly custom… My uncle didn't let him finish the sentence and replied: the only ones who ate human flesh were sorcerers, and not everyone was a sorcerer (…) you are the sorcerer of your tribe, and that's why you eat the flesh and drink the blood of your God. What's wrong with our doing the same with our venerated figures?[50]

Ndongo-Bidyogo equates African and European traditions and beliefs repeatedly, disrupting the hierarchical dichotomy between the colonizer and the colonized. In other occasions, the author goes even further to accuse the colonizer of being the problem in need of solution. In the following exchange, Father Ortíz asserts that 'the world advances, and it's important for your tribe to leave its primitive ways behind. We've brought civilization, we cure your sickness, we've brought peace, and we've fought your barbarity.'[51] To refute this cultural paternalism which legitimizes the needs for maintaining the colonization, Uncle Abeso, once again, pairs both civilizations, 'You say you have brought medicine, but you found medicine here too. You say you have brought peace, but you were the ones who incited war.'[52] And 'tell me, don't the tribes of white people fight among themselves? The only problem I see with you is that you want us to give up our customs. And that can't be.'[53] These words resonate as the central message throughout the novel expressing his rejection to a white transculturalization of Africa. 'I believe' – Ndongo-Bidyogo declares – 'that we have the obligation to reflect upon these problems, and to transfer them to the Rest (of Humanity) so that the heavy stereotypes which fall on us stop being clichés, so that the reality is known.'[54] Thus, Ndongo-Bidyogo consciously privileges literature as the tool for social, and cultural, transformation leading to the ultimate change of mentalities and power relations' framework. With this book, Ndongo-Bidyogo restores the long-silenced black voice in Hispanism. That is, after the Empire is buried, shadows of your black memory are born.

---

50   Ibid., 91–92.
51   Ibid., 91.
52   Ibid., 92.
53   Ibid.
54   (Ndongo-Bidyogo interviewed by Tènon), Tènon, "Site du Geal,"1. 'Creo que tenemos la obligación de reflexionar sobre estos problemas, y trasladar esas reflexiones al resto de la Humanidad para que los estereotipos que pesan sobre nosotros dejen de ser tópicos y se conozca la realidad.'

3   Playing in the Shadows of Your White Walls

Wherever there is power, there is resistance.[55]

Shadows of Your Black Memories offers us a portrayal of the colonial past as well as a glimpse into the future. Ndongo-Bidyogo's text is both History and an annunciation of an individual and collective black liberation. From his privileged position between two cultures – like his biological father occupies in the novel – he exposes the fallacy of Western dichotomies, tropes and discourses of moral, material, and spiritual superiority. As an "Other" from the Rest *in* the West, his mission is to contest the West's hegemonic ideology which creates reality. His critical eye transforms both in a panopticon and an oracle for the Rest to envision alternative narratives against the dominant consciousness, thus demystifying the narcissistic fantasies of the white West.

Although Ndongo-Bidyogo's novel deals with the Spanish colonialism, his text extrapolates the lessons to the Rest due to the shared experiences that all Africans have had in relationship with every European country. Whether it is the Portuguese slave trade, the Spanish system of casts in Mexico and enslavement of blacks across Latin America including the Caribbean, the British Empire in Africa, the West Indies, Oceania, and Asia, the French, the Germans, the Dutch, the Belgians in Africa… all the way long to slavery, segregation and police brutality in the History of the United States, or the apartheid in South Africa… Ndongo-Bidyogo's counter-discourse is acutely applicable. The latter statement is factual simply because every emerging power in the West has found a vehicle through which to build itself as a separate, superior entity aiming to preserve a set of material wealth as well as spiritual values, whilst justifying the actions carried out against those who do not conform. Stuart Hall defined this Western attitude which Ndongo-Bidyogo also exposes in his novel as an ideology which seeks to emphasize European uniqueness and non-western inferiority.

According to Hall (1992), the "West" functions as a thinking tool, which sets a certain structure of thought and knowledge.[56] Nonetheless, such a category cannot be built in isolation, but rather to the contrary, it must function as part of a language, a system of representation. In turn, the system of representation provides a standard or model of comparison, helping to explain the difference. As a

---

55   Michel Foucault, *The History of Sexuality: The Will to Knowledge*. (Harmondsworth: Penguin Books, 1998), 95.

56   Stuart Hall, "The Rest and the West," in *Formations of Modernity*, eds. Stauart Hall & Bram Gieben. (Oxford, Polity Press in association with Open University, 1992), 184–227.

result, this process of differentiation will produce a certain kind of knowledge.[57] Knowledge always expresses power relations because discourse is the production of knowledge. When knowledge becomes naturalized as common sense a hegemonic discourse of domination establishes hierarchies. This knowledge-is-power transforms ideology into facts, 'The hegemonic discourse becomes a Regime of Truth – When power operates as to enforce the truth of any set of statements, then such a discursive formation produces a regime of truth.'[58] To explain the solidification of this Regime of truth, Hall outlines four discursive strategies: a) an idealization; b) the projection of fantasies of desire and degradation; c) the failure to recognize and respect difference; d) the tendency to impose European categories and norms, to see difference through the modes of perception and representation of the West.[59] The greatest success of Ndongo-Bidyogo's counter-discourse is precisely to expose thus neutralizing all four strategies of Western's regime of truth about Africans.

Nevertheless, following Michel Foucault's and Edward Said's theoretical frameworks regarding discourse, power and orientalism, Hall concluded that 'terms like the west and the rest are historical and linguistic constructs whose meanings change over time.'[60] What becomes clear for Hall in every case is that the making of binary oppositions appears to be central to the production of all linguistic, symbolic and material systems of domination regarding the formation of meaning itself, as well as its circulation. We should perhaps pause here the reading of this essay to reflect upon the implications on the fact that many peoples of the (Rest of the) world learn their own Histories with books printed in Cambridge and Oxford and see their global images defined by a narrow set of representations from Hollywood. In other words, especially Africans, Asians and Latin Americans learn who they were, are, with books and movies manufactured in Western ideological centers of power. Or as Chimamanda Engozi Adichie (2009) claims, 'Power is not just to tell the story of a person but to make it the definitive story of that person.'[61] In short, Power has the force to impose its truth, to shape consciousness and condition the individual's subjectivity. Power creates truth and has the means and ability to both reproduce it consistently and to circulate it widely. Thus, it is an unequivocal consequence that these cultures, the views of themselves and, ultimately, their very lives become much westernized, that is, subsumed by whiteness.

---

57   Ibid., 186.
58   Ibid., 208.
59   Ibid., 215–216.
60   Ibid., 188.
61   Chimamanda Engozi Adichie, *The Danger of a Single Story*. TED [Video File], (2009).

Certainly, the West is by no means monolithic and – as Ndongo-Bidyogo reveals – possesses internal fragmentation, hierarchies, and contradictions. Nonetheless, Western discourses have proven to converge throughout history in two variants of – what I may call now – the same pattern of a defensive mentality. The first variant of it would establish a line of soft power which implies a partition between Us *and* Them: the white West *and* the Rest. However, in moments of crisis where either Western hegemony is challenged, or material scarcity becomes staggering for the middle class, the latter benign divisor line may turn into a second variant of this defensive mentality that entails a hard power division that confronts Us *vs.* Them: the white West *vs.* the Rest.[62]

If anything, to cite a few, the convergence of Greek, Spanish, British, and American hegemonic discourses into the two variants of a single defensive pattern over six centuries helps us gain a historical perspective. It evidences of the trajectory of European domination and encapsulates the polymorphism of the white West in imposing its religious, cultural, linguistic, symbolic, material, racial, economic systems of differentiation upon the rest of the world.

For instance, by constructing their citizenship, the Greeks sought to establish a fundamental distinction between Hellenes and all other men. Heraclitus, for example, attested that there existed a clear demarcation between Greek and non-Greek mentalities when he stated, 'eyes and ears are poor witnesses for men with barbarian souls.'[63] Although Heraclitus was not the only one – quite to the opposite Greek classic literature and philosophy present a plethora of references to the *barbaros* – his statement sheds light on the vital importance of understanding the logos as a part of the soul.[64] For Greeks, not understanding the logos meant the observer's condemnation to fail in any observations he would make of the world. Consequently, any perceptions and interpretations of reality made by such individual would become a meaningless, irrational, expression of a distorted reality; the expression of an inferior

---

62   "Soft power" refers to the diplomatic capacity to influence, attract and co-opt with other nations decisions, culture, values, and national and foreign policies. In opposition, "Hard power" entails the coercion using force, the threat of military action, or money compensation as a means of persuasion. For a contemporary analysis of the terminology and an insightful perspective, please see Thomas L. Ilgen, *Hard Power, Soft Power and the Future of Transatlantic Relations*. Ashgate, 2006.

63   Heraclitus. The Fragments of Heraclitus, Fragment, DK B107. Heraclitus Fragments. [κακοὶ μάρτυρες ἀνθρώποισιν ὀφθαλμοὶ καὶ ὦτα βαρβάρους ψυχὰς ἐχόντων].

64   This conception of the 'Barbarians' could have been passed down by the Arabs' understanding of 'Barrio;' note that in Hispanic Arabic bárri meant exterior and in Classic Arabic بَرِّي [barrī], 'savage.' Please consult the three volumes of Black Athena: The Afroasiatic Roots of Classical Civilization published in 1987, 1996 and 2006, where Martin Bernal discusses the perception of Ancient Greek in relation to Greece's African and Asiatic neighbors, their knowledge and influence in Ancient Greek civilization.

self. Rooted in this linguistic, philosophical principle, broadly speaking Barbarians were deemed to be all men who neither spoke nor understood the Greek language properly or did so with grotesque phonetics and grammar.[65] Henceforth, the foundational myth of Greek identity for the development of Western Civilization came to be deeply ingrained in a defensive mentality.

Likewise, the Spanish Empire established a dichotomy between the civilized Catholics and its savage others in the same fashion that the Greeks had done between Hellenes and barbarians. It is significant how Spain justified its territorial expansion between the 15th and the 19th centuries using a discourse whose mission was the evangelization of Indians in the Americas to "save their souls."[66] Whilst the Spanish model became hegemonic in the West and agglutinated immense power and wealth, we find a parallel form of control compete in northern Europe. This other ideology showed disdain towards the notions of political control through marital alliances and cultural, racial assimilation through *mestizaje*. This alternative discourse became more evident with the decay of the Spanish Empire and the growing dominance of a Protestant British Empire in the 19th century, when the British redefined the West drawing two thick lines: a religious line to the south between Protestants with Catholics, and a racial one with its others in the East. Whilst the first one was nurtured by the longstanding Black Legend, the second one originated an orientalist discourse of differentiation to exercise control over the sexualized bodies of people who held strange, irrational rites and uncivilized costumes. Similarly,

---

65   However, Benjamin Isaac (2017) nuances that the term *barbaro* has often been misinterpreted as indicating an original linguistic basis, 'in the *Iliad* the term may mean no more than the people mentioned spoke a foreign (barbarian) language. Generally speaking, all *barbaroi* are undoubtedly *barbarophonoi*, but that does not mean that the essence of being barbaros is the difference in language. It may be just one of the characteristics of *barbaroi*' (p. 198). According to Isaac's findings in his analysis of classical literature, 'several texts account how barbarians do not know sexual restraint (...) Barbarians' laws are no standard for a Greek city (...) their music is strange, their rites are foolish. Acculturation is possible, but, it seems, almost for deterioration. One can become a barbarian, but barbarians becoming Greek are exceptional' (p. 207). What is more, the term *barbaro* seemed to always transpire in connection with land, which would be indicative of the existence of an intrinsic relationship between cultural, spiritual, and territorial senses of belonging. For further details, please see Benjamin Isaac, *Empire and Ideology in the Graeco-Roman World: Selected Papers*. Cambridge, Cambridge University Press, 2017.

66   This ecumenical mission derived from an agreement between the Pope Alexander VI and the King Ferdinand of Aragon and Queen Isabella of Castilla. The Pope issued the Papal Bull Inter Caetera in 1493 -known as The Doctrine of Discovery- granting Spain the right to conquer the New World in exchange for the sacred commitment of the monarchs to evangelize, thus incorporating the vast indigenous populations to the Catholic faith and Church. (The original manuscript of this Papal Bull is preserved in the Archivo de Indias in Seville).

these discourses would be exacerbated by France, Germany and all other European nations which had colonies in Africa and other parts of the globe.[67]

In the wake of the 20th century and after two world wars, the paradigm to differentiate between the West and the Rest morphed once again. By the middle of the century, the United States pushed for the decolonization of the British and French colonies – meaning dismantling their gross Empires – in the implementation of a New World Order through the creation of institutions like the United Nations in 1945. This new international order resulted in the emergence of the United States as a superpower. Alongside the emerging hegemony came a new system of division between first and third world countries: a capitalist terminology which would soon thereafter be replaced by a euphemism that distinguished between developed economies and developing countries during the political correctness movement of the 1990s.

Hence, as I have concisely outlined in this section regarding the Western polymorphism of power, the West must be understood as an ideal which requires the "Rest Other" to continue to be construed as barbarian, savage, irrational, strange, tribal, undeveloped, and an ever-present point of reference for the west to be able to construct its atemporal self as rational, developed, industrialized, urbanized, capitalist, secular, modern, and, in short, morally, spiritually, and materially superior. In the latter sense, the white West's ideals remain a conflation of facts and fantasy which condemns the Rest (non-whites, non-Christians, non-modern, non-civilized, non-developed, non-industrialized, non-capitalist, non-secular) to be hierarchized into inferior statuses.

4   Conclusion: Rewinding Globalization, Rebuilding White Walls

I am going to build a wall:
A beautiful, tall, thick as hell,
huge as well, unbreakable wall...
And Mexico is going to pay for it.
[...] Hey!
Look at them, they exist:
They are the great wall.[68]

PERSÁNCH, 2018, p. 51

---

67   Consider the Orientalist Congresses organized and celebrated in Europe as of 1873 to articulate colonialism in Africa as well as in the East. For an analysis of Spanish differential attitude against Europeans' interests, see the exhaustive overview of Bernabé López García (1990) in "Arabismo and orientalismo en España: Radiografía y diagnóstico de un gremio escaso y apartadizo. Africanismo y orientalismo en España 1860–1930."

68   JM. Persánch, "The Wall," in *Moments Before Midnight*, ed. Amalie Rush Hill. Oregon: Bob Hill Publishing, 2018.

President Trump admitted certain inspiration by Medieval settlements when he publicly acknowledged how 'They say it's a Medieval solution of wall. That's true. It's Medieval because it worked then and it works even better now.'[69] However, the greater wall ever made – the most persistent, and unbreakable – was the white one the Europeans imagined and imposed upon the Rest by separating, dividing humanity with the invention of the race. If President Trump's words can provide evidence of anything, it is that they certify how rapidly the West can shift its discourse from the "West *and* the Rest" to the "West *vs*. the Rest" in a globalized world. In the highly intertwined world in which we live today, racial ideologies circulate transnationally between diverse cultures more than ever before, triggering global responses and effects: as I argued elsewhere, consider as just one example of many, the response to the terrorist attacks of the 21st century and, as a recent exemplar, the Paris terrorist attack of November 13th, 2015. The killings of innocent people in Bataclan mobilized Western civic societies and political leaders under the motto "*Je suis Paris*." Over the course of events, the Western discourse produced a palpable racial undertone that equated "terrorism" with "radical Islam" -or just Islam – over the subsequent weeks. Such discourse was absorbed quickly by the global imaginary, having the immediate effect of racializing violence as an irrational feature of Arab countries. This transnational example is significant to illustrate how today, racial ideologies circulate transnationally between diverse cultures, making local events global, and in turn, serve to unify Western principles, ideologies and goals through the lenses of whiteness faster than ever before.[70]

In fact, as John Hartigan (1997) informed us, 'the fact of whiteness is based on its historical duration and its ideological coherence and effective power.'[71] If this is so, what might be the implications of the re-emergence of white populisms, white nativism across the globe? We might find indeed the answers in capitalism as it seems condemned to cause systemic crises every time a model of production perishes; but this is not limited to it as Antonio Escohotado has proven in his three volumes of Los enemigos del comercio. There can be only crises where there is wealth, and certain periods of stability and growth. Thus Communism, for example, is con-substantial to capitalism's ability to generate wealth and well-being.[72] In the 21st century capitalist logic, this means there

---

69   Please see Tim Marcin, 'Donald Trump Says Border Wall Is a 'Medieval Solution' but Claims it Still Works,' Newkweek, January 9 2019. Available at https://www.newsweek.com/donald-trump-border-wall-medieval-solution-1285670.

70   JM. Persánch, "From Impurity of Thought to the Glocalization of Whiteness in Spain," Transmodernity, Special Issue, 8 (2) (2018): 132–133.

71   John Hartigan, "Establishing the Fact of Whiteness," *American Anthropologist*, 99(3) (1997): 498.

72   Antonio Escohotado, Los enemigos del comercio, Espasa Forum, Volumes I, 2017, II, 2018, III, 2019.

will be a crisis each time technology and techniques are fully globalized – meaning being absorbed and mastered by the Rest – thus reducing the gap with the West, followed by a resurgence of Western push to mutate seeking to regain control the situation. In the latter sense, for example, China has absorbed and mastered the speculative economy – manipulating its currency as well as leading in patents and expanding investment overseas – posing a challenge to the US hegemony in turn rehabilitating the invigoration of whiteness across the globe.

In Europe, the picture is no different. Europe appears to be imploding like the Soviet Union did three decades ago. The Brexit might be just the first symptom of a seriously ill patient. Nonetheless, looking beyond the Brexit, the rise of Scottish and Catalan nationalism, together with both left and right populisms across Europe, express how deeply the dissatisfaction is with the European project. In all case scenarios the West truly transpires a sentiment of staggering nostalgia, and they all want to rewind globalization whether this erupts into slogans like "Make America Great Again" in the States and to "Take Control Back" in Britain, or shown in successful alt-right movements across Europe including the Front National (National Front) in France and Alternative für Deutschland (Alternative for Germany) in Germany obtaining their best electoral results to date, as well as in Sweden, and for the first time since the restoration of democracy in Spain.

It is in this context when the white West is looking for a formula that would enable them to morph again, thus retaking control over the growing Rest. What, then, could be the role of the Rest if any at all? What appears unquestionable is that the contemporary self of the West, as much as its persona have most definitely been subsumed and devoured by the abundance of their material goods. Subsequently, it would be no prediction, but rather an assertion to say that both current and future generations will see themselves urged more and more to resituate the human experience in the center of modernity over the illusive ethos of endless progress. All in all, what becomes clear is that if the Rest chooses to mirror the West's attitudes, the world will witness a global tragedy. Given that modernity, capitalism, progress, globalization, go hand in hand with pollution, scarcity, inequality, greed, power, it should not be taken as an exaggeration either to sustain that the need for rehumanizing the West will seem more acute in the aftermath of globalization than it was in the wake of twentieth-century's Fascism and Nazism. If anything, the generations to come in the 21st century will more than ever have to face a single mission, that of turning the West as brutally human, as far as they possibly can to save it from self-destruction, thus dragging the Rest with it. To carry out this mission – as Ndongo-Bidyogo's novel predicted – the presence of Rest *in* the white West appears indeed essential.

Bibliography

Achebe, C. *Things Fall Apart*. Heinemann, 1958.

Aponte Ramos, D., & Rizo, E. *Guinea Ecuatorial como pregunta abierta: Hacia el dialogo entre nuestras otredades*. Pittsburgh, University of Pittsburgh, 2014.

Baldwin, J. Interview Néelandaise de James Baldwin – 1981 (sous-tirée en français). *Vpro Zomer Gasen*. [Video file]. (1981). Retrieved from https://www.youtube.com/watch?v=nonAlJptCQY 11 August 2017.

Bernal, Martin. *Black Athena: The Afroasiatic Roots of Classical Civilization*. Volumes I Free Association Books, 1987, II Rutgers University Press, 1996, III Rutgers University Press, 2006.

Driver, A. "The Construction of National Identity in Donato Ndongo's *Las tinieblas de tu memoria negra*." *Divergencias: Revista de estudios lingüísticos y literarios*, 7(2) (2009): 3–12.

Escohotado, Antonio. *Los enemigos del comercio*, Espasa Forum. Volumes I, 2017, II, 2018, III, 2019.

Expansión. Datos macro de Guinea ecuatorial. Retrieved from https://www.datosmacro.com/paises/guinea-ecuatorial.

Feger, H. *Handbuch Literatur und Philosophie*. Stuttgart, Springer-Verlag, 2012.

Ferguson, N. *Civilization: The West and the Rest*. New York: The Penguin Press, 2011.

Foucault, M. *The History of Sexuality: The Will to Knowledge*. Harmondsworth: Penguin Books, 1998.

Fra-Molinero, B. "La educación sentimental de un exiliado africano: Las tinieblas de tu memoria negra de Donato Ndongo-Bidyogo." *Afro-Hispanic Review*, 19(1) (2000): 49–57.

Gautier Carmona, J. "Un viaje a las tinieblas de tu memoria." *Siglo XXI*, July 17, (2011). Retrieved from http://www.diariosigloxxi.com/texto-diario/mostrar/72827/un-viaje-a-las-tinieblas-de-la-memoria-negra#.VhRPNvlViko.

Hall, S. "The Rest and the West." In *Formations of Modernity*, edited by Stuart Hall & Bram Gieben. (Oxford, Polity Press in association with Open University, 1992), 184–227.

Hartigan, J. "Establishing the Fact of Whiteness." *American Anthropologist*, 99(3) (1997): 495–505.

Helmut, H. "Western Identity, Barbarians and the Inheritance of Greek Universalism." *The European Legacy*, 10(7) (2006): 725–739. DOI: 10.1080/10848770500335800.

Heraclitus. The Fragments of Heraclitus, Fragment, DK B107. *Heraclitus Fragments*. Retrieved from http://www.heraclitusfragments.com/files/ge.html.

Hulme, P. *Colonial Encounters: Europe and the Native Caribbean*, 1492–1797. London, Methuen, 1986.

Ilgen, L.T. *Hard Power, Soft Power and the Future of Transatlantic Relations*. London & New York, Routledge, 2006.

Isaac, B. *Empire and Ideology in the Graeco-Roman World: Selected Papers.* Cambridge, Cambridge University Press, 2017.

Las Heras, A. *Sueños: El lenguaje onírico desvelado.* Buenos Aires: Alhue, 2005.

Liniger-Goumaz, M. *De la Guinée Equatoriale Nguémiste. Eléments pour le dossier de l'Afrofascisme.* Genève, 1983.

López García, B. "Arabismo y orientalismo en España: Radiografía y diagnóstico de un gremio escaso y apartadizo." *Awraq*, Madrid, Instituto Hispano-Arabe de Cultura, XI (1990): 36–69.

Mann, M. "European Development: Approaching a Historical Explanation." In *Europe and the Rise of Capitalism,* edited by Baecheler, J. et al. Oxford, Basil Blackwell, 1988.

Marcin, T. "Donald Trump Says Border Wall Is a 'Medieval Solution' but Claims it Still Works." *Newsweek,* January 9 2019. Available at https://www.newsweek.com/donald-trump-border-wall-medieval-solution-1285670.

Mbembe, A. The Banality of Power and the Aesthetics of Vulgarity in the Postcolony. *Public Culture, 4*(2) (1992): 1–30.

Mommsen, T.E. "Petrarch's conception of the 'Dark Ages.'" *Speculum,* 17 (2) (1942): 226–42.

Ndongo-Bidyogo, D. *Las tinieblas de tu memoria negra.* Barcelona, Ediciones del Bronce, 1987.

Ndongo-Bidyogo, D. *Shadows of your black memory.* (M. Ugarte Trans.) Chicago, Swan Isle Press, 2007.

Ngom, M. "Afro-fascismo y creación cultural en Guinea ecuatorial: 1969–1979." *Revista Canadiense de Estudios Hispánicos, 21*(2) (1997): 385–395.

Ngozi Adichie, C. The Danger of a Single Story. *TED* [Video File] (2009). Retrieved from https://www.ted.com/talks/chimamanda_adichie_the_danger_of_a_single_story.

Otabela, J-D. & Onomo-Abena, S. *Entre estética y compromiso: La obra de Donato Ndongo-Bidyogo.* Madrid, Universidad Nacional de Educación a Distancia, 2009.

Persánch, JM. "The Wall." *In Moments Before Midnight,* edited by Amalie Rush Hill. Oregon, Bob Hill Publishing, 2018.

Persánch, JM. "From Impurity of Thought to the Glocalization of Whiteness in Spain." *Transmodernity,* Special Issue, 8 (2) (2018): 110–137.

Roberts, J.M. *The Triumph of the West.* London, British Broadcasting Corporation, 1985.

Rodríguez Núñez, Á. "La antigua Guinea Española: Análisis y perspectivas." *Semanario del centro superior de Estudios de la defensa nacional (CESEDEN).* Compostela, Universidad de Santiago de Compostela, (n.d.). Retrieved from http://www.cmeyanchama.com/Documents/Guinee/trabajoceseden_Seminario.pdf.

Tènon, K. *Site du Geal.* March 9, (2013). Retrieved from http://sitedugrenal.e-monsite.com/medias/files/entrevista-a-donato-ndongo-1.pdf.

Ugarte, M. "An Introduction to Spanish Post-Colonial Exile: The Narrative of Donato Ndongo." *Arizona Journal of Hispanic Cultural Studies, 8* (1) (2010): 177–184.

CHAPTER 8

The Topography of Nostalgia: Imaginative Geographies and the Rise of Nationalism

Andrew Ridgeway

José Arcadio Segundo did not speak until he had finished drinking his coffee.
"There must have been three thousands of them," he murmured.
"What?"
"The dead," he clarified. "It must have been all of the people who were at the station."
The woman measured him with a pitying look. "There haven't been any dead here," she said. "Since the time of your uncle, the colonel, nothing has happened in Macondo."[1]

∴

1 Introduction

The beginning of the 21st century has been marked by a resurgence of 'new' nationalism, which includes but is not limited to right-wing populism, anti-immigrant sentiment, anti-globalization and nativism. The rise of neo-nationalism is marked by political nostalgia – a fugue state that invokes historical amnesia to establish new cartographies of displacement and erasure. Former U.S. presidential candidate Newt Gingrich's 2011 claim that 'Palestinians are an "invented" people' and U.S. President Donald Trump's more recent promise to 'make America great again' illustrate how political nostalgia suppresses the traumatic memory of colonialism in the name of a reconstituted nationalism that effaces difference. This essay analyzes the Israeli occupation of Palestine and President Trump's promise to build a wall on the U.S. – Mexico border through the lens of postcolonial literature to interrogate how political nostalgia "remaps" the political imaginary to strengthen geopolitical commitments to colonial

---

1 Gabriel García Márquez, *One Hundred Years of Solitude.* New York: Avon Books, [1967] 1971.

knowledge-production. I use Gabriel García Márquez's *One Hundred Years of Solitude* (1967)[2] and Teju Cole's *Open City* (2012)[3] to highlight how postcolonial literature can establish (or re-establish) "imaginative geographies" to articulate ways of knowing and remembering that call attention to the epistemological foundations of nationalism and the violent history of colonialism.

I begin by examining the relationship between literature and cartography. Drawing on the idea of imaginative geographies, I argue literature and cartography can be read as "useful fictions" that inform fantasies of collective identity rooted in the nation-state. These fantasies often invoke nostalgia, which manifests as a desire to restore the past to redeem the present. While many people who witness or feel nostalgia think of it as a uniform experience, I build on the work of Svetlana Boym (2007) to argue there are actually different kinds of nostalgia with different political implications.[4] The nostalgia President Trump invokes when he promises to "make America great again" is very different from the nostalgia that permeates novels like *Open City* and *One Hundred Years of Solitude*. The former seeks to restore the past, while the latter reflects upon the past without trying to return to it. Analyzing nationalism through the lens of literature juxtaposes these different types of nostalgia to highlight how desire and longing map what Edward Said (1979) called *imaginative geographies*, spatial representations that define both the difference and the distance between the self and other.[5] I argue that *Open City* and *One Hundred Years of Solitude* reveal how imaginative geographies are often predicated on historical amnesia. This is especially true when imaginative geographies are approached through the lens of nostalgic nationalism: the desirability of the past is often contingent on a sanitization of history.[6] In other words, nationalism invokes nostalgia to romanticize the nation-state by erasing or revising the violence of its history and its origins. The promise to "make America great again," for example, ignores that America has never been great for everyone who lives within its borders. In fact, Cole's *Open City* specifically emphasizes how "American greatness" always comes at the expense of people who exist outside normative definitions of American identity.

Fantasies of collective identity, which often invoke nostalgia to justify xenophobic nationalism, are imagined, but not necessarily imaginary. They have material implications. They contribute to the construction of *architectures of enmity*, imaginative geographies that invoke "us/them" binaries to normalize

---

2   Ibid.

3   Teju Cole, *Open City*: A Novel. New York: Random House Trade Paperbacks, 2012.

4   Svetlana Boym, "Nostalgia and Its Discontents." *The Hedgehog Review*, (2007):7–18.

5   Edward Said, *Orientalism*. New York, NY: Random House, 1979.

6   Boym, "Nostalgia and Its Discontents"; Michael J. Shapiro, *Violent Cartographies: Mapping Cultures of War*. Minneapolis, MN: University of Minnesota Press, 1997.

state-sanctioned violence.[7] I employ *Open City* and *One Hundred Years of Solitude* to examine the Israeli occupation of Palestine and the militarization of the U.S.-Mexico border to argue architectures of enmity are not merely ontological. They are also quite literal: structural violence is often a product of physical structures (walls, fences, detention centers, etc.) designed to inflict violence against individuals who exist outside nostalgic representations of national identity. These "immigrant others" embody what Zygmunt Bauman (1990) refers to as the figure of the stranger – the ambiguous subject who is neither friend nor enemy.[8] Expanding on Bauman's (1990) theory of the stranger, I argue nationalist appeals to restorative nostalgia suppress native histories to facilitate political alienation and transform the colonized subject into a trespasser inhabiting enemy territory. In short, colonization is a process of estrangement that supplants the imaginative geography of the colonized with the imaginative geography of the colonizer to exclude colonized subjects from the narrative of the nation-state.

The disparity between the spatial representations of the colonizer and those of the colonized emphasizes the variable nature of imaginative geographies. The difference is often a question of how nostalgia is employed. An imaginative geography framed as a restoration of the past lends itself to an architecture of enmity and often requires a corresponding physical infrastructure to secure the fantasy of collective identity rooted in the nation-state. An imaginative geography that simply reflects upon the past – like the imaginative geographies present in Cole's *Open City* and García Márquez's *One Hundred Years of Solitude* – can establish or resurrect stories that call into question the epistemological foundations of the nation-state. Literature and cartography are useful fictions that challenge the "postcolonial melancholia" of contemporary nationalism by presenting alternative representations of the past that highlight the historical contingency of national identity. I conclude by arguing that novels like *Open City* and *One Hundred Years of Solitude* are not merely ways of mapping the postcolonial present but can also articulate imaginative geographies that function as sites of subject-formation and resistance.

2   Literature and Cartography

At first glance, fictional literature and cartography seem like fundamentally different forms of knowledge production. Cartography aspires to objectivity, accuracy, and utility, whereas literature is marked by subjectivity, ambiguity

---

7   Shapiro, *Violent Cartographies*.
8   Zygmunt Bauman, "Modernity and Ambivalence," *Theory, Culture & Society*, 7 (1990): 143–169.

and enjoyment. A map is created so it can be *used*. People turn to maps in moments of necessity: when they are lost or need to find the most direct route
to their destination. People read literature to *get* lost; they lose themselves in
stories. A person with a map is interested in its functionality. But literature has
no definite function. The best thing about literature is that it is useless. No one
needs literature. Maps transform unfamiliar territory into sterile grids that can
be marked and measured. As Viktor Shklovsky (1917) observed, literature is an
exercise in defamiliarization; common things are re-presented as strange and
unfamiliar.[9] Maps wait patiently until they are needed. Literature rarely waits
to be consulted. It has a habit of poking its nose where it does not belong – into
politics, history, psychology and a whole host of other disciplines that do not
bother with it.

There is another important difference: reading literature is often considered
an exercise in empathy. Cartography, on the other hand, is implicated in the
production of enmity; it delineates friends from enemies.[10] In a later section,
I discuss how maps are complicit in the creation of fantasies of collective identity that determine how people understand themselves in relation to those they
consider threatening. For now, it is enough to say maps are the epistemological bedrock of mass violence; the constant companion of military strategists,
security analysts and drone operators alike. Maps are instruments of war.[11]
They target enemies with incredible accuracy and disastrous consequences.
They have the potential to fundamentally alter the landscape they aspire to
represent: a coordinated air strike that levels a building or demolishes a village
necessitates the creation of new maps. Literature humanizes difference. Derek
Gregory (2004) explains how the very logic of cartography produces,

> high-level, disembodied abstractions...and a discourse of object-ness
> that reduces the world to a series of objects in a visual plane. Bombs then
> rain down on the co-ordinates on a grid, letters on a map, on 34.518611N,
> 69.15222 E, on K-A-B-U-L; but not the city of Kabul.[12]

Any comparison of literature and cartography must consider literature's capacity to produce empathy, while recognizing how cartography is implicated
in the production of enmity.

---

9   Viktor Shklovsky, "Art as Technique," in *Critical Theory: A Reader for Literary and Cultural
      Studies,* edited by R. Daly. (New York, NY: Oxford University Press, [1917] 2012): 48–58.
10   Shapiro, *Violent Cartographies.*
11   Ibid.; Derek Gregory, *The Colonial Present*. Malden, MA: Blackwell Publishing, 2004.
12   Gregory, *The Colonial Present,* 54.

Despite all this, cartography and literature *do* have many characteristics in common. Both are systems of knowledge production that lend themselves to close reading and are subject to interpretation. Neither are capable of representing the world in its totality, but both produce textual artifacts that seek to render the world more intelligible. Literature "maps" the world, insofar as it helps readers navigate the mental and emotional landscapes of their lives. Similarly, a map is a document that tells a story. Neither is objective or neutral. Both cartography and literature express a series of political, cultural, and epistemological commitments which vary according to the dominant assumptions of the time period in which they are produced. A sixteenth-century map of the United States, for example, will often treat indigenous people with the same disregard as the literature written during that period.[13] This will be addressed later, as part of a larger discussion about how the shifting coordinates of the U.S. – Mexico border are naturalized by epistemic practices that frame former natives as strangers in colonized territory. In the meantime, it is sufficient to say books and maps are both ways of knowing, which means they are limited by what people know (or think they know) when they produce them.

There are other similarities that stem, in part, from the relationship between form and content and operate at the level of interpretation. Literature and cartography both inhabit the "no man's land" between the digital and the analog. Digital maps are a constellation of floating signifiers that rearrange themselves as the subject moves through physical space in real time. The transition from analog maps to digital maps is analogous to the transition from structuralism to poststructuralism in literary criticism; a shift from evaluating each text as a static, self-contained object to understanding a text as a shifting network of signifiers. Subjects no longer locate themselves on the map. Instead, maps restructure themselves around the subject. The same is true of literature, which reorganizes itself around the subject's social location. No two people will ever have the same digital map, because no two people can occupy the same coordinates at the exact same time. Similarly, no two people will interpret a literary text the same way; at best they will establish overlapping trajectories, degrees of intersection. Like a digital map, a literary text changes as the reader moves through space and time. Reading *Ulysses* (1922)[14] in Santa Fe is not the same experience as reading *Ulysses* in Dublin and, to paraphrase Heraclitus, one cannot step into the same book twice.

Considering the extent to which literature and cartography trespass into one another's territory, it seems only natural to read maps as literary texts or,

---

13   Shapiro, *Violent Cartographies*.
14   James Joyce, *Ulysses*. London: Penguin Books, [1922] 2000.

alternatively, to read literary texts as maps. Literature and cartography are "useful fictions" implicated in the production of imaginative geographies. As such, they are operative lenses through which political subjects construct their understanding of affinity and difference.[15] Imaginative geographies are fantasies that combine the utility of cartography with the enjoyment literature engenders. As my reading of Boym (2007) and Shapiro (1997) will demonstrate, the imaginative geographies expressed in literature can affect the shift from restorative nostalgia (with its non-critical, self-referential topography of enmity) to reflective nostalgia (with its self-reflexive topography of affinity). Literature can evoke new imaginative geographies to "remap" the political imagination and challenge cartographic representations of national identity that lend themselves to violence and xenophobia. As a closer examination of García Márquez's *One Hundred Years of Solitude* and Cole's *Open City* will demonstrate, postcolonial literature, with its emphasis on memory, ambiguity and the politics of enemy-construction, is particularly well-suited to this task.

3   Imaginative Geographies

On the surface, García Márquez's *One Hundred Years of Solitude* and Cole's *Open City* are very different texts. The former, published in 1967 by a Columbian author, uses magical realism to tell a story about several generations of the same family living in the fictional town of Macondo. The latter, published in 2011 by an American author of Nigerian descent, surveys the post-9/11 landscape of New York City through the eyes of a melancholic intellectual who immigrated to the United States as a teenager. While it might seem counter-intuitive to juxtapose such radically different texts against one another, both examine the spatial coordinates of memory; the relationship between cartography and history. They articulate imaginative geographies; spatializations which 'fold distance into difference'[16] and delineate the self from the other. In *One Hundred Years of Solitude*, this imaginative geography is explicit: Macondo is a fictional town in an unnamed country where history repeats itself across successive generations. In *Open City*, imaginative geographies are both manifold and implicit. Cole's map of history traces versions of New York City that used to exist and suggests spatial arrangements that might have come into existence if events had gone differently. The purpose of bringing these two texts together is to articulate *new* imaginative geographies and, in doing so, reveal

---

15   Gregory, *The Colonial Present.*
16   Gregory, *The Colonial Present,* 17.

how maps are the product of our imagination and the extent to which they are invested with specific political desires.

Literature and cartography are not merely disparate ways of producing knowledge. According to Gregory (2004), they also produce a series of spatializations that distinguish friend and foe, self and other, native and foreigner.[17] He observes how geography is 'literally earth-writing.'[18] As it is often the case with processes of representation, all geography is imaginative, insofar as it is arbitrary, historically contingent and subject to fluctuation. In fact, Gregory (2004) suggests thinking of imaginative geographies as 'fabrications,' a word which suggests 'imaginations given substance.'[19] The term imaginative geographies (as distinct from the term geography) denotes the extent to which nations are formed by ideas and fantasies of collective identity. Gregory (2004) is careful to point out these ideas have no positive content. Rather, they are *negative* ideas. The implications are twofold. First, a nation like America is defined primarily by what *it is not*. It can only be defined in relation to other fantasies of collective identity, i.e. "America is *not* Ecuador, it is *not* communist, it is *not* Muslim." Second, the negative content of these ideas establishes an empty space where contesting fantasies can assert themselves – the same way a hollow signifier like "freedom" can be linked to a variety of potentially conflicting meanings.

For a fantasy to assume primacy within this empty space, it must be performed to the exclusion of others. The claim that America is the "land of the free," for example, only assumes meaning in relation to other geographical regions which are *not* considered free. It also implies a willingness to remove or eliminate anything that threatens freedom. James Der Derian writes that 'more than a rational calculation of interests takes us to war. People go to war because of how they see, perceive, picture, imagine and speak of others.'[20] In other words, the fact that imaginative geographies are 'performances of space'[21] does not detract from their very real consequences. In fact, the immateriality of imaginative geographies is *why* borders must be policed and violently enforced – violence is what lends them material substance. Without violence, borders would be reduced to the status of mere representation; a fantasy that reveals itself as fantasy. The result is a vicious cycle: violence lends geography

17   Gregory, *The Colonial Present.*
18   Derek Gregory, "Imaginative Geographies," *Progress in Human Geography,* 19(4) (1995): 449.
19   Gregory, *The Colonial Present,* 17.
20   James Der Derian, "9.11: Before, After and In-Between." *Social Science Research Council,* (n.d.).
21   Gregory, *The Colonial Present,* 19.

substance, while preserving the substance of geography by "protecting the bor-der" becomes a pretext for violence.

For Gregory (2004), the performance of imaginative geographies is simulta-neously a means of reaffirming the colonial present *and* a potential method of resistance. While he does not focus explicitly on how literature organizes and performs alternative spatializations of difference, his decision to introduce imaginative geographies with a passage from Giles Foden's novel *Zanzibar* (2002)[22] is a telling example of how imaginative geographies blur the ever-shifting border between factual narratives and fictional narratives. The Bush administration, for example, articulated the imaginative geography of Iraq through a narrative about weapons of mass destruction which presented itself as factual but turned out to be fictional. When it comes to constructing (and deconstructing) imaginative geographies, it is not a question of determining the objective "truth" about a place so much as interrogating the psychic and political investments that undergird a particular series of spatial representa-tions. The nation-state is a fantasy that maintains its coherence through a col-lective commitment to a cultural and political narrative of national identity.[23] A map is a spatial representation of the nation-state that preserves this narra-tive's claim to objectivity by eclipsing the representations that preceded it.[24] A contemporary map of the United States, for example, supplants older maps that recognize Texas as part of Mexico or refer to landmarks by indigenous nomenclature.[25] A nation like the United States seems like a fixed entity; it is only by examining maps as a historical sequence that we begin to see how borders shift and change. Shapiro (1997) explains how, when an older spatial arrangement is replaced by a new constellation of spatio-political coordinates, the latter frames itself as apolitical and ahistorical; an objective description of "the way things are."

Literature, by its very nature, calls into question the way things are. It estab-lishes a space where authors can depict non-existent versions of the past or rearticulate the past in ways that render it unrecognizable to inhabitants of the present. Literature reveals how the present could have turned out differently. Like a series of maps viewed concurrently, literature brings the contingency of history to the forefront. This is especially true of novels like Cole's *Open City*, which excavates geographies of the past and juxtaposes them against the spa-tial arrangements of the present, or García Márquez's *One Hundred Years of*

---

22   Giles Foden, *Zanzibar*. Faber & Faber, [2002] 2003.
23   Gregory, *The Colonial Present*; Shapiro, *Violent Cartographies*.
24   Shapiro, *Violent Cartographies*.
25   Ibid.

Solitude, which reimagines the spatial coordinates of memory to challenge linear conceptions of history. These novels perform imaginative geographies as a means of resisting the dominant colonial narrative and the cartography this narrative seeks to normalize. *Open City* and *One Hundred Years of Solitude* challenge postcolonial melancholia by shifting the emphasis from restorative nostalgia, which uses the fantasy of collective identity to naturalize nationalism, to reflective nostalgia, which privileges critical reflection and a diasporic politics of intimacy and affinity. In my reading of Boym (2007), reflective nostalgia does not accept nationalism at face value: it refuses to conflate "home" with "homeland." Instead, it establishes an understanding of "home" as a shifting network of people who take care of one another, while simultaneously recognizing how such networks rarely correspond to the lines of a map.

4   Political Nostalgia

According to Boym (2007), the word "nostalgia" is a combination of the Greek word *nostos*, which refers to a return home and *algos*, the Greek word for pain.[26] It was coined in 1688 by the Swiss doctor Johannes Hofer to refer to pain that results from the desire to return to one's country of origin. As Marcos Piason Natali (2004) points out, the term nostalgia is a product of modernity.[27] Nostalgia was used with increasing frequency as technological advances and changing political and economic conditions made immigration more likely. As the word entered common parlance, the definition expanded to include any pathological attachment to distant times or places. Sigmund Freud (1915/1953) refers to this definition in his essay "Mourning and Melancholia," which linked nostalgia to melancholia, an intense state of longing for an object or individual that can never be recovered.[28] For him, melancholia was an obstacle to healthy grief; a psychic block that prevented individuals from recognizing and accepting loss. The melancholic subject refuses to accept the impossibility of returning to a time before the loss occurred. Nostalgia is a symptom of melancholia. It is a mentality the melancholic subject adopts to avoid confronting the trauma of an irrevocably altered existence. The subject who cannot accept the reality of the present seeks refuge in the past.

---

26   Boym, "Nostalgia and Its Discontents."
27   Marcos Piason Natali, "History and the Politics of Nostalgia." *Iowa Journal of Cultural Studies*, 5 (2004): 10–25.
28   Sigmund Freud, "Mourning and Melancholia," in *The standard edition of the complete psychological works of Sigmund Freud*, trans. J. Strachey. (London: Hogarth Press, Vol. XIV 1953): 243–258.

Natali (2004) explains how nostalgia has typically been construed as a coun-terproductive political imperative. He argues that, for thinkers like Kant, Hegel and Marx, the desire to return to the past was antithetical to an understanding of history as empirical, rational, and inherently emancipatory. It contradict-ed the notion that history is a sequence of successive stages that build upon each other; a process of gradual self-improvement for the human race.[29] Natali (2004) contends that, for Marx especially, nostalgic representations of history were not just backwards and antiquated. They were anti-revolutionary. Marx advised those seeking social emancipation to 'let the dead bury their dead.'[30] Natali (2004) claims that devotion to the past, for Marx, was a desire for a world that was less just. Nostalgia was a form of false consciousness. Marx condemned it in the name of historical progress.[31] In Natali's (2004) reading of Marx, his-tory is linear, progress is irreversible and nostalgic sentiment merely prolongs inequality. The melancholic nostalgia Freud describes and the political nostal-gia Marx condemns are parallel. Both refuse to recognize the irretrievability of the past. Both seek an impossible return. As melancholic nostalgia functions as an obstacle which prevents the subject from moving forward with the griev-ing process, so too, does political nostalgia interfere with the political subject's ability to put the past behind them.

Natali (2004) is justifiably skeptical of this leftist critique of nostalgia as po-litically counterproductive. As he points out, the interpretation of 'nostalgia as politically sinister' is based on a linear conception of time and a series of false dichotomies: 'conservativism and progressiveness…reaction and progress…fic-tion and fact, irrationality, and rationality.'[32] The risk is the devaluation of af-fect; the possibility that historiographic evidence is seen as the only legitimate way to represent the past. While Natali is correct to interrogate false binaries that privilege historiographic evidence over emotive and affect-oriented rep-resentations of history, he does not fully consider the political consequences of the latter. He concedes that injustice can be concealed in idealized repre-sentations of history but does not address how nostalgia can be weaponized to rewrite the past to achieve the political objectives of the present moment. Nostalgia does not merely conceal inequality. It can also be invoked as a means of political erasure. Disdain for political nostalgia might be the product of false binaries, but that should not preclude recognizing how nostalgia can be used

---

29   Natali, "History and the Politics of Nostalgia."
30   Karl Marx, "The Eighteenth Brumaire of Louis Bonaparte," in *The Communist Manifesto and Other Writings,* authored by K. Marx & F. Engels. (New York, NY: Barnes & Noble Books, [1852] 2005), 66.
31   Natali, "History and the Politics of Nostalgia."
32   Ibid., 20.

to efface difference or justify ongoing structural violence against marginalized people. Natali is not wrong to challenge the leftist critique of political nostalgia, but he understates the extent to which distorted representations of the past shape and inform the political landscape of the present.

It is important to distinguish between different *kinds* of political nostalgia. Not every form of political nostalgia presupposes linear time or relies on the false dichotomies Natali correctly criticizes. As Boym (2007) observes 'nostalgia, like globalization, exists in the plural.'[33] She distinguishes between "restorative nostalgia" and "reflective nostalgia" and argues the two have vastly different political implications. *Restorative nostalgia* is anchored to a static interpretation of national identity. It is inherently populist, obsessed with preserving traditional values, selective in its presentation of the past and does not think of itself as nostalgia but, rather, as a series of objective historical facts. With uncanny precision, Boym (2007) anticipates the rise of contemporary neo-nationalism in the United States,

> Restorative nostalgia knows two main plots: the restoration of origins and the conspiracy theory. The conspiratorial worldview reflects a nostalgia for a transcendental cosmology and a simple premodern conception of good and evil. This worldview is based on a single transhistorical plot, a Manichean battle of good and evil, and the inevitable scapegoating of a mythical enemy. Ambivalence, the complexity of history, the variety of contradictory evidence, and the specificity of modern circumstances are thus erased and modern history is seen as a fulfillment of ancient prophecy.[34]

This description of restorative nostalgia preempts both President Trump's promise to "make America great again" *and* the "deep state" conspiracy theories circulated by President Trump's political allies. Restorative nostalgia is closely tied to what Paul Gilroy (2006) refers to as *postcolonial melancholia*, a romanticization of an imperial past that minimizes the violence of colonialism in the name of a reconfigured nationalism that obliterates difference.[35]

Boym (2007) explains how reflective nostalgia differs from restorative nostalgia, in that the former does not romanticize the past or seek to restore a mythical concept of national identity.[36] *Reflective nostalgia* invokes compassion,

---

33   Boym, "Nostalgia and Its Discontents," 17.
34   Ibid., 14.
35   Paul Gilroy, *Postcolonial Melancholia*. New York: Columbia U.P., 2006.
36   Boym, "Nostalgia and Its Discontents."

humor, irony, critical reflection and a variety of different identities to establish political narratives that acknowledge the complexity of history. While restorative nostalgia concerns itself with securing borders, reclaiming lost territory, preserving national identity, and restoring imperial powers to their former glory, reflective nostalgia seeks to establish a 'diasporic intimacy' that 'cherishes non-native, elective affinities'[37] and disrupts the imaginative geographies that sustain contemporary nationalism.

5   Historical Amnesia

In García Márquez's *One Hundred Years of Solitude*, José Arcadio Segundo Buendía, the lone survivor of a government-sponsored massacre of striking banana workers, returns to Macondo, the scene of the crime, only to discover the events have been erased from the collective memory of the city's inhabitants. There is no sign of any massacre. Macondo is already immersed in the process of forgetting; a self-imposed historical amnesia from which it will never recover. As he wanders from house to house, the traumatized José Arcadio Segundo is told the same thing by the inhabitants of each home he visits: nothing has happened in Macondo. There was no massacre – he was hallucinating, or dreaming, or both. Even his family doubts his sanity. His twin brother, Aureliano Segundo, ignores José Arcadio and defers to an official proclamation which claims the workers voluntarily dissolved the protest and returned home to preserve the peace. José Arcadio Segundo's experiences are at odds with official history; he exists outside the dominant narrative – an exile, a ghost, an object of pity and doubt.[38]

Anne Marie Taylor (1975), in her analysis of *One Hundred Years of Solitude*, observes how the reader is witness to Macondo's 'persistent, almost ritualistic failure to remember.'[39] But this failure to remember is not unique to the inhabitants of Macondo. As Cole's novel *Open City* demonstrates, *historical amnesia* is endemic to politics; it informs (and misinforms) procedures of knowledge production that shape the political subject's commitment to national identity.[40] In *Open City*, Cole's narrator – a melancholic, half-German, half-Nigerian psychiatric resident named Julius – explores New York City during the final year

37   Boym, "Nostalgia and Its Discontents," 15.
38   Márquez, *One Hundred Years of Solitude*.
39   Anne Marie Taylor, "Cien Anos de Soledad: History and the Novel." *Latin American Perspectives,* 2(3) (1975): 98.
40   Shapiro, *Violent Cartographies*.

of his medical fellowship. His mental map of New York reveals how specific historical events are inscribed through reference and repetition into the geography of the collective imaginary, while other events are buried beneath new narratives or disappear 'into an onrush of time.'[41] In other words, Julius recognizes history as a process of selection, informed by *erasure* and *revision*. Taken together, these techniques constitute an epistemological apparatus that works to 'map a non-knowing grounded specifically in white racial privilege.'[42] They are two parts of 'the forgetting machine.'[43] Erasure and revision reinforce one another: what people omit from a historical narrative is as important as what they choose to add or include. The historian, like the cartographer, is actively involved in the creation of the spatiotemporal constructions of "the West" that 'underwrite and animate its constructions of the other.'[44] History can be understood as a kind of map-making, whereby the topography of memory is measured, organized, labeled, delineated, and interpreted according to the demands and political objectives of the present moment.

In the urban landscape Julius inhabits, the spatial and temporal coordinates of history blur together and become indistinguishable from one another. Julius surveys the gap in the New York City skyline and remembers 'a tourist who once asked...how he could get to 9/11: not the site of the events of 9/11 but to 9/11 itself, the date petrified into broken stones.'[45] The hole in the skyline establishes space for remembering; space that is not offered to other instances of violence, which have been obscured by the constellation of parks, streets, monuments and buildings that serve as a physical manifestation of the city's active, or short-term, memory. For Julius, the site of the World Trade Center was a palimpsestic reminder of how many times the map of New York City had been written, erased, and rewritten. Contemplating the destruction of the Twin Towers, Julius observes that it was not the first time the site had been subject to erasure. The towers themselves had replaced a bustling neighborhood filled with immigrants, whose homes had been demolished in the 1960s in the name of progress. Those neighborhoods had been swept into the ash heap of history and forgotten. The fact that the people of New York do not remember the Syrians, the Lebanese and the other immigrant communities who had been pushed into Brooklyn by the construction of the towers or the

41   Cole, *Open City*, 152.
42   Charles W. Mills, "Global White Ignorance," in *Routledge International Handbook of Ignorance Studies.* (Taylor and Francis Inc., 2015), 217.
43   Aimé Césaire, *Discourse on Colonialism.* trans. J. Pinkham. (New York, NY: Monthly Review Press, [1950] 2000), 52.
44   Gregory, *The Colonial Present*, 5.
45   Cole, *Open City*, 52.

indigenous Lenape people who had inhabited the area before the arrival of settlers is not incidental. Rather, it reflects a colonial geography that establishes
its objectivity and benevolence through a process of selective memory. Julius
traces an alternative imaginative geography that stands in contrast to the post-
9/11 landscape he inhabits. This is an example of reflective nostalgia: Julius
does not take the map for granted – he questions how it could have turned out
differently. In doing so, he establishes an affinity for communities that are not
his own; an affinity that transcends the spatial and temporal constraints of his
own location.

García Márquez's *One Hundred Years of Solitude* and Cole's *Open City* reveal how imaginative geographies produce, and are produced by, historical
amnesia, a self-imposed forgetting that sanitizes the past. Shapiro (1997) explains that depictions of United States history which locate the "discovery"
of America with the arrival of European settlers are one obvious example of
how systems of knowledge-production are used to erase the violence that at-
tends colonial encounters.[46] He observes how '[t]he disappearance of most
of the indigenous Americans here is handled by having them not exist in the
first place...the Euro-American narrative of space leaves the aboriginal people
in prehistory.'[47] In other words, history is not a series of "objective" events so
much as the product of epistemic practices that stem from specific political
commitments. Shapiro (1997) describes how seventeenth-century intellectuals like Cotton Mather facilitated historical amnesia via a process of renaming
that displaced the original inhabitants of what is now known as the United
States.[48] Mather's 'Exact Map of New England and New York'[49] was not a politically neutral document: by renaming landmarks 'Mather was involved in
the making of a new 'spatial history,' transforming space into a place of re-
settlement while erasing prior naming practices.'[50] Like José Arcadio Segundo,
indigenous people were trapped outside the "official" historical narrative and
exiled to the margins of the past.

6   Mobility and Erasure

Imaginative geographies signify *what* and *how* people choose to remember
and forget, which has implications for how they understand the historical

---

46   Shapiro, *Violent Cartographies*.
47   Ibid., 28.
48   Shapiro, *Violent Cartographies*.
49   As cited in Shapiro, *Violent Cartographies*.
50   Ibid., 27.

narratives that frame their political reality. Ian Bickerton (2012) writes that since the Palestinian exodus of 1948, when approximately 700,000 Palestinians were killed or forcibly exiled and hundreds of Palestinian towns and villages were either depopulated or destroyed, Israel has engaged in an extended campaign of revision and erasure.[51] Israel has "remapped" the territory under its control by expunging many Arab landmarks and replacing them with new towns and historical markers bearing Israeli nomenclature. The Arabic names of more than 9,000 villages, ruins and geographic features have been renamed since 1948. Much like the process of epistemic erasure inflicted against the indigenous people of the United States, the renaming of Arab landmarks and settlements creates historical amnesia; a displacement of Palestinians that is simultaneously geographic *and* temporal. This process extends into the present: when the Trump administration formally recognized Jerusalem as the capital of Israel in December of 2017, CNN's Oren Lieberman (2017) reported that 'Trump-naming frenzy' had taken hold of Israel.[52] Multiple infrastructure and municipal projects are expected to bear President Trump's name, including a new high-speed rail station. This naming trend is significant for two reasons. First, the "naming frenzy" was punctuated by calls to rename *existing* Arab landmarks. In other words, President Trump's decision to rearrange the existing geopolitical landscape was accompanied by a corresponding attempt to alter the epistemic coordinates of the city itself. Second, the rail station in question is part of a contested Tel-Aviv – Jerusalem line that runs *through* and *beneath* the West Bank – a crystal clear example of 'the politics of verticality'[53] which splinters Palestinian sovereignty and transforms both the airspace above and the ground beneath the West Bank into sites of occupation. The vertical topography of the Israeli occupation can be conceptualized as a series of layers that overlap, but never intersect.[54] The Tel-Aviv–Jerusalem line is part of a larger network of roads, tunnels, bridges, walls, and checkpoints that reinforce what Franz Fanon calls 'the dictates of mutual exclusion'[55] – an artificially fragmented landscape that separates the colonizer from the colonized.

In *One Hundred Years of Solitude,* García Márquez illustrates this process of fragmentation with his depiction of the new railroad and the 'innocent

---

51   Ian J. Bickerton, *The Arab-Israeli Conflict: A Guide for the Perplexed.* London: Continuum, 2012.

52   Oren Liebermann, "Israel plans a Trump station as Trump-naming frenzy sweeps country." December 28, (2017).

53   Eyal Weizman, "Introduction to The Politics of Verticality." June 23, (2002).

54   Ibid.

55   Frantz Fanon, *The Wretched of the Earth.* Trans. R. Philcox, Trans. (New York, NY: Grove Press, [1961] 2004), 4.

yellow train'[56] that bring the banana company to Macondo. The first wave of banana company employees is a slew of 'engineers, agronomists, hydrologists, topographers and surveyors'[57] who immediately set to work changing the layout of the town. The foreigners alter the physical properties of the landscape and the climate to suit their own purposes. Then they build a company town with shady streets and beautifully manicured lawns surrounded by an electric fence. The revised geography of Macondo is reminiscent of the 'compartmentalized world' Fanon describes in *The Wretched of the Earth* when he claims the sector of the colonizer is 'built to last, all stone and steel…a sector of lights and paved roads.'[58] The land inhabited by the colonized, on the other hand, is 'a world with no space, [where] people are piled on top of each other.'[59] In Macondo, the electric fence that separates the luxurious houses of the foreigners from the 'miserable huts'[60] of the workers establishes disconnected geographies that occupy the same topography. Within this divided space, the colonizer enjoys unrestricted mobility, while the movement of colonized subjects is restricted.

This discrepancy of mobility speaks to the importance of the infrastructure the colonizer uses to divide the occupied territory into different sectors or compartments. In both Macondo and the West Bank, the train is more than a means of transportation; it is a physical manifestation of the colonizer's complete control over the relationship between time and distance. The railroad that comes to Macondo collapses the distance between Macondo and the rest of the world. It introduces a standardized measurement of time and re-maps the geography of Macondo by changing the temporal coordinates of travel. A journey which used to take weeks or even months is compressed into the space of a few hours. This is also true of the Jerusalem–Tel-Aviv line: it facilitates the mobility of Israeli citizens (who can cross occupied territory quickly) while the mobility of Palestinians is restricted by the walls, tunnels, armed guards and checkpoints they encounter when they move from one location to another. The colonizer and the colonized use the same map, but the scale of the map varies. In the imaginative geography produced by the colonizer, distance becomes a physical expression of difference.

As the "naming frenzy" illustrates, the infrastructure which expands or collapses distance to establish the materiality of the colonial hierarchy does not

---

56   Márquez, *One Hundred Years of Solitude*, 215.
57   Ibid., 218.
58   Fanon, *The Wretched*, 4.
59   Ibid.
60   Márquez, *One Hundred Years of Solitude*, 282.

exist in a vacuum. It must be supplemented with an assemblage of epistemic techniques that normalize the spatiotemporal coordinates of colonization. In Macondo, for example, a variety of state-sanctioned discourses conspire to efface the banana company workers, wiping them from the collective memory of Macondo's inhabitants and from the pages of history itself. The banana company's 'sleight-of hand lawyers'[61] use clever legal maneuvers to deny the workers any formal recognition until 'by a decision of the court it was established and set down in solemn decrees that the workers did not exist.'[62] Significantly, these legal decrees *precede* the banana company massacre. They do not "cover up" violence which has already occurred; they establish an epistemic framework in which the massacre can take place. The epistemic erasure *anticipates* the violence inflicted on the workers. When the massacre occurs, it merely confirms what everyone already knows: the banana company workers do not exist. Evaluated in this context, comments about the non-existence of the Palestinian people assume a new significance. When former U.S. Presidential candidate Newt Gingrich claimed in 2011 that Palestinians are an "invented people," he was not simply arguing that Palestinians have no right to the territory they inhabit. He was establishing an imaginative geography – a blank spot on the map – that rendered violence against Palestinians thinkable. An imagined people can be erased without consequence. In short, he was articulating *a self-fulfilling prophecy that erases its own remainder.*

The "blank spot" on the map is not the product of bulldozers demolishing Palestinian homes and buildings but, rather, the inevitable fate of all political fantasies, which dissolve when juxtaposed against "real" history. It is the logical conclusion of an epistemic procedure that sanitizes the Israeli occupation, insofar as it manages to convey the impression that the history of Israel is an unbroken line stretching all the way back to antiquity. This is precisely what Israeli Prime Minister Benjamin Netanyahu claimed in 2011 when he told the United States Congress that Israelis are,

> not the British in India [or] the Belgians in the Congo [because] this is the land of our forefathers, the land of Israel, to which Abraham brought the idea of one God, where David set out to confront Goliath, and where Isaiah saw a vision of eternal peace.[63]

---

61   Márquez, *One Hundred Years of Solitude*, 289.
62   Ibid.
63   Text of PM Binyamin Netanyahu's Speech to the US Congress. May 24, (2011). Please see http://www.jpost.com/Diplomacy-and-Politics/Text-of-PM-Binyamin-Netanyahus -speech-to-the-US-Congress.

Golda Meir, the fourth Prime Minister of Israel made a similar, albeit more explicit, claim when she said: 'there was no such thing as Palestinians…They did not exist.'[64] Meir and Netanyahu's comments bring us, once again, back to José Arcadio Segundo and the massacre of the striking banana workers. One can easily imagine one of the 700,000 "nonexistent" Palestinian refugees returning to Haifa, only to be told by the Israeli settler living in his home that 'there haven't been any dead here. Since the time of Abraham, nothing has happened in Israel.'

7   Architectures of Enmity

The Israeli infrastructure projects being named after President Trump invite a comparison to the infrastructure President Trump promised to build: namely, the proposed wall on the U.S.-Mexico border. In fact, the Israeli constructed wall in the West Bank could be considered a blueprint for the wall President Trump described during his 2017 presidential campaign. The West Bank separation wall is a 708 km long "security fence" consisting of barbed wire, radar, cameras, checkpoints, trenches, 8-meter concrete blocks, watchtowers and armed guards.[65] The wall does not prevent Palestinians from crossing (legally and illegally) into Israeli territory,[66] but it *does* serve as an expression of Israeli sovereignty that produces a psychic division between a "civilized" interior and an "uncivilized" frontier. In other words, it serves to make intangible "us/them" distinctions more concrete. In the United States, the political rhetoric that frames Mexican immigrants as criminals, drug traffickers, potential terrorists and rapists suggests President Trump's proposed border wall would serve a similar purpose, lending substance to a fantasy of collective identity that frames Mexican immigrants as a threat to American greatness.

Infrastructure projects like the West Bank separation wall are a physical manifestation of what Shapiro (1997) calls architectures of enmity, ontological constructs which determine how 'territorially elaborated collectivities…provide the conditions of possibility for regarding others as threats or antagonists.'[67] Architectures of enmity are imaginative geographies that partition the world into categories of "us" versus "them" to mobilize public support for war and

64   Sunday Times, (1969).
65   Rachel Busbridge, "The wall has feet but so do we: Palestinian workers in Israel and the 'separation' wall." *British Journal of Middle Eastern Studies*, 44(3) (2017): 373–390.
66   Ibid.
67   Shapiro, *Violent Cartographies*, xi.

normalize international conflict. While Shapiro (1997) speaks of architectures of enmity in primarily ontological terms, he is acutely aware of how fantasies of collective identity – and the processes of threat construction they engender – have material consequences. Ontology does not exist in a vacuum; it shapes how people act in the world and determines which forms of violence they consider legitimate. As Julius observes towards the end of *Open City*, 'we are not the villains of our own stories. In fact, it is quite the contrary: we play, and only play, the hero...we are never less than heroic.'[68] The word "play" is significant: like all imaginative geographies, architectures of enmity are *performed*.[69] Moreover, they are performed at the expense of an enemy who stands outside civilization and cannot be extended moral consideration: criminals, terrorists and other "bad guys" who must be destroyed and whose monstrosity makes us heroic by default.

Shapiro (1997) focuses explicitly on the ontological foundations of inter-state conflict. He does not elaborate on how architectures of enmity can be expressed as systemic violence. When President Trump, for example, positions Mexican immigrants as a threat to American greatness, he establishes the discursive scaffolding of an architecture of enmity that normalizes the structural violence which occurs near the U.S.-Mexico border. Structure, in this context, has two meanings: it refers to configurations of power which inflict violence against vulnerable populations and to the actual "brick and mortar" buildings that restrict mobility, impose spatial hegemony, and separate the colonizer from the colonized. In other words, this architecture of enmity is not merely a series of ontological coordinates which make threat construction politically feasible. It is also, quite literally, an architectural configuration that inflicts violence on people who are designated threats or enemies. This is identifiable at every level of government, from the "defensive architecture" and "hostile design" urban planners use to push homeless populations out of public spaces to the expansive system of roads, gates, walls, fences, guard posts, checkpoints and detainment centers the federal government uses to secure national borders.

As a structural manifestation of structural violence, a wall on the U.S.-Mexico border would be nothing if not redundant. The militarization of the U.S.-Mexico border has created a hostile topography that pushes migrants away from settled areas and into desolate regions, where they are more likely

68   Cole, *Open City*, 243.
69   Gregory, *The Colonial Present.*

to die of exposure.[70] In 2017 alone, 412 migrants died trying to cross the U.S.-Mexico border.[71] If, as Massey et al. (2003) suggest, border enforcement represents a 'ritualistic performance'[72] of American identity, the imaginative geography of the U.S.-Mexico border is a fantasy of restorative nostalgia performed at the expense of a disposable immigrant other. President Trump's proposed border wall (and his corresponding promise to "make America great again") will merely lend substance to an architecture of enmity that casts migrants as a threat to national security. If President Trump builds a wall on the U.S-Mexico border, the structural violence engendered by this architecture of enmity will become a physical structure which expresses violence through its architecture.

In other words, while the border wall would be unique as a visible expression of "us/them" dichotomies, it would be a mere extension of a violent topographical configuration *that already exists*. The constellation of Immigration Customs Enforcement (ICE) detention centers lurking like a glacier beneath the surface of U.S. immigration policy is a ruthless barrier that prevents hundreds of thousands of people from entering the country every year. In *Open City*, Julius visits one of these detention centers, a remarkably unremarkable 'gray metal box' that blends seamlessly into a series of prefabricated buildings that 'seemed designed not to be noticed.'[73] The detention center is located on the outskirts of the city, far from areas of human habitation. It takes Julius an hour to get there by chartered bus. The political marginalization of the immigrants is reflected by this physical marginalization; this expulsion from the city proper. Politically, legally, and cartographically, the detained immigrants inhabit an industrialized "no man's land" as bare and desolate as the Arizona desert that claims the lives of hundreds of immigrants per year.

Julius soon discovers the gray, metal box is actually a warehouse that stores unacknowledged imaginative geographies *and* the unwanted people who cling to them. Julius speaks to a prisoner named Saidu, who maintains a mental map that presupposes a special affinity between the United States and his own home country of Liberia,

> [Saidu] had been taught about the special relationship between Liberia and America, which was like the relationship between an uncle and a

---

70   Douglas S. Massey, Jorge Durand & Nolan J. Malone, *Beyond Smoke and Mirrors: Mexican Immigration in an Era of Economic Integration.* New York: Russell Sage Foundation, 2003.

71   US-Mexico border migrant deaths rose in 2017 even as crossings fell, UN says. Please see The Guardian, February 6, (2017). Retrieved from https://www.theguardian.com/us-news/2018/feb/06/us-mexico-border-migrant-deaths-rose-2017.

72   Massey, Durand & Malone, *Beyond Smoke and Mirrors*, 103.

73   Cole, *Open City*, 62.

> favorite nephew. Even the names bore a family resemblance: Liberia, America: seven letters each, four of which were shared. America had sat solidly in his dreams, had been the absolute focus of his dreams.[74]

The imaginative geography that equates Liberia with America is an expression of Saidu's fantasy of belonging. Such fantasies are incompatible with the restorative nostalgia of the post-9/11 landscape: Saidu dreams of America, but America does not dream of *him*. Saidu assumes a "special relationship" between the United States and Liberia because he is conscious of the shared history between the two countries. Liberia was established by citizens of the United States as a colony for former African American slaves and their descendants. Unfortunately for Saidu, U.S. immigration policy does not formally acknowledge this shared history. The "special relationship" between the United States and Liberia is not part of the imaginative geography that determines who qualifies for citizenship. As far as the United States is concerned, any "family resemblance" between itself and Liberia is merely coincidental. Any shared history has been forgotten. In other words, Liberia is not a "favorite nephew" so much as an estranged second cousin.

8   The Politics of Estrangement

As a legal immigrant visiting a detention center, Julius occupies a unique position. On the one hand, he is skeptical of the way nationalism invokes restorative nostalgia to idealize normative interpretations of American citizenship. On the other hand, his status as a legal resident puts him in a position of relative privilege that makes him unwilling to fully identify with Saidu's predicament. Julius knows the imaginative geography Saidu subscribes to is as much of a fantasy as the myth of citizenship from which Saidu is excluded. His own memories of Nigeria make him aware of the extent to which *all* geography is imaginary; an illusion that precludes recognizing affinities that transcend the constraints of national identity. At the same time, while Julius recognizes "friend/enemy" distinctions rooted in nationalism are fictional, he cannot bring himself to discard those distinctions and fully empathize with Saidu. Instead, Julius preserves the clinical distance he maintains with his own patients. Julius treats Saidu's narrative as an object of analysis and skepticism. Julius suspects Saidu is lying when he says he was not a soldier, noting the man 'had

---

74   Ibid., 64–65.

months...to perfect his claim of being an innocent refugee.'[75] His skepticism and detachment reflect U.S. immigration policy, which formalizes doubt and suspicion in the name of national security. The humanizing narrative of the immigrant is always held at arm's length and scrutinized as a trick or a ploy. By adopting this attitude, Julius preserves the power differential that prevents him from being grouped with undocumented residents like Saidu. He knows Saidu is not an enemy who threatens national security but is simultaneously unwilling to consider Saidu a friend – a label which carries a corresponding ethical obligation Julius is unwilling to accept. Julius resolves this crisis of categorization by identifying Saidu as a stranger.

The figure of the stranger resists being assimilated into architectures of enmity, which are predicated on the ability to classify people as either friends or enemies. According to Zygmunt Bauman (1990), the ambiguity of the stranger disrupts this process of classification.[76] The stranger is the non-enemy who inhabits territory traditionally reserved for friends but cannot be incorporated into fantasies of collective identity rooted in restorative nostalgia. The stranger is indeterminate; the unfamiliar "other" who lives next door. The ambiguity of the stranger undermines architectures of enmity by disrupting the 'fought-after co-ordination between moral and topographical closeness.'[77] Saidu might insist he is a Christian and friend to America, but, according to Bauman (1990), the stranger's claim of commonality is always overshadowed by uncertainty.[78] The stranger's ambiguity feeds xenophobic fantasies of "the enemy within" who poses as a friend but uses duplicity, subversion, and sabotage to undermine the nation-state. The fact that Saidu comes from a nation where the historically dominant minority is descended from American citizens, and thus feels as though he has a special kinship with the United States, only underscores estrangement as a process of political alienation inseparable from colonialism.

As Saidu's experience demonstrates, the stranger is the end-goal and the unintentional byproduct of the nationalist project; a symptom of erasure and revision, but also an unclassifiable other that undermines nationalism by calling architectures of enmity into question. On the one hand, nationalism is most successful when it invokes restorative nostalgia to impose a process of forgetting that repositions colonized subjects as strangers in their own land: native Americans who are "off the reservation" or Palestinians who find themselves detained by Israeli security forces in their own neighborhoods. In the United

---

75   Ibid., 67.
76   Bauman, "Modernity and Ambivalence."
77   Ibid., 150.
78   Bauman, "Modernity and Ambivalence."

States, for example, conservative politicians have established an imaginative geography that frames Mexican people as strangers and invaders of annexed territory; territory that belonged to Mexico long before it belonged to America and to indigenous people long before it belonged to Mexico. They reinforce this imaginative geography by actively suppressing histories that highlight the contestability of the U.S.-Mexico border. In 2010, Arizona passed House Bill 2281, which banned teaching Mexican-American studies in public schools.[79] Laws like H.B. 2281 (which was struck down by a federal judge in 2017) work in conjunction with English-only education initiatives to position Mexican-Americans and Mexican immigrants as strangers trespassing in colonized territory. Any claim to kinship between Mexican people and territory that was formerly part of Mexico is obfuscated by the process of estrangement. The resulting imaginative geography is characterized by historical amnesia that divorces the ongoing violence at the U.S.-Mexico border from the legacy of American colonialism: 'there haven't been any dead here. Since the time of the general, Santa Anna, nothing has happened on *la frontera*.'

On the other hand, the process of estrangement produces ambiguities that destabilize nationalism by calling into question architectures of enmity. In Israel, for example, approximately 40,000 refugees from Eritrea and Sudan have created a rift between Israeli nationalists who prioritize border security and Israelis who invoke Israel's history as a haven for people fleeing persecution.[80] According to NPR's Daniel Estrin (2018), the Israeli government's official term for these refugees is 'infiltrators,' a label reminiscent of the conspiratorial worldview Boym (2007) references in her definition of restorative nostalgia.[81] Critics of the Israeli government's deportation policies frequently cite Leviticus 19:34, which reads: 'the stranger who resides among you shall be to you as one of your citizens; you shall love him as yourself, for you were strangers in Egypt.'[82] The presence of these strangers has created a schism between the restorative nostalgia of Israeli nationalists like Netanyahu, who has claimed the refugees represent a threat to the state, and the reflective nostalgia of Israelis who seek to establish 'diasporic intimacy'[83] that transcends nationality. The two sides have articulated imaginative geographies that are completely at odds with one another; conflicting maps of the same territory. The stranger's

---

79   Edwin Rios, "Arizona Republicans banned Mexican American studies. The fight is now back in court." August 23, (2017).

80   Isabel Kershner, "Israel Moves to Expel Africans. Critics Say That's Not Jewish." February 2, (2018).

81   Daniel Estrin, "African Refugees in Israel Face Deportation." January 27, (2018).

82   As cited in Kershner, "Israel Moves to Expel Africans."

83   Boym, "Nostalgia and Its Discontents," 15.

failure – or refusal – to be assimilated into the dominant architecture of enmity has created space for multiple stories to articulate themselves at the same time.

9   Conclusion

The presence of the stranger destabilizes architectures of enmity. It interrupts processes of enemy construction, which are predicated on mapping practices that cannot endure ambiguity. In other words, the figure of the stranger introduces a moment of hesitation that calls the spatiotemporal coordinates of postcolonial melancholia into question. The stranger belies the historical amnesia that sanitizes the violence of the colonizer. The stranger's very presence in colonized territory resists tactics of erasure and revision that establish and sustain the imaginative geographies of contemporary nationalism. In short, the figure of the stranger necessitates the creation of *new* imaginative geographies; spatializations of difference that consider both the violence of colonialism and historical contingency of national identity. As my examination of *Open City* and *One Hundred Years of Solitude* demonstrates, literature is uniquely suited for this "remapping" of the political imagination. It can initiate a shift from restorative nostalgia, which oversimplifies history to conceptualize identity as static and determinative, to reflective nostalgia, which acknowledges identity as complex, conditional and fluid. While restorative nostalgia lends itself to the type of nationalism that promises to reestablish American greatness, imaginative geographies that constitute themselves through reflective nostalgia render such nationalism unintelligible. Reflective nostalgia begs the question: when President Trump promises to "make America great again," which America is he referring to? Which imaginative geography is he seeking to restore?

While novels like *Open City* and *One Hundred Years of Solitude* cannot directly answer these questions, they do offer a point of departure for rethinking restorative nostalgia and the architectures of enmity it legitimizes. To paraphrase Der Derian, the violence that stems from the militarization of the U.S. – Mexico border and the Israeli occupation of Palestine is the result of more than a rational calculation of interests. It is also the product of how we *see*, *perceive*, *picture*, *imagine* and *speak* of others. In other words, it is closely tied to stories that affect how we perform our understanding of space; the narratives that influence how we map both the distance and the difference between self and other. Examining imaginative geographies through literature reveals how fantasies of collective identity acquire political substance to become architectures of enmity that are ontologically and structurally implicated in the production of colonial violence. Literature and cartography operate as "useful fictions" that blur the border between political fact and political fantasy, calling into question how history and nostalgia are invoked to establish barriers that separate friends from enemies, natives from foreigners and citizens from "infiltrators." Consequently, literature that supplants restorative nostalgia with reflective nostalgia does more than suggest two different ways of reading the maps we use to orient ourselves in the world. It also determines whether we read each other as strangers deserving hospitality or legitimate objects of systemic violence.

Bibliography

Bauman, Z. "Modernity and Ambivalence." *Theory, Culture & Society, 7* (1990): 143–169.

Bickerton, I.J. *The Arab-Israeli Conflict: A Guide for the Perplexed.* London: Continuum, 2012.

Boym, S. "Nostalgia and Its Discontents." *The Hedgehog Review,* (2007): 7–18.

Busbridge, R. "The wall has feet but so do we: Palestinian workers in Israel and the 'separation' wall." *British Journal of Middle Eastern Studies, 44*(3) (2016): 373–390. DOI: 10.1080/13530194.2016.1194187.

Césaire, A. *Discourse on colonialism.* (J. Pinkham, Trans.). New York, NY: Monthly Review Press, 2000.

Cole, T. *Open City: A Novel.* New York: Random House Trade Paperbacks, 2012.

Der Derian, J. "9.11: Before, After and In-Between." (n.d.). Retrieved February 28, 2018, from http://essays.ssrc.org/sept11/essays/der_derian.htm.

Estrin, D. "African Refugees in Israel Face Deportation." January 27, (2018). Retrieved April 05, 2018, from https://www.npr.org/2018/01/27/581343553/african-refugees-in-israel-face-deportation.

Fanon, F. *The Wretched of the Earth.* (R. Philcox, Trans.). New York, NY: Grove Press, [1961] 2004.

Foden, G. *Zanzibar.* Faber & Faber, [2002] 2003.

Freud, S. "Mourning and Melancholia." (J. Strachey, Trans.). In *The Standard Edition of the Complete Psychological Works of Sigmund Freud* (Vol. XIV). (London: Hogarth Press, 1953), 243–258.

Gilroy, P. *Postcolonial Melancholia.* New York: Columbia U.P., 2006.

Gregory, D. "Imaginative Geographies." *Progress in Human Geography, 19*(4) (1995): 447–485. DOI:10.1177/030913259501900402.

Gregory, D. *The Colonial Present.* Malden, MA: Blackwell Publishing, 2004.

Hofer, J. "Medical Dissertation on Nostalgia." *Bulletin of the Institute of the History of Medicine,* (1688): 376–391. Retrieved February 28, 2018.

Joyce, J. *Ulysses*. London: Penguin Books, [1922] 2000.

Kershner, I. "Israel Moves to Expel Africans. Critics Say That's Not Jewish." February 2, (2018). Retrieved April 05, 2018, from https://www.nytimes.com/2018/02/02/world/middleeast/israel-migrants-african.html.

Liebermann, O. "Israel plans a Trump station as Trump-naming frenzy sweeps country." December 28, (2017). Retrieved April 05, 2018, from https://www.cnn.com/2017/12/27/politics/israel-trump-train-station-rail-name-naming/index.html.

Liebermann, O. "Israel Plans a Trump Rail Station as Trump-naming frenzy sweeps the country." December 27, (2017). Retrieved February 28, 2018, from https://www.cnn.com/2017/12/27/politics/israel-trump-train-station-rail-name-naming/index.html.

Márquez, G.G. *One Hundred Years of Solitude*. New York: Avon Books, [1967] 1971.

Marx, K. "The Eighteenth Brumaire of Louis Bonaparte." In *The Communist Manifesto and Other Writings,* authored by K. Marx & F. Engels. (New York, NY: Barnes & Noble Books, [1852] 2005), 63–169.

Massey, D.S., Durand, J., & Malone, N.J. *Beyond Smoke and Mirrors: Mexican Immigration in an Era of Economic Integration*. New York: Russell Sage Foundation, 2003.

Meir, Golda. (n.d.). Retrieved February 28, 2018, from https://en.wikiquote.org/wiki/Golda_Meir.

Mills, C.W. "Global White Ignorance." In Routledge International Handbook of Ignorance Studies. Taylor and Francis Inc., 2015. https://doi.org/10.4324/9781315867762 doi:10.1093/acprof:oso/9780190245412.003.0004.

Natali, M.P. "History and the Politics of Nostalgia." *Iowa Journal of Cultural Studies, 5,* (2004): 10–25.

Netanyahu, B. "Text of PM Binjamin Netanyahu's Speech to the US Congress." May 24, (2011). Retrieved February 28, 2018, from http://www.jpost.com/Diplomacy-and-Politics/Text-of-PM-Binjamin-Netanyahus-speech-to-the-US-Congress.

Plato. *Cratylus*. (B. Jowett, Trans.). (n.d.).

Rios, E. "Arizona Republicans banned Mexican American studies. The fight is now back in court." August 23, (2017). Retrieved April 05, 2018, from https://www.motherjones.com/politics/2017/07/arizona-republicans-banned-mexican-american-studies-the-fight-is-now-back-in-court/.

Said, E.W. *Orientalism*. New York, NY: Random House, 1979.

Shapiro, M.J. *Violent Cartographies: Mapping Cultures of War*. Minneapolis, MN: University of Minnesota Press, 1997.

Shklovsky, V. "Art as Technique." In *Critical Theory: A Reader for Literary and Cultural Studies,* edited by R.D. Parker. (New York, NY: Oxford University Press, [1917] 2012), 48–58.

Smith, B. "Gingrich: Palestinians 'invented,' promises Netanyahu-style foreign policy." December 9, (2011). Retrieved February 28, 2018, from https://www.politico.com/blogs/ben-smith/2011/12/gingrich-palestinians-invented-promises-netanyahu-style-foreign-policy-041411.

Taylor, A.M. "Cien Anos de Soledad: History and the Novel." *Latin American Perspectives, 2*(3) (1975): 96–112.

The Guardian. "US-Mexico border migrant deaths rose in 2017 even as crossings fell, UN says." February 6, (2018). Retrieved February 28, 2018, from https://www.theguardian.com/us-news/2018/feb/06/us-mexico-border-migrant-deaths-rose-2017.

Weizman, E. "Introduction to The Politics of Verticality." June 23, (2002). Retrieved April 05, 2018, from https://www.opendemocracy.net/ecology-politicsverticality/article_801.jsp.

Index

CPSIA information can be obtained
at www.ICGtesting.com
Printed in the USA
JSHW011420010620
5985JS00005B/13

9 781642 591941